T0325308

Books by Hillel Halkin

Letters to an American Jewish Friend (1977)

*Grand Things to Write a Poem On: A Verse
Autobiography of Shmuel Hanagid* (2000)

Across the Sabbath River (2002)

A Strange Death (2005)

Yehuda Halevi (2010)

Melisande! What Are Dreams? (2012)

Jabotinsky: A Life (2014)

*After One-Hundred-and-Twenty: Reflecting on Death,
Mourning, and the Afterlife in the Jewish Tradition* (2016)

The Lady of Hebrew and Her Lovers of Zion (2020)

Lives of the Children of Manasia (With Isaac Thangjom, 2021)

A
COMPLICATED
JEW

Selected Essays

Hillel Halkin

WICKED SON

A WICKED SON BOOK
An Imprint of Post Hill Press
ISBN: 978-1-64293-810-4
ISBN (eBook): 978-1-64293-811-1

A Complicated Jew:
Selected Essays
© 2021 by Hillel Halkin
All Rights Reserved

Cover Design by Tiffani Shea

This is a work of nonfiction. All people, locations, events, and situations are portrayed to the best of the author's memory.

No part of this book may be reproduced, stored in a retrieval system, or transmitted by any means without the written permission of the author and publisher.

Post Hill Press
New York • Nashville
posthillpress.com

Published in the United States of America
1 2 3 4 5 6 7 8 9 10

Table of Contents

Preface: A Complicated Jew

The eighteen essays selected for this book were published over a period of nearly half a century, the first of them in 1974, the last in 2021. Most appeared in *Commentary*, my writing for which was inseparable from my long association with Neal Kozodoy, the magazine's second-in-command throughout the 1970s and '80s and editor in chief from 1995 to 2009. I started contributing to *Commentary* soon after Neal went to work for it and stopped when he retired, and I am deeply grateful for his prolonged aid and support. Subsequently, I wrote for the internet magazine *Mosaic*, which Neal helped found, and for the *Jewish Review of Books* and its editor Abe Socher. Essays published there appear in these pages, too.

I have not arranged these essays in the order in which they were written. Rather, I have sought to give them an autobiographical sequence. Thus, the book's first entry deals with my family's origins in Eastern Europe, its second and third with my New York childhood and adolescence, and so on. This was an imprecise method, since some pieces touch on, or have as their background, more than one time of my life, but I thought it better than any other.

Deciding what to choose for this volume, whose length was a preordained given, was not always easy. Essays like "Holy Land," "Rooting for the Indians," "Either/Or," "Driving Toward Jerusalem," "My Uncle Simon," "Sailing to Ithaca," and others of a personal nature were never in doubt. Nor were many that I had no qualms about omitting, occasion-driven pieces on books, events, and political developments that belong to the past. The borderline cases tended to be those in which there was a mixture of the two things. If I included "Feminizing Jewish Studies" (1998) and "How Not to Repair the World " (2008), it was because, though the books discussed there may no longer be of much interest, they gave me an opportunity to say things that I felt strongly about and still do. Conversely, while they have passages that I value, I left out essays like "Whose Palestine? An Open Letter to Edward Said" (1979), and "The 'Waltzing with Bashir' Two-Step" (2009), which contained more detail about the book and film they reviewed than I thought it fair to subject readers to today.

In some cases it was hard to decide about a piece because it was one of several on the same subject. Although I've written on various issues having to do with the Bible, for example, there was only so much that I felt this book could accommodate. Similarly, I excluded otherwise worthy essays on Israel and Zionism because there were already enough of these. In one case, I dropped an entire category. I've published literary essays that I think have stood up well over time—ones on Saul Bellow, Philip Roth, Henry Roth, Cynthia Ozick, and Salman Rushdie, to mention some—but there would have been room at most for just one of them and I preferred to single out none.

I sometimes found myself wishing that I could take the best parts of different essays written on related themes and combine them. Although this was not, of course, possible, I did take the liberty in several places of borrowing a few lines from a piece I excluded and weaving them into one I included. I also allowed myself to make a small number of cuts and stylistic revisions in essays written, often in haste, many years ago. Nowhere have I changed matters of substance.

The titles of magazine articles are almost always given them by their editors. The author is rarely consulted, and although I was not always happy with the titles my essays received (some I thought excellent), I have let them stand. By now, whether I originally liked them or not, they have adhered to what they were stuck on and I would not try to peel any of them off. Book titles, on the other hand, are jointly decided on by the

HILLEL HALKIN

author and the publisher. When it came to a title for this one, neither its publisher Adam Bellow nor I had any bright ideas. "I suppose it should have something to do with being Jewish," I said to Adam. All this book's essays, after all, were written for Jewish publications and touch on some aspect of Jewish life or thought.

"Well," Adam asked, "what kind of a Jew would you say you were?"

"A complicated one," I said.

Which is how, quite spontaneously, the title of this book came about. I will not try to justify it in this preface. The essays themselves, I believe, do that well enough.

The Road to Naybikhov

After a while, it went away. For a day or two, though, driving the long, straight roads on which we were often the only car for miles, it kept coming back, far down the road, like a mirage or a defect in my retina: a wagon with a Jew in it.

Horse-drawn wagons are plentiful; Jews are rare. This is the paradox of the modish pursuit of Jewish roots in what were once the shtetls, the towns and villages, of the Pale of Settlement of the Russian empire. Nowhere else in Europe can one see so unchanged the physical world in which Jews lived one hundred years ago. The Jews alone are gone from it.

I had been to Russia and Ukraine once before, as a correspondent, in 1995, spending a week in Moscow and a week in Kiev—long enough to glimpse from close up the utter destruction of Russian Jewry's own roots (to glimpse, too, the devastation wreaked on Russia by seventy years of Soviet rule). I had wanted to get to the countryside, especially to the little village in White Russia—Belarus, as it now is called—in which my father lived until he was twelve, but there had not been time.

Late last spring I went.

Naybikhov, the place was called in Yiddish, Novibychov in Russian, and it had taken me a long time to get there because already as a child I was prepared to set out. Not so much because of anything my father told me. The youngest of seven brothers and sisters, he did not like to talk about his childhood, the mere mention of which made him

1

melancholy—a response not in keeping with the fact that the poverty he was raised in was never dire and my aunts and uncles claimed he was the family pet. Nor, when it came to their family, did the Holocaust throw a dark shadow, practically all of their close relatives having, like them, left for America before World War I.

It was my aunts and uncles who told me most of the little I knew about Naybikhov, and although they never spoke of it nostalgically, something in me stirred to what I heard. No doubt this was a result of growing up on a fifth floor in Manhattan, from the parqueted heights of which I yearned instinctively for the country. Anything smelling in my imagination of dirt, soil, rotting leaves, manure, cows, horses, tool-sheds, woodpiles, the smoke of fireplaces excited me, the son of a college professor who could not swim but had lived in a log cabin overlooking the Dnieper, with a wood-burning stove, and a yard, and a cow that was milked every day, and a vegetable garden on top of a hill that sloped steeply down to the river from which water was fetched in buckets, and the boats heading downstream from Mogilev to Gomel, or even all the way to Kiev, and sometimes tying up to take on passengers. I loved rivers, lakes. High and dry between one summer vacation and the next, I would have traded my childhood for my father's. I would have made better use of his than he did.

So I had dreamed of Naybikhov. But children do not travel to the lands of their dreams, and as I grew older, there were other places to visit. Besides which, one could not tour freely under the Soviets. Nor was I even sure that Naybikhov still existed, having been told by a Russian Jew I met in Israel that it was leveled during the war. By the time it was possible to reach it unchaperoned, and I found a map establishing that it was there (some twenty-five miles from Bychov, on the road to Rogachov, the *rogachove gass* my aunts and uncles remembered), along came the meltdown at Chernobyl. Naybikhov was less than 200 kilometers to the north. Better not, I was warned.

In any case, long before then, I had begun traveling to the shtetl in other ways. With no conscious connection to Naybikhov, I had drifted, at first quite inadvertently, into being a translator of Hebrew literature, and the Hebrew literature I loved most, and was (on the rare occasions when a publisher could be found for it) happiest translating, was of the early modern period—the literature produced in Eastern Europe in the late nineteenth and early twentieth centuries by writers like Mendele Mokher Sefarim, Mordecai Ze'ev Feierberg, Micha Yosef Berdichevsky, Yosef Hayim Brenner, Uri Nisan Gnessin, and Hayim Nahman Bialik. Born and raised in the Pale of Settlement, all of these men wrote extensively about its towns and villages—many of whose names I knew as well from another Hebrew genre, nineteenth-century collections of Hasidic tales like *The Praises of the Baal Shem Tov* and *The Life of Our Master Nahman of Bratslav*.

Eventually, I began to translate from Yiddish too: Sholem Aleichem, I. L. Peretz, Mendele once again—and once again, the shtetl was the venue. And so when, each of us in pursuit of his family's past, I flew last May with a friend to Kiev, where we were met by a car with a driver and an interpreter and driven off into rural Ukraine and Belarus, I was not stepping into an entirely unknown world. I had lived in it, on and off, for a long time.

Spread out on my knees, the road map, despite its strange spellings, confirmed this: Berdičev, Polonoje, Braclav, Vinnica, Mežibož, Skvira, Nemirov, Satanov, Šargorod—I had been to them all. In Bojarka, alias Boiberik, I had spent four months with Sholem Aleichem's Tevye the dairyman; Žitomir was the site of Bialik's mischievous and mournful adolescence; on a frozen winter day in Kamenka the Baal Shem Tov had warmed his disciples by lighting a tree with a touch of his finger; Uman was where Rabbi Nahman went to die, and more mysteriously, to befriend heretics; in the company of the narrator of Sholem Aleichem's *Railroad Stories*, I had passed through Žmerinka, Gajsin, Teplik, Tulčin, Beršad, Obodovka.

One of our first stops was Zhitomir. Bialik's low, one-story house, looking like all the others on its block, was for sale. The owners wanted

$7,000. Yes, they knew a famous Jew had lived in it. Two or three tourists had been there before us.

We were not invited inside, and I did not get to see the kitchen and bedroom that were probably all there was of it. But it would not have surprised me to hear a cricket shrilling there like the one that had moved in when Bialik was a boy.

> A retiring fellow, he kept out of sight
> And fretted in chinks of the gloom-blackened night,
> A poet who had only one song to sing
> And sang it, and sang it, and sang it.

It would not have surprised me because of the backyard. It was the exact same yard as the one described in Bialik's story "Behind the Fence," written in Odessa in 1909. Nothing—the rotting timbers, the collapsing sheds, the piles of junk—had been removed. No one had bothered to fix the hole in the fence through which Noyekh, the teenage son of Hanina-Lipa and Tsipa-Leah, had arranged his trysts with Marinka, who lived next door with her Jew-hating stepmother, the jawbreakingly-named Shkuripinshchtikha.

It was that way everywhere. I recognized it all: the pine forests and the birch forests, the enormous fields of pale green wheat, the vast, flat distances, the sandy dirt roads, the tin roofs of the houses, the picket fences, the chickens pecking by the roadside, the lilac bushes tall as trees, the high fur hats of the storks' nests, the kerchiefed women on the benches. "I know that goat!" I cried as we passed through Chmelnik. It had a white beard and was straining to reach, its head between two pickets, the neighbor's cabbages. "It's just a goat," said my friend, who had thought the chickens were just chickens. But it wasn't. It was Mendele's.

On a hilltop in Medzhibozh, where the Baal Shem Tov lived and is buried, I stood looking down at the Bug River; on its far bank, in the village of Trebikhabtsi, rose a white Orthodox church. Once the Baal Shem Tov was asked by a Gentile why the Jews shake back and forth in prayer. "Do you see that man swimming?" he asked, pointing to the river. "If you didn't know what he was doing, you would think he was just waving his arms, but unless he waved them he would drown. We pray to keep our souls from drowning."

I knew the river, then, too.

It was the first generations of Hasidim with their rabbis and disciples who sacralized the geography of Eastern Europe. Until then, apart from the land of Israel, Jews had their holy places—tombs and synagogues, for the most part—but not their holy regions; the road from the grave of one *tsaddik* to the next, the street between two houses of prayer, were an ordinary road and street. Except for historical chronicles and the titles of rabbis—Meir of Regensburg, the Maharal of Prague, and so on—places had little importance in Jewish literature. A people in exile, the Jews lived where they lived and made little of it.

Beginning in the eighteenth century, Hasidism changed that:

> Once the Baal Shem Tov was traveling from the village of Chertri, and when he came to a forest where several Jews had been murdered he stopped for the night to banish the evil spirit of murder from the place. "I mean to sleep," he told his disciples, "but you stay awake and say Psalms, because my Christian servant plans to kill us here." . . . And again, before Nemirov, his servant sought to kill him and confessed. "What made you think such a thing?" asked the Baal Shem Tov. "Don't you know I can't be outwitted?"

The road from Chertri to Nemirov now marked a religious drama. Every Jew who knew this story felt a tremor as he passed the forest in which the Baal Shem Tov had slept—and if he did not know which exact forest it was, every one along the way shone darkly with numinous possibility.

It has been claimed by searchers for Jewish continuity that the earliest modern Hebrew and Yiddish fiction grew out of the genre of the Hasidic tale. This may be, although such fiction would have developed under the impact of Russian and Western culture in any event. The first Hebrew novel ever written, Joseph Perl's wackily brilliant *Revealer of Secrets,* published in 1819, was in fact an anti-Hasidic tale, a wild parody of Hasidic writings. But what Hasidism certainly did do for the Jewish writer in Eastern Europe was to invest the everyday with a significance even greater than Judaism—a religion notorious for its attention to life's minutiae—had given it until then. A Jew had always had a blessing to say for washing his hands, for whatever he ate or drank, for a rainbow or a thunderclap. He did not have one for tying his shoelaces, but who did not know the story of the Hasidic disciple who never took his eyes off his rabbi because even the way the rabbi tied his shoes conveyed profound and holy mysteries?

The belief that all things are pregnant with meaning underpins modern European fictional realism too; and if today we know more about the daily life of the shtetl's Jews than we do about any other Jews before them, this is not only because it is closer to us in time, or because we have photographic and other documentary evidence of it, but because it fully engaged the imagination of the literature that it engendered. When Mendele, in his early Hebrew story, "In the Hidden Place of Thunder," describes with Breughelesque comedy a Sabbath afternoon in the shtetl, its old men and women sitting on their stoops, "sneezing, belching, yawning, and trumpeting their noses, or else munching on chickpeas and beans," its children, "their faces covered with slime," splashing "in the moldy water running out of a broken pipe," its "nursing mother [who] bares a breast for her bawling baby and wipes the juices running from its nose while venting her aches, pains, and peeves on all her enemies," and so on, he is doing what no Jewish writer did before him: painting a broad canvas of a community from which nothing, as it were, is left out. His reported boast that, were the shtetl to vanish, it could be reconstructed in its entirety from his books, was not entirely bravado.

There was something unique about this. Prior to post-World War II America, no other Jewish society in the Diaspora took this kind of interest in itself. It did not happen in Germany, or in England, or in Italy, or in France, let alone among Ladino-speaking Jews in Turkey, Greece, and the Balkans, or among Arabic-speaking Jews in the Middle East. And with it came a degree of self-awareness that was unprecedented too. Unlike our perceptions of other historical Jewish communities, which are often quite different from the ways they viewed themselves, our perceptions of the shtetl, however inconsistent or contradictory, tend to be the shtetl's own. Whether we think of it as a place of great material poverty and spiritual riches; or as a hopeless quagmire of pettiness, zealotry, squalor, and ennui; or as the scene of a mighty struggle for the Jewish soul among religion, revolution, and Zionism; or as the home of a vital secular Yiddish culture tragically nipped in the bud by Hitler and Stalin; or, on the contrary, as an exhausted form of life that had no future, we are saying nothing about it that it did not say volubly about itself.

When we talk about the specialness of the East European Jewish experience, it is this, then, that we are talking about. Other Jewish communities knew extremes of poverty and piety, others experienced the conflict between tradition and modernity, others fought over the same responses to this conflict, had their Orthodox, their Zionists, and their Communists, and were at most a generation or two behind. The Jewish Baghdad of 1940 was in many ways remarkably like the Jewish Warsaw of 1900. It did not, however, have a literature. Today we can read the fiction of Baghdadi-born Israeli writers like Sami Mikha'el and Eli Amir and learn a great deal about it. Yet retrospective literature about a society, even by those who grew up in it, is not the same as the literature *of* a society. The Baghdad of the 1940s is mute. It will always need our interpretation. The shtetl preempts it.

Before it can be rediscovered, the past must be lost. Once, most people could safely assume that the world they grew up in closely resembled their great-grandfathers'. Today we are into roots.

But there are other reasons for the increased interest of Jews in the shtetl and for the growing number of books about it—books that, happily, have joined Mark Zborowski and Elizabeth Herzog's saccharine *Life is with People* (1952), for years the subject's standard, and practically only, text on the library shelves.

One reason has been mentioned: the fact that, starting with the liberalization of the Soviet Union and its satellites in the 1980s, the rural regions of western Russia and Poland have become increasingly accessible. Not that tourism there does not frequently still run to the bizarre. In Kamanetsk-Podolsk—a middle-sized Ukrainian city with a shambles of an old acropolis that, properly restored, could vie in charm with any Italian hill town—my friend and I stayed for a pittance in a three-room suite in the best hotel, with fancy carpets, mirrored walls, armoires full of old porcelain, no hot water, and no elevator to take us and our luggage to the fourth floor. But with many more Jewish travelers visiting and writing about the places from which most American Jews descend, there has developed not only an acquaintance with them, but an entire genre—the shtetlogue—complete with its stock scenes and situations. The successful or disappointed hunt for the family house and graves, the forlornly untended Jewish cemetery, the old synagogue turned into a pizzeria or discotheque, the elderly Gentile recalling Jewish neighbors, the visit to the field, ravine, or ditch in which the town's Jews were shot, the last surviving Jew of Dobroslavka or Podorosk—when so little is left, it cannot but repeat itself.

Concurrently, over fifty years after the Holocaust, the number of Jews who were actually raised in shtetls and remember them is dwindling rapidly; soon the last of them will be gone. This has led to a last-minute rush to record what can still be gotten down, a collective effort ranging from mammoth undertakings like Steven Spielberg's oral interview project at Yale to individual attempts to document the memories and knowledge of the survivors of specific communities.

Nor has the Holocaust itself, as might perhaps have been expected, gradually receded with time to the peripheries of American Jewish consciousness. Rather, it seems to become more central every year. One can only speculate why. The extremely slow wearing-off of the protective numbness of the first post-Holocaust years? The still-festering wound of guilt in an American Jewish community that might have brought more pressure to bear on its leaders to try mitigating or obstructing Hitler's genocide? A liberal identification with the earth's oppressed that, discomfited by American Jewish affluence and Israel's long rule over the Palestinians, has turned to the Holocaust to reassert Jewish victimhood and reclaim a Jewish place, as it were, out of the sun? The shtetl, in any case, accounted for over two-thirds of the Nazis' Jewish victims.

Not unrelatedly, the shtetl is also much on the minds of those assertive proponents of a new Diasporism who have become steadily more vocal on the American Jewish scene. Their disillusion with both Israel and suburban synagogue Judaism has caused them to regard the shtetl—its material simplicity, its religious passion, its human solidarity and strong labor movement, its rich folklore, its humor, even (as demonstrated by the current popularity of *klezmer* bands and Yiddish clubs) its music and its language—as an alternative model of Jewishness. What cannot be brought back to life can, or so it is claimed, be emulated.

Different reasons, different books.

It was for the new Jewish seeker of roots that Chester G. Cohen published his *Shtetl Finder* back in 1989. A gazetteer skimpy in information, it nevertheless provides a helpful list of over 2,000 once heavily Jewish localities in Eastern Europe. Naybikhov, I noticed in planning my trip, was not on it. Dovsk, some twenty miles farther south, the village my father was born in and his family left when he was a year old, was. The *Shtetl Finder* said of it:

> Located east of Rogatchov. 1894—Volf Braginski was local deputy for the Eretz Israel farmers and workers support association. Birthplace of Simon Halkin, born 1899, who moved to the United States in 1914 and was a Hebrew poet and author.

This was curious because my Uncle Simon once wrote some verse about Dovsk that described it as a tiny hamlet compared to Naybikhov:

> Twelve houses and a half—all this
> Was yours, Dovsk, and a station, too;
> A child's isle in an endless blue
> Of sky and of hushed, murmured bliss.

Dovsk, though, turned out to have developed into a sizable town, possessing, besides what looked like its original twelve and a half houses along the Naybikhov road, extensive clumps of Soviet apartment blocks further on. But where was the station? "The nearest railroad runs through Gomel," an old woman told me. But an even older one knew. "It's gone now. Yekaterina slept there." Of course. My aunts and uncles had told me Dovsk stood at the crossroads of the Moscow-Warsaw and Odessa-Petersburg carriage ways. Catherine the Great's horses were changed at the Dovsk relay post while she slept.

So it goes with the voyager to the shtetl: equipped with a map that may contain no more than a single street, house, or landmark, the contribution of a lone photograph or memory salvaged from parents or relatives asked too late or too little—or else, assembled with the help of numerous informants, with a detailed grid of a place that existed sixty or ninety years ago—he matches it against a reality to which it may bear great or small resemblance. He has traveled thousands of miles to somewhere that few or no foreigners ever get to in the hope of seeing not, like the adventurous tourist, what could never have been imagined, but what has always been imagined; so that, drawing near at last, he cannot help feeling, like the South African-born English writer Dan Jacobson upon visiting his grandfather's native Lithuanian town of Varniai in his fine family memoir *Heshel's Kingdom* (1998), "a strange nervousness," soon to be "replaced by a misgiving in nature. What threatened me now was anticlimax merely."

Theo Richmond, also an English Jew and the author of *Konin: One Man's Quest for a Vanished Jewish Community* (1996), had similar forebodings. On the train from Warsaw to his mother's shtetl in Poland, his temples began throbbing insistently. "The pressure had been there since breakfast, a tremulous apprehension, a fear knotting my stomach. And now, getting closer to Konin by the minute, I felt the knot tighten." Suppose he were to discover, as Jacobson feared doing, "that I had come here for nothing?"

Indeed, apart from two Jewish women, one living alone and one married to a Gentile, nothing is what Jacobson found. A few hours after arriving in Varniai, he was ready to depart. "So, like the site of my grandfather's grave," he writes,

> the whereabouts of his house and *shul* remain hidden from me. Should I hunt for them further?... To what end? I find a shrinking in myself from the prospect of hunting around the town and eventually gazing at a street of unplastered brick houses like all the others; or some little apartment block, or group of shops, or clinic, or set of school buildings.

Richmond, on the other hand, found a great deal, not only because Konin, unlike Varniai, was physically unharmed by the war, but because he had spent years interviewing its locatable survivors and meticulously plotting its geography. And yet after spending several days in it, he feels even emptier than Jacobson:

> From the beginning I had known I would have to come here. Now the journey was done. Curiosity was satisfied, an ache assuaged. To say I felt regret leaving this place would be false and sentimental. I felt no emotion. Maybe it was spent. Or maybe the town was releasing me from its grip, for I knew now that it was not the place that held meaning for me but the people who once lived here. Their Konin would stay with me always, a persistent echo.

It was not the place that held meaning but the people: how many pilgrims to the shtetl must have made this ruefully enlightening discovery! A few days after my visit to Naybikhov I attended a conference of Russian Jewish intellectuals in Samara, an industrial city on the Volga. Invited to speak, I told them of my pilgrimage and asked, "How many of you have been to your family's shtetl?" Not one of thirty people raised a hand.

At first this amazed me. Why, they could have gotten there and back in a weekend! But that was precisely the point. Had my father grown up in Scranton or Des Moines, would I have taken a weekend to visit it? Probably not. What might I have expected to see there that I had not seen a thousand times before? Without its Jews, without its literature, their parents or grandparents' shtetl was, for the conference's participants, just another hick town in a landscape—as a survivor of Polish Brańsk says to Eva Hoffman, author of *Shtetl: The Life and Death of a Small Town and the World of Polish Jews* (1997)—"soaked with blood." In the final analysis, so it struck Jacobson and Richmond, too.

No, it is the Jewish life once lived in the shtetl that astounds by its intensity and its variety. Richmond, who laboriously constructs, piece by piece, a diorama of this life in the Konin of the 1920s and '30s, paints a vivid picture: Hasidim and Misnagdim, religious Jews and secular Jews, Yiddish-speaking Jews and Polish-speaking Jews, brainy Jews and tough Jews, Jews who were doctors, lawyers, teachers, tailors, porters, stonemasons, upholsterers, athletes, musicians, Bundists, Communists, Zionists of every stripe, Jews with names like Stein the Cossack, Simcha Schnorrer, Moishe Pot-of-Semolina, and the Red Rebbe, Jews who had Jewish soccer teams, Jewish ballroom dances, and Jewish theater groups performing Ibsen.

Richmond observes that Konin, in western Poland, was in some ways not a typical shtetl. Of it, one informant says, "We were more emancipated than many others in Poland because we were near Germany." But no shtetl was entirely typical; every shtetl was nearer to or farther from somewhere; every shtetl was a place that had evolved in time and was changing. The Konin of 1910, had Richmond found anyone to remember it, was not the Konin of 1930. Nor would the Konin of 1950 or 1990, had the Holocaust not taken place, have been the Konin of 1939.

It is important to keep these obvious truths in mind because, in thinking and speaking about the shtetl, we sometimes treat it as a timeless essence located in an East European Everywhere. This pitfall is avoided by Richmond and Hoffman, as it is by Yaffa Eliach in her newly published *There Once Was a World: A 900-Year Chronicle of the Shtetl of Eishyshok*, a book that follows the development of one community—the Lithuanian town of Eisiskes, some fifty miles south of Vilna, just across the Belorussian border—over nearly a millennium. A native of Eisiskes, Eliach, in her vast ambition to recreate "the vanished Jewish market town I had once called home," has written a compendious work, the equivalent of a one-volume encyclopedia that makes massive use of archives and historical documents no less than oral sources and that deals with every conceivable aspect of a shtetl's life.

But the literature of the shtetl is something else. Here is a passage from Eliach's chapter on Eisyshok's *heders* or schoolrooms:

> With or without the aid of their teachers, the little children who sat in the *heder* from dawn to dusk looked to their imaginations for help in memorizing their lessons, seeking to associate the letters of the *aleph bet* with all the sights and sounds of the world that was just outside their windows, yet ever far away.

And here, in a story written in 1897, is Feierberg's description of a young boy looking out one such window as evening descends in late autumn:

> The mud in the streets seemed neck-high. Beneath an overcast sky, the wind whipped thin drops of rain that beat furiously against the passersby, who walked bent beneath the sufferance of their torn, ragged coats, which were soaked through with rain and grime. I, Hofni,

loved to stand at such times on a bench by the window of the *heder* and look out; I loved to watch the spray and the pockmarks that formed on the surface of the puddles when the rain spattered down on them; I loved to look at the doleful faces of the people as they fought their best with the flagstones and planks of wood that had been strewn about to make footpaths. Mire and muck, figures in silhouette, houses like sepulchers, wet stone, bits of broken glass, snow and rain mixed together —all were engraved on my heart by a grim and terrible hand.

In Feierberg's story, we are *in* the shtetl as we are not in Eliach's book; there is no way her writing could convey as does his the chill, damp feel of a poor Ukrainian town pelted at dusk by a November sleet. But we are not just there, we are also in the consciousness of a boy, and it is a particular consciousness, already gloomy and fearful at a young age and taking what pleasure it can in its gloom. In a word, it is profoundly melancholic.

This is the melancholy that was my father's when made to talk about his childhood, and it is the dominant tone in the Hebrew and Yiddish literature of the age. Pervasive even in works ostensibly comic or defiant, it is largely ignored by today's writers on the shtetl, who view life there in a more a positive light. Their need to mourn the shtetl, or to mobilize it for ideological purposes, or to respect it as an ancestral past, or simply their unawareness of the literature it produced has caused them to overlook the latter.

Although Eliach's chapter on the *heder*, for instance, is a first-rate summation of a shtetl education, one would never guess, despite its section on "Punishment," its mention of the *heder's* onerously long hours and annual months of study, and its statement that "the method of teaching was monotonous and boring," how many unforgivingly bitter accounts of such an education were written by men who felt that their childhoods were stolen or destroyed by it. In hundreds of additional stories, poems, memoirs, and essays, these same men portrayed the shtetl as an asphyxiatingly dreary and provincial place in which the sheer struggle to keep body and soul alive ground its inhabitants brutally down. Considering that some two and a half million of these inhabitants fled to the United States and other countries between the early 1880s and the outbreak of World War I, we must take the literary evidence at face value.

—⟋⟍—

We must also, of course, heed our warning against generalizing across time. It may well be that this period was a particularly bad one for the shtetl's Jews, one in which overpopulation caused by a soaring birth rate and falling death rate that tripled their numbers in the nineteenth century, and the steady growth of the anti-Semitism nourished by this demographic explosion, created an unprecedentedly grim reality.

Certainly, in the immediate aftermath of World War I, life in the shtetl changed for the better—at least once the Ukrainian massacres of 1920-21 were over. (It forms a strange lacuna in contemporary Jewish historical awareness that accounts of anti-Jewish violence in Eastern Europe tend to go straight from czarist pogroms to the Holocaust, skipping over the murder of 100,000 Ukrainian Jews during the Russian Civil War.) To take the case of education again, by the early 1920s, a boy in independent Poland or Lithuania, or even in Soviet Russia, could pick from a wide range of excellent secular Jewish schools that were open to girls as well. The temporary cessation of government anti-Semitism, the introduction of the radio, the cinema, and motor transport, the decline of religious observance and authority, and the growth of movements like Zionism and Bundism with their many social organizations and activities—all this made shtetl life more open, less isolated, and less oppressive, especially for young people who did not have to support a family. That is why Richmond and Hoffman, whose informants grew up in these years, can paint a credible picture of the shtetl as a not unattractive place. Born thirty years later, Feierberg's Hofni might have felt the same way.

But there is a catch to all this that American Jews are only too familiar with. For the freer the atmosphere of the shtetl grew, and the more Jewish creativity was released in it, the more Russianized, Polonized, or Lithuanianized its Jewish residents became. Although comprehensive figures are unavailable, the statistics show that throughout Eastern Europe, the percentage of Jews speaking Yiddish as a first language or at all declined sharply in the interwar years, while the rate of intermarriage, though low by current American standards, steadily rose—two highly accurate gauges of social and cultural assimilation.

It is impossible to know exactly what would have happened to places like Konin and Eisyshok had Polish and Lithuanian Jewry not been destroyed. Had they been shielded from the blight of Communism as well, they certainly would have remained more Jewish than the shtetls of the Soviet Union, which by the late 1930s had practically no public Jewish life left. But today, after six more decades of accelerated assimilation, such life would not necessarily have been more intense or ethnically distinctive, let alone characterized by a vigorous Yiddish culture, than small-town Jewish life in contemporary America.

Moreover, not only was there mass overseas emigration from the shtetl in the years before 1914, and not only did this resume (albeit, due to new immigration restrictions in the United States and Europe, more slowly) after 1918, when it also turned to Palestine, but there was an additional population drain to the large cities of Eastern Europe—places like Warsaw, Vilna, Kovno, Lodz, Lvov, Minsk, and (after the Bolshevik Revolution) Moscow, Kiev, and Leningrad—where Jewish communal structures were less encompassing and assimilation greater.

Richmond's statistics for a middle-sized town like Konin show that its Jewish population peaked at about 3,400 in 1883 and had declined to 2,700 on the eve of the Holocaust. (Some of these 2,700, moreover, must have moved to Konin from small nearby villages that were emptying of their Jews even faster.) More dramatically, since the town itself was growing all this time, the proportion of Jews in it dropped from 52 percent to 23 percent. Everything we know about Jewish demography in the modern age tells us that, left to take its course, this trend would have continued.

The new Diasporists have it backward, then, when they urge us not to be misled by the finality of the Holocaust into thinking that the shtetl was historically doomed, since it was, after all, in its prime at the time of the German invasion. Rather, as an integral, tightly-knit world of secular Yiddishkeit, it *was* doomed by the very forces of modernization that created it in the first place, and that were changing and diminishing it well before the Holocaust. Only the Holocaust's blinding glare permits the illusion that, in its absence, we would see this world still intact before us. What most likely we would have seen in Jewish communities like Konin, Bransk, Eisyshok, and Varniai had they survived to this day would be an East European version of Scranton or Des Moines.

—⟋⟍—

The road from Bychov ran parallel to the Dnieper, which was hidden from sight. At times it was possible to make out far away the low bluffs across the river. We passed fields and forests and an occasional car or wagon but no dwellings.

"My God, it must have been lonely here," said my friend.

Sheep were grazing by a pylon at the entrance to Naybikhov. The village ran along the main road in two rows of painted wood houses, each with one story and two windows facing the street, a triangular attic beneath a gabled tin roof, and a picket fence.

I asked Sergei, our driver, to continue to the village's end. When we reached it we drove slowly back, looking for a bench with women on it. In front of every house in rural Ukraine and Belarus is a bench, and on it sometimes sit kerchiefed women, and it was these women we had learned to ask whatever it was we wanted to know.

We found three of them. Although they asked no questions themselves, their scrutiny was intense. Halkin? Galkin? They pronounced the name in both its Belorussian and Russian fashions. No, they had never heard it. Nor did I have any chance of finding my father's house. The village was destroyed in heavy fighting in the war and rebuilt. The Russians were pushed across the river by the first German attack, then counterattacked, then were driven across the river again.

So the man I had met in Israel had been right. Still, Naybikhov did not look rebuilt. It looked old. Its rebuilders had rebuilt it the only way they knew, the way their fathers and grandfathers had built, trimming the wood in the same patterns, painting it the same colors. That was a comfort.

Not enough of one, of course. And yet I had been prepared for this. Given the years since 1914, when my father's family left for America, finding any trace of it would have been miraculous. I wandered off to look for a view of the river.

The houses on the hill behind the main street were less brightly painted. Some were plain log cabins like the one my father grew up in. The Dnieper was below. Not the huge river I had seen in Kiev, to which it came swollen by tributaries, it was nonetheless wide, flowing softly between grassy banks.

When I returned to the street, my companions were talking to a heavyset man. He had the florid face of a drinker and smelled like one although it was not yet noon. Anatoly. Halkin? Galkin? Anatoly had an idea. There was an old man—the oldest in the village—he was ninety-four years old, this old man—and he lived in that house over there—no, that one, the red one with the blue trim. He was the person to ask. If anyone would know, it was him.

It took some banging on his blue window frames to get Mikhail Yosifovich Skobov, who was a bit hard of hearing, to come to his front gate. Once there, however, he stood plumb-line straight, hardly leaning on the cane that he held with the proud, quiet bearing of a man who has shouldered his end of life squarely. A battalion commander in the war. Shaggy eyebrows and high cheekbones like my Uncle Simon's. Halkin? Galkin? He remembered no such family. But in 1914 he was only ten.

Well, that was that, then.

And then I remembered something myself. One of the few things my father had told me about Naybikhov was that his family had a next-door neighbor, a man named Potap. Potap was their *shabbes goy*, the Christian who performed tasks forbidden to Jews on the Sabbath like lighting fires and shoveling snow. He was paid in vodka, and one Sabbath, having drunk more of his pay than usual, he pointed to the large knife that hung on the wall—my father's father was a slaughterer—and said good-naturedly, "You *zhidi* are fine people. Someday I'll take that knife and cut all your throats."

That should have been quite enough, it now struck me, to make any small boy melancholic.

"Potap?" said Mikhail Yosifovich. I had omitted the throat-cutting incident from my account. "A devil of a fellow! I'll show you where his house was."

He took us down a lane to a green hillside overlooking the river. There was no sign it had ever been lived on, no ruins or foundations. "Here." He halted by a circular depression in the ground. "We called this Potap's pool. It was a carp pond that he made."

The river flowed below and disappeared around a bend. Although I did not know if my father's house had been to the left or right of Potap's, the scene was just as he had described it. No, not just: the slope to the river, down which two fishermen, a father and his son, were now descending with their poles, was not at all steep. It was gentle and inviting. But that was what a child's memory would have made of it.

Wild flowers grew in the grass. Further on was a hedge of blossoming lilacs.

So this was it. This was where we had come from.

"I've never seen you look so happy," said my friend.

Actually, it seemed to me that I had been crying. There was a rusty tin can on the ground. "I'd like a shovel," I said.

Sergei brought a shovel from somebody's yard, and I dug up a bit of gray, sandy soil, roots and all, and filled the can with it. Then I walked to the river.

—⚏—

Two goats were tied to a pole halfway down. They circled one way and then the other as I approached. Nearer the water, in the hushed bliss, a horse cropped grass on a knoll.

By the water's edge, pulled up on the bank, was a rowboat. I knew that boat. It was Gnessin's.

Uri Nisan Gnessin. Born in Gomel, a rabbi's son. Dead at thirty-two, in 1913, of heart disease. In a novella of his, a man lies at night by the Dnieper, on the hilltop above which some young people have been sitting around a campfire. Now, as they make their way down to the riverside, one of their voices reminds him of an old love's:

> It was remarkable. What, suddenly, had happened—
> what had happened to make his heart ache, ache as hotly
> as it did long ago in the frozen glitter of the moon?... No
> one was left on the hilltop; but from the gulley winding
> down to the water through the blackness between the
> hills, a murmur of voices reached him. Subdued, it drew
> near until he made out, assured and daintily affected,
> the speech of a woman.... There: already at the side
> of the empty boat that stood waiting on the bank, its
> crossed oars aslant, she sprang into it. Its sides splashed in
> the smooth water, splashed and splashed again, the oars
> knocking in the great silence of the night. Had his soul
> heard it all in a dream it had dreamed long ago?

1998

Rooting for the Indians

S hortly before my ninth birthday, in the spring of 1948, as the
British were preparing to leave Palestine and let the Jews and Arabs
fight it out between themselves, I became a Cleveland Indians fan.
Although I was born and raised on the West Side of Manhattan and had
never been in Cleveland in my life, this struck me as no impediment.
A new enthusiast for professional sports, I wanted to be different from
the Yankee, Giant, and Dodger fans around me. When the major league
teams went south for spring training, I drew up a list of them and casually picked a favorite. The two teams whose names I liked best were the
Indians and the Pittsburgh Pirates, the catchy alliteration of which appealed to me. In the end, though, I settled on the Indians, lighting a torch
for Cleveland that burned bright until, sometime in adolescence, my
interest in baseball flickered out almost as suddenly as it had caught fire.

Yet perhaps not so casually after all. Jerusalem lay under siege while
I followed the news from a distance, its lifeline of convoys ambushed on
mountain roads. Was not choosing the second exile of being a Cleveland
fan in New York (I was never to encounter another) like the vain attempt
of a neurotic sufferer to lighten his burden by broadening its base? And
had not the Indians had their land stolen by the white man just as mine
had been stolen by the Roman, the Arab, and the Englishman? Ever since
I saw my first Western, roped into a boisterous children's section that

cheered at every red man toppled from his horse, I had rooted for them with the instinctive sympathy of like for like.

My cousin Jonathan, who lived a few blocks away, was a Yankees fan, adding to the rivalry with which we played slug and Chinese with a spaldeen on the sidewalk. (You won't find it in any dictionary, but there was no New York boy in those years who couldn't have told you that a spaldeen, made by the same Spalding company that manufactured baseballs, was the pink core of a tennis ball and the regulation playing ball of the city's streets.) Scared of the Irish boys who came looking for fights from across Broadway, we mostly went in for indoor sports. In one of these contests, a heavyweight boxing match featuring my cousin, who was a half foot taller and forty pounds heavier than I was, as Joe Louis, he knocked me, Jersey Joe Walcott, out for the count on my bedroom floor with a gash that required stitches.

When our fisticuffs were stopped by the downstairs neighbors knocking on the radiator pipes, we took out the dice. Long before the advent of the binary computer we had discovered that, by combining the values of two randomly rolled cubes, each with one to six dots on its sides, and aided by a Monopoly board, we could represent practically any athletic event: track-and-field meets, tennis matches, seven-day bike races, the Kentucky Derby, nine-inning baseball games. These we broadcast live, one of us assuming the role of announcer while the other supplied the sound effects. The professional version of this old ticker-tape technique, sometimes still used in those years when New York teams played in far-off places like Chicago or St. Louis, could be heard nightly on Marty Glickman's *Today's Baseball*, which I never missed. We were in the last glory days of radio, no more aware of their rapidly approaching end than were the passengers of the great nineteenth-century clipper ships of the coming of the oceanic steamer.

One day the Irish boys caught us.

We were walking home on a Saturday morning from the junior service at the Anshei Chesed synagogue on West End Avenue and 100th Street when I spotted a gang of them coming toward us. Taking advantage of my size I turned to my cousin and said, "Look, I'm smaller and faster than you, so I'll run for help." And without waiting for an answer I was weaving through the traffic and heading for the other side of West End.

Too clever for my own good! No sooner had I gained what I thought was the safe ground of the opposite sidewalk than I found myself surrounded by more young Irishmen, three or four urchins led by a freckled commander. I was trapped—and without my cousin's broad back to hide behind.

"Hey, kid! What's your name?"

"Harold," I lied.

"How come you're all dressed up?"

I bit my lip.

"You Jewish, Harold?"

"No," I said. Which would have been bad enough had I not gilded the lily by adding, "I'm Catholic."

"Yeah?" A flicker of interest tinged with disappointment ran through the circle of boys. "What church d'ya go to?"

What church? There was a big one on Amsterdam Avenue and 96th Street—or was it Protestant?

"I don't go to church," I said. "I mean yet. I'm new in the neighborhood."

There was a skeptical silence. Clearly, the first thing a Catholic did in a new neighborhood was go to church. The commander asked:

"Where d'ya go to school?"

I went to a Jewish day school called Ramaz on the East Side.

"The Ramsey School," I said. "On Lexington Avenue."

"There ain't no such place," a boy said.

"There is too," said another. "It's across the park."

"Alright, Harold," said the commander. "Let's see what's in your pockets."

I was in luck. Because it was the Sabbath, I didn't have a wallet or any money. All I had was…my yarmulka. I was done for.

"Come on, turn 'em inside out."

I turned them inside out.

"That one too."

Out it came.

"What's this?" He held it up by the button, the cotton lining bellying down from the black satin top.

"It's a handkerchief," I said.

"That ain't no handkerchief," said a boy. "It's a bra for his titties."

Guffaws.

"It's a handkerchief," I insisted, fighting back the tears.

"If it's a handkerchief," the commander said, handing it back, "let's see you blow your nose in it."

I blew my nose in it.

"Harder."

I blew harder.

Solomonic, he looked around. There were no more questions. "Okay, Harold," he said, patting my head, "you can go now. Tell your momma to buy you a nice white handkerchief. And don't let us catch you again without you been to church and seen the Father."

—⟋⟍—

I was free, the sickening taste of self-betrayal in my mouth. It was the bitterest moment of my life, and it would have made a Zionist of me on the spot, as the Dreyfus case had made one of Theodor Herzl, had I not already been one by parentage, education, and conviction. In Palestine it could never have happened. There I would have stood tall, even if I were hanged for it by the British like the Irgun fighter Dov Gruner.

Of course, Jews could fight back in New York, too. Hadn't I heard of a place called Borough Park, where Jewish gangs roamed the streets beating up Christians? But Borough Park was a mythical kingdom to me, its Jewish gangs as distant as the Ten Lost Tribes who lived beyond the Mountains of Darkness. It would no more have occurred to me that I could get there by subway than that I could take the IRT line to the far bank of the Sambatyon River, whose deadly torrent kept the tribes from being reached.

Palestine was real. I knew the map of it better than I knew the map of Manhattan, could draw it with my eyes shut—its gently curving coastline that fish-hooked at Haifa Bay, its three lakes strung in order of size on the thread of the River Jordan, its wide-hipped Negev with its toe in the Red Sea. Among my most precious possessions was a viewer with a box of slides, given me as a birthday present, which showed me, when held to the light, Tel Aviv and Jerusalem, the Plain of Sharon and the Valley of Jezreel, in colors brighter than any around me. In times of sorrow I solaced myself with these scenes like a thumb sucker, braced by the sight of orange groves and cypress trees, the Western Wall and Rachel's Tomb. Their dirt had clung to my ancestors' feet in ancient times—the same dirt I had once seen in my grandmother's apartment on the day she had beckoned me mysteriously into her bedroom, which smelled of heavy drapes and nitroglycerin pills, opened the bottom drawer of a chest, pulled out a cloth bag no bigger than a change purse, and confided in a whispered mixture of Yiddish and English that she would be buried with its contents, leaving me too embarrassed to ask how even such a small thing as herself could fit into so little soil.

The map I could draw was that of the British Mandate, which I had the chance to study whenever my family sat down to eat, since it appeared on the blue and white Jewish National Fund box that stood on a sideboard in our kitchen. This box had a slot at the top big enough for a half dollar and said "Fight for a Free Palestine" in flowing script; on Friday afternoons, before the Sabbath began, we emptied our pockets of coins and dropped them into it. It was still only half full when the state of Israel was declared in mid-May, after which the Fight for a Free Palestine went on being waged in our kitchen long after the slogan itself had fallen, like a captured flag, into enemy hands—the major Arab victory, as it turned out, of the 1948 war.

But now I became more interested in other maps: those of the fighting that appeared in *The New York Times*, showing the clashing armies as curved arrows with boxes on their tails, crescent moons in them for the Arabs, stars of David for the Jews. Haifa and Jaffa had fallen to the Jews, the Egyptian advance on Tel Aviv had been stopped, the Syrians, too, were held at Degania, but Jerusalem was still besieged and all attempts to dislodge the Arab Legion from its blocking position at Latrun had ended in failure. I took Latrun myself one June night while lying in bed, filling my room with the *tyuuu-tyuuu* of rifle fire, the *ta-ta-ta-ta-ta* of machine guns, and the *pkkhhhkhhh* of heavy mortars before bringing in an old British Spitfire for a strafing run to drown out the laughter from the living room where my parents were entertaining.

Things were off to a good start in the American League, too. The Indians, who had finished fourth the year before, were battling the Yankees, the Boston Red Sox, and the Philadelphia Athletics for first place. Yet in the night games I played, imitating the sound of a roaring crowd with a throaty *hrrrrhrr* and the crack of a bat with a cluck of my tongue, they were never sure winners, for while I was pitcher, batter, fielder, and ball all rolled into one, none of these was under my control any more than were the dice I threw with my cousin. As my eyes followed the loop of a fly ball to right field or the dotted line of a grounder to third, I no more knew what would happen next, whether the Indians' Allie Clark would make the catch or Ken Keltner would throw the batter out, than I had known whether Latrun would be taken until I saw its Arab defenders break and run.

Bored in school, I also played day games. Toward the end of the school year, my fourth-grade teacher Mrs. Olitsky called my mother to say she feared I had a nervous disorder since I was twitching my face, rolling my eyes, and making strange noises in class. I was hurried to the doctor, who pronounced me physically fit but recommended I see a psychologist. Luckily, it was the end of June. The psychologists were going away on vacation, and I was about to be sent off for the first time to summer camp.

If the miniature Zion in the Poconos to which we were bused from New York resembled in some ways the enlightened dictatorship that most summer camps aspire to be, it was in other ways a full-fledged police state, its tyranny meant to ensure that the campers spoke only Hebrew during their waking hours and, if possible, in their sleep. This was made clear on the first evening. Gathered at sunset around a pole with two flags, the blue and white one above the red white and blue, we were handed our copies of a small brown English-Hebrew dictionary, compiled under the guidance of the camp's director. This, we were told, would suffice for our daily needs. Henceforth, at this time of day, every day, a letter Ayin, which stood for Ivrit, meaning Hebrew in Hebrew, would be awarded or denied every camper on the basis of how much of the language—or how little English, itself now a prima facie offense—he or she had used in the preceding twenty-four hours. Campers would be graded by their scores, the ultimate prize being a sweatshirt with an Ayin on its front, which we could see being sported like varsity letters by the veterans of previous years. And since this incentive might prove insufficient, a penal code existed as well, whereby a camper or bunk might be docked from an activity, or assigned extra clean-up duty, should the quota of Ayins not be met.

In practice, as we were to find out, no counselor having enough ears to keep track of every word his campers uttered, the entire system depended on an army of lookouts, informers, and *agents provocateurs*. It was also not free of counselors who might be prevailed upon to award an unmerited Ayin or even a whole bunkload of them, much as a Soviet factory manager might fake production figures or fabricate a heroic worker for the sake of his career. Like any totalitarian regime, my new environment functioned by means of a fine balance of repression and deceit, each needed to keep the other in check.

I thrived in it. Not only was I a better Hebraist than most boys my age, but English, now that it was outlawed, assumed a cleansing flavor I had previously savored only in dirty words. In a society where speaking one's native language was a crime, friendship was—had to be—a gesture of unequivocal trust. How lackluster all ordinary relationships would later seem as compared with the solidarity I shared that summer with my bunkmates, whose names and faces I still remember: Freddy Ashkenazi... Boruch Dunn...Roger Fein...Sammy Weinstein...West Virginia.

West Virginia's real name I probably never knew. He was one of a small number of boys who hailed from beyond the Eastern Seaboard and whose names—Omaha, Alabama, Big Detroit and Little Detroit, Wyoming, Kansas City—testified to the impression made on us by their curious accents and the fact that Jews lived in such places at all. What drew me especially to West Virginia was that he was a Cleveland fan, and a luckier one than I was, for he had seen the Indians play. It was he who taught me how Bob Feller went into his windup, kicking his left foot almost over his head; instructed me in the hook slide of Larry Doby, the first Negro player in the American League; and showed me the jack-in-the-box crouch, promptly appropriated by me for my own, from which Lou Boudreau, the Indians' shortstop-manager, batted.

He gave me another lesson, too. One evening we were walking through the woods that bordered the camp grounds, arguing whether Feller or Bob Lemon should start against the White Sox in Chicago the next day, when in the path ahead of us two fallen logs rose hastily, snatched up various articles of clothing from the ground, and disappeared into the dusk. Counselors!

West Virginia was the first to reach the scene, from which he held up an abandoned trophy, a double-coned object whose unfamiliar smell of honeyed sweat made me swoon.

"What is it?" I asked.

"A bra," he said.

The Irish bastards!

The two of us had fled into the woods to seek refuge from the dancing that was held every Friday evening in the long mosquito-ridden hour between Sabbath services and dinner. Boys in white shirts and creased white ducks with buttoned flies, girls in blouses and skirts, we were shepherded from prayer to a field beneath the dining room where a fat Israeli dance counselor made us join hands in a circle. A limp semblance of one having been achieved, we commenced a round of galopades, in the most mortifying of which a boy or girl had to skip within the enclosure we had formed and choose from it a member of the opposite sex, whereupon the two circled together hand in hand until the chooser retired and it was the chosen's turn to choose.

Y'mina, y'mina,
Smola, smola,

"Rightward, rightward, leftward, leftward," the fat counselor sang as the circle revolved in one direction and its orbiting couple in the other, the boys roughly pushing each other into it to avoid being chosen themselves. Amended by them to

Y'mean her, y'mean her,
Smell her, smell her,

this caused the girls to shrink back with the already martyred expression of their sex.

These Sabbath eve dances, in which we did the jigs and hops that had been popular among the *halutzim*, the pioneers in Palestine, a generation earlier, much as the quadrille and the reel continued to be danced in the colonies of the New World long after being abandoned in the mother countries of the Old, were but one of many activities designed to transmute the base alloy of exilic existence into a higher reality. The entire camp was one vast symbolic enterprise, a *minutus mundus* of arcane correspondences, starting with the director himself who, with his khaki shorts and cotton-candy puffs of graying hair on either side of a balding head, could have doubled for David Ben-Gurion were it not for the thoughtless omission of a paunch.

The wooden cabins in which we lived were not ordinary bunks but collective settlements, kibbutzim and moshavim bearing the names of Nahalal, Beit-Alfa, Tel-Hai, and Ein-Harod. The walks we took every week around the lake, at the far end of which we stopped to eat the peanut butter and jelly sandwiches we had prepared after breakfast to give the kitchen staff the day off, were hikes by the Sea of Galilee. The barren patch of ground behind the basketball court in which, by some reverse miracle of nature, even weeds would not grow, was not just a vegetable garden but a desert tract of the Negev magically transported to the green hills of Pennsylvania. In response to our complaints about being brought to this vest-pocket wasteland to tend the radishes and cucumbers we had planted during the first week of camp and seen no subsequent sign of, the gardening counselor—a mournful man with a limp and a Russian accent who sometimes accompanied us on his harmonica while we scratched aimlessly at the ground—could only repeat incomprehensible phrases about the sanctity of labor and the return to the soil. Years later I came across these very words in the writings of A.D. Gordon, the great apostle of Labor Zionism. Once recovered from my impression that he had plagiarized our gardener, I was delighted to discover in them the moral of a parable over whose bare text I had sweated unfruitfully the summer I was nine.

The hieroglyphics of our existence extended to the athletic field as well, where we were encouraged to play soccer, the Jewish national sport. Yet this game proved to be based on so perverse a conception of the human body, treating the feet as though they were hands and the hands as vestigial tails, that we soon broke out our bats and gloves. Even so, however, every moment of the games we played had to be conducted in Hebrew; the only permissible exceptions were words not found in the little brown dictionary, which had a whole section of baseball terms.

It was during one of these games that I struck out and was bounced by my counselor Sammy Sonnenschein, who was umpiring behind home plate. The count was two and two as I coiled myself into my Lou Boudreau stance and waited for the pitch. It was low and outside.

"*Kadur!*" called Sammy. Three and two. The next pitch was down the middle but even lower. I flung away my bat and headed for first base.

"*Hakhta'ah!*" Sammy cried. Strike three. I couldn't believe my ears.

"Fug you!" I said—in English. My mispronunciation of the word was a consequence of having been reading Sammy's copy of Norman Mailer's newly published *The Naked and The Dead*, sneaking it from the shelf above his bed and returning it with each finished installment. Unaware that its spelling was a concession to the censor, I assumed it to be the correct form of a word I had been garbling all my life.

"You're out of the game!" Sammy said. "And you've lost your Ayin for the day."

I was resigned to the heave-ho; it happened in the major leagues for less. But the Ayin was unfair. I had spoken more Hebrew on the field than the rest of my team combined.

"So how do you say it?" I challenged.

"Say what?"

"What I just said. Show me in the dictionary."

Sammy Sonnenschein scratched his head. The fat Israeli dance counselor was unavailable for consultation. "You little son of a bitch!" he said—in English too. That evening around the flagpole I was given my Ayin, extending my winning streak. The sweatshirt would soon be mine.

My Hebrew also entitled me sometimes to broadcast the daily news bulletin that was featured every evening in the dining room. After reviewing the situation in the Middle East, where an Arab-Israeli truce was precariously holding, and announcing such events as the Soviet blockade of Berlin and the nomination for the presidency of Henry Wallace by the Progressive party, I read out the day's baseball scores to a tumultuous audience. First came the National League. Then, ha-Liga ha-Amerikayit:

Ha-Yankim mi-New York 11, ha-Humim mi-St. Louis 2.

Ha-Garbayim ha-Adumim mi-Boston 4, ha-N'merim mi-Detroit 1.

Ha-Indiyanim mi-Cleveland 2, ha-Atletikayim mi-Philadelphia 0.

The White Sox and the Senators were rained out. It was the middle of August and the American League was witnessing the closest pennant race in its history, with New York, Boston, Cleveland, and Philadelphia all still within a few games of each other.

Yet whatever enduring fame I acquired that summer came not as an announcer but as an actor. Alone among the boys in my bunk, I was cast in a dramatic pageant staged by the waterfront in the last week of camp. Its subject was the Jewish state's heroic struggle to defend itself against seven invading armies, and I had the part of a Haganah intelligence scout who, having penetrated enemy lines disguised as an Arab, appears out of the darkness to inform his comrades of an imminent attack. Cloaked in a white sheet, a checked towel on my head, I waited for my cue by the dim flicker of torches and shooting stars. A mournful flute played the hymn of the Palmach.

The music stopped; I was on. Gathering the folds of my sheet, I stepped onto the dock, thinking it was the wooden ramp that led to the stage, and plunged into the lake. As the Arabs were beaten back without benefit of my warning, I was fished from the water like a slice of wet bread, comforted by the stagehands that my spectacular entrance would be remembered long after all else was forgotten.

—⚏—

I came home from camp with my Ayin sweatshirt and a fever and was put to bed, surrounded by pillows, sucking candies, the morning *Times*, the afternoon *Post*, and a Howard Pease sea novel brought home from the public library by my father. Mostly I listened to the radio, an old wooden table model with leather knobs and a large, fibrous speaker that was placed near me on a serving cart and tolled my day more faithfully than church bells. In the morning there was *The John Gambling Show*, *The Breakfast Hour*, *Queen for a Day*, *Quick as a Flash*, *Strike It Rich*, and *The Sixty-Four-Dollar Question*, followed by *Luncheon at Sardi's* and my own pillow-propped lunch, after which came a baseball game: Mel Allen and the Yankees on WINS, Red Barber and the Dodgers on WHN, or Russ Hodges and the Giants on WMCA at the bottom of the listening dial. (Ah, gentlemen, where is the CD that will bring back to me your voices? Yours, Russ Hodges, as crackling and warm as a log fire; yours, Red Barber, as purringly sly as a cat's; and yours, Mel Allen, Caruso of the diamond, golden tenor of my youth, whose tones had more body and flavor than the beer they promoted and a milder, smokier aroma than the cigar they deigned to praise!)

After the game, if I hadn't dozed off during the seventh-inning stretch, came the last of the afternoon soap operas, *Lorenzo Jones* or *Mary Noble, Backstage Wife*, followed by the early-evening thrillers: *The Green*

Hornet, Captain Midnight, Sky King, Jack Armstrong, Sergeant Preston of the Yukon. Dinner was brought on a tray while I listened to the news commentaries delivered with the evangelical gloom of Gabriel Heatter or the patrician smugness of Fulton Lewis, Jr. At seven there was *Today's Baseball,* followed from out of the thrilling days of yesteryear by *The Lone Ranger* and afterward, if I was lucky, by a night game.

Then, however, the lights were turned out and the radio was returned to its place in the corner. I had to get out of bed and tiptoe across the room, where I crouched with my ear to the speaker in the orange glow of the tubes at the back of the set, ready to shut it off and dive back into bed like a runner beating a pick-off throw if I heard my parents' footsteps in the hallway. How, then, did I allow myself to be caught off-base by my mother, who came to check that I hadn't thrown off my blankets in my sleep and found me standing in my bare feet, my cough not yet gone, the telltale tubes still fading in the dark?

It was because the Indians, neck and neck in the homestretch with the Yankees and Red Sox, were playing New York in Cleveland; because, down six to four in the bottom of the ninth, they had loaded the bases with one out; and because…but I would have to wait for the morning paper to learn the outcome. Cleveland had scored one more run before switch-hitting Dale Mitchell, batting right-handed against lefty reliever Joe Page, grounded to Rizzuto at short to end the game. The Indians had slipped to third place.

After that summer, I didn't go back to the junior service. From then on I joined my father on Saturday mornings on a mile-long walk to the synagogue of the Jewish Theological Seminary on Broadway and 122nd Street, where he taught.

We were accompanied by his friend and colleague, the Bible scholar H.L. Ginsberg, who lived nearby. While the two of them argued about Ginsberg's latest proposals for emending verses in the Bible, which he regarded as an inexhaustible compilation of scribal errors, I concentrated on the cracks between the paving squares on the sidewalk, alternately avoiding or stepping on each of them, or quizzed myself on the cars parked along Broadway. Although you could walk the entire distance in those days without coming across a foreign make, there were, beside those of the Big Three manufacturers, numerous automobiles as extinct today as the woolly mammoth: Packards, Hudsons, Nashes, Kaiser-Frazers, Crosleys, and Studebakers, the last with its 1948 model whose back looked so like its front that drivers were said to have climbed into the rear seat before noticing the absence of a steering wheel.

Ginsberg was a nervous man with a rapid-fire stutter that disappeared when he sang, which may have been why, despite a shrill, reedy voice, he was compassionately tolerated on the High Holy Days as the synagogue's cantor for the *shaharit*, the opening part of the morning liturgy. In the second row in which, when he wasn't at the lectern, he sat with my father alongside other senior faculty members like the homiletics teacher Max Arzt, the medieval Hebrew literature professor Shalom Spiegel, the rabbinics scholar Max Kadushin, and the theologian Abraham Joshua Heschel, he was known as "Blitz" because of the speed with which he led the prayers.

These were my father's social cronies. The third row was occupied by junior faculty, while the first was mostly empty, its long pew reserved for four eminences: the Seminary's chancellor Louis Finkelstein, the renowned Judaica scholar Louis Ginzberg, the great Talmudist Saul Lieberman, and the legendary librarian and bibliographer Alexander Marx. A tall man with twinkling eyes and a goatish beard on which he chewed, Marx sat in front of me and sometimes playfully spun around to grab and twist my ear. He had served, I was told, in the German cavalry in World War I, which further heightened his stature in my eyes.

Lieberman, who sat next to him, was my uncle, the husband of my mother's sister. A Lithuanian Jew with a no-nonsense attitude toward religion, he once, when I was a college student, startled me by saying that he considered prayer a waste of time, since it interrupted his study of Talmud and he had nothing to say to God. I did not contradict him by remarking that, standing diagonally behind him as a boy on Yom Kippur, the only day of the year on which he covered his head with his prayer shawl, I had glimpsed beneath it the tears running down his cheeks.

Had he believed on that occasion that his fate for the coming year was about to be sealed in the great Book of Life? Until recently I had conceived of this volume as a heavy ledger with lines ruled in gold. Now, old enough to understand that it was a metaphor, an all-knowing God having no need to keep records like a school principal, I asked myself how, if God knew in advance what would happen to me, I could have any choice but to do what He knew I would. Why reward my good deeds or punish my bad ones if I only performed them because I had to?

I did not know that, from Augustine to Spinoza, there wasn't a philosopher who had not wrestled with this problem—that in fact there wasn't a major philosophical question that most children had not asked themselves by the age of ten, after which it was a matter of either refining or forgetting it. The best I could do was hypothesize that, if my actions originated as thoughts in God's mind, He had left me a thin margin of freedom, just as the players in the baseball games that took place in my head retained the ability to surprise me.

The Indians had bounced back from their loss to the Yankees and were now going into the last game of the season on October 3 a game ahead of the Red Sox. They had only to beat fifth-place Detroit to win the title and open the World Series on the sixth against the Boston Braves. This was perfect timing. The Jewish New Year fell on the fourth and fifth, and I would not have to miss an inning.

But it was not to be. Cleveland lost, shut out by Hal Newhouser, while the Red Sox beat the Yankees. The season had ended in an unprecedented dead heat. A one-game playoff would be held in Boston the next day.

At dinner that night, my father recited the blessings over the wine and hallah, which we ate dipped in honey to make the new year sweet. A guest from Israel had brought a pomegranate, a first fruit from the Jewish state, in a diplomatic pouch, and my father's voice shook as he held it and said, "Blessed art Thou O Lord our God, King of the Universe, who hath given us life and sustained us and brought us to this day." Our guest showed me how to eat it, scooping the blood-red seeds from its rind and spitting them out when sucked clean of their flesh. "I remember one Rosh Hashanah," he reminisced, "when I was a *halutz* in a work gang on the Afula-Tiberias road. We didn't work that day, but we didn't pray, either. Although we all came from religious homes, work had become the only prayer we knew. We were sitting outside our tent, not knowing what to do with ourselves, when I picked up my violin and started to play. First I played all the sad tunes I could think of, and then I played the quiet ones, and then I played the happy ones. Before I knew it we were all dancing on the Afula-Tiberias road."

The service in the Seminary's synagogue the next morning was a lengthy one. I kept looking at my watch. Apart from the prayers, there was the blowing of the shofar to draw things out. The shofar blower had a bad day, producing an arpeggio of false starts and muffled squeaks for every true note that he sounded, wiping his mouth with his jacket sleeve and peering down the opening of his horn as though expecting to find a dead mouse. As soon as the prayers ended, I asked my father for the key to our apartment and raced home ahead of my parents.

I ran the whole mile, arriving in the bottom of the second inning with the score tied one to one, in plenty of time for Ken Keltner's three-run homer in the top of the fourth. After that, it was the Indians all the way. Boudreau homered twice, the knuckleballing Gene Bearden kept Boston at bay, and Cleveland took the game and the pennant. As Keltner charged Birdie Tebbetts's grounder in the ninth and fired it to Eddie Robinson for the last out, I pounded a triumphant fist into my palm to make the sound of ball meeting glove. Then I ran to the window of my room and flung it open. In the waning autumn light I watched the dusk-crazed pigeons circle and wheel over the buildings between West End Avenue and Riverside Drive, the chrome-colored sunset glancing off their pale wings.

Given that it took the Indians six more years to win their next pennant, during which they broke my heart every summer, you could call it beginner's luck.

—m—

The new year started off with Cleveland winning the World Series four games to two, the last of them on the day before Yom Kippur.

Though not yet required to by Jewish law, I decided to fast. Now that I was attending an adult synagogue, I would do as the adults did.

I was to regret it. Hunger came and went in sharp spasms, leaving me now grim and resolute, now drained and past caring. Each time the congregation recited the *Al Het*, the public confession of sins arranged in alphabetical order by some liturgical bureaucrat, I beat my breast until it hurt. The roster was endless, interminable; to each sin, whether guilty or not, I had to confess with the other defendants as though in a purge trial. And as if hunger were not torture enough, I was made to rise to my feet each time the Ark was opened and stand there on stiff, weary legs as though I were in a courtroom whose judge kept leaving it on other business and returning.

Although the *shaharit* was tossed off at his usual pace by H.L. Ginsberg, even he could not make it any shorter. Then my father, the Seminary's regular Torah reader, chanted the day's portion about the scapegoat sent to die in the wilderness; in the notes of his delivery, famed for its exactitude, there was a great sadness. H.L. was relieved and a new cantor took his place for the Musaf, the next round in the day-long devotions; fresh from the bullpen, he lingered over each page of the prayer book as if in hopes of wearing God out. The airless synagogue had a smell like that of rotting leaves—the debris, so I imagined, of fallen prayers.

Minhah, the afternoon service, was recited and with it the story of Jonah, who bolted in a panic from God to end up in the belly of a fish. Then the entire congregation rose to its feet once more for Ne'ilah, the closing service of the day. One last time the list of sins was recited, sin by alphabetical sin. Now I took no part in it but listened numbly, overwhelmed by my physical ordeal and the magnitude of my iniquity, my sole concern being to stave off the impending levitation of my body. The prayers unfolded in turn: the *shemoneh esrei* was behind us, *avinu malkenu, aleinu*, the final *kaddish*, and the congregation repeated seven times "the Lord is God," each repetition more ragged than the one before, like breakers collapsing on the shore.

Then the shofar was blown—this time loud and clear—and everyone exclaimed hoarsely, "Next year in Jerusalem!" while hurriedly putting away his prayer shawl. It was—I knew it, half-dead though I was—the most sensible prayer of the day.

2007

Either/Or

If we can't stay eternally youthful for ourselves—"for ever panting and for ever young," as Keats put it in his "Ode on a Grecian Urn"—we can at least stay that way for one another by not going to reunions. Such was my first thought when the email invitations began arriving last winter. They came from former classmates at the two New York schools I went to as a boy, the Ramaz School and the Bronx High School of Science, and both were for the same 50th-year gathering. This was because Ramaz, at whose elementary school I studied from 1947 through 1952, when I finished eighth grade, had a high school I didn't attend. The high school class I would have belonged to graduated in 1956, the same year as did my class at Bronx Science—and since half a century later I still seemed to be considered an honorary member of it, I was included in the guest list.

The two events were of different sizes. My class at Ramaz—the school's name had been formed from the first three initials of Rabbi Moses Zevulun Margolies, the grandfather-in-law of New York rabbi Joseph Lookstein, who founded it in 1937—had some thirty students; my class at Bronx Science, 750. At the Science reunion I might have known few people. At the Ramaz one I would have known almost everyone. Yet since the I who would have known them was born, as it were, in the act of leaving them, they belonged to a period of my life now hardly recognizable to myself. In the end, I went to neither affair. Let us remember and be remembered as we were.

The fact that Ramaz, in the late 1940s and early '50s, was so small, and that there were, to the best of my knowledge, only two or three other Jewish private schools like it in all of New York City, and probably not a dozen in the entire United States, says something about the strides that American Jewish education has made since then. Of course, in those days there were also more old-fashioned places in New York like Mesifta Torah Ve-Da'as, or the Talmudical Academy, which were halfway between a traditional East European yeshiva and an American-style institution. Although they taught secular subjects, and their students took New York State Regents exams, they were for boys only, had a rigidly Orthodox orientation, and heavily emphasized, on the Jewish side, the study of Talmud above all else.

Ramaz did not stress Talmud. While most of its students came from religiously observant homes, the school was coed and prided itself on the high quality of its education. It charged what were, by the modest standards of the times, high tuitions, and the parents who paid them expected their children to be eligible for the best colleges. The image it cultivated, in keeping with its location on Manhattan's Upper East Side, was of a progressive Jewish prep school, a kind of Fieldston or Horace Mann for Modern Orthodox boys and girls.

The preppiness meant that the boys had to wear shirts and ties to school, the girls blouses and skirts; that we had school caps with an "R" on them, with which we were supposed to cover our heads in the East Side streets near our building in place of the yarmulkes we wore inside; and that our curriculum included a class in "social dancing" in which we learned to foxtrot and rhumba and to ask politely for the next dance and to cut in. As for the progressiveness, it consisted largely of a course called "Hygiene" that taught us, with a thoroughness I found eye-opening, the facts of life. (It is astonishing how much, compared to youngsters today, we didn't know then.) Nor were we disciplined with any great rigor, my harshest experience being made to sit through a class as a nine-year-old with a piece of gum I had been chewing affixed to the tip of my nose. The nearest thing to corporal punishment I recall was administered by a scowling Hebrew teacher who, when we stepped out of line, hurled well-aimed erasers at us from the blackboard that exploded in puffs of chalk upon hitting their target.

On the whole, the education I received at Ramaz was solid and pedestrian. Although there wasn't a teacher who excited me or broadened my horizons, my one rebellion was unrelated to our studies. One year the school issued "prayer cards" on which, in columns marking the days of the week, our parents were asked to vouch for our having said *shaharit*, the morning prayer, at home before leaving for school. I led a mutiny that ended with several members of my class rising to their feet and tearing up the cards. Eventually, the experiment was rescinded.

What I suffered most from at Ramaz I couldn't blame on the school. This was growing up in a neighborhood—my family lived at West End Avenue and 104th Street—that I was not really a part of. I didn't know the boys on my block who went to the local public school, and by the time I came home every day on the double bus ride from 86th Street and Lexington Avenue, it was too late, and I was in any case too shy, to befriend them. I was living, not in a foreign land, but in one I had never been naturalized in. Instead of returning every night to a ghetto as did Jews in the Middle Ages, I set out for one every morning.

Still, in those years, I did not feel inwardly split between the Jew and the American in me. Most probably, this was because the American was less developed. It was there, of course. I was, after all, an American boy—I played American sports, memorized major league batting averages, never missed a Western at the movies, and listened to the hit parade on the radio. New York was a city that, even then, before the word "multicultural" had been invented, was among the most multicultural the world had ever known. The only anti-Semitism I encountered came from the tough Irish boys who sometimes drifted over from across Broadway to pick fights.

I didn't question being sent to Ramaz. It was part of the way things were. I neither liked nor disliked it with any fervor. My single most vivid memory of it is of the day I decided to leave.

That day began with the intention of staying at Ramaz for four more years through high school.

When I took the exam for Bronx Science midway through eighth grade, it wasn't with the expectation of changing schools. I had only wanted to prove that I was as smart as my sister. Science, which had the reputation of being one of the best academic high schools in the country, was one of five elite New York institutions that took students on the basis of citywide tests, and my sister had been accepted three years previously and had gone there.

I might have thought more seriously of following in her footsteps had I not, in the course of my eighth-grade year, become quite devout. Until then I had performed the commandments of Judaism because I had been taught to. Now, as my bar mitzvah approached, I found myself doing so as God's votary. I had a newborn consciousness of service, a feeling of purity and rectitude, as if every act or utterance—a blessing before food, a bedtime prayer, the washing of hands on rising in the morning—was like sweeping the floor or making the bed of a master who employed me well. How could I be a shirker at such a task? Yehuda ben Tema says, "Be fierce as a leopard, quick as an eagle, swift as a deer, and brave as a lion to do the will of your Father in Heaven." So began the Shulhan Arukh, the authoritative code of Jewish law compiled by the mystical sixteenth-century rabbi Joseph Caro. Much was expected from me. I would prove equal to it.

My parents regarded this outbreak of pietism with bemusement mixed with some concern. They were sophisticated people for whom Orthodoxy was a pleasantly regulated way of life shared with a social circle composed largely of my father's academic colleagues at the Jewish Theological Seminary, the rabbinical training institution of Conservative Judaism, and their wives. God, as far as I could see, had little to do with it. (Certainly not for my mother, who had shocked me that year when, unaware that I was watching from the kitchen doorway, she violated the Sabbath laws by relighting a flame that had gone out beneath the tin stove guard on which lunch was being warmed for expected guests.)

When I took to wearing an *arba kanfos*, the ritually fringed undergarment that more moderately observant Jews forgo, my mother made a face; my father, though he complied with my request to turn on the radio for me so that I could listen to college football games on Saturday afternoons, let me know he thought it was absurd. Yet he was not unhappy, I think, to see me become a serious Jew, and he was pleased when I accepted his invitation to study Talmud with him one or two evenings a week.

Those evenings brought me closer to him than I had ever been. We sat at the desk in his study, the huge folio volume that had belonged to my grandfather, with its treasure-chest scent of stored wisdom, opened in front of us. We were studying the tractate of Bava Metzia, the laws of torts traditionally assigned to beginners, and my father had chosen not chapter one, "Two Who Hold," but rather chapter three, "He Who Entrusts," which began, "He who entrusts a friend with a farm animal or tools that are stolen or lost…" Together we followed the twists and turns of the Aramaic discussion. Why, if the friend confessed negligence, did Rav Papa say he acquired ownership of the property in question? To whom did it belong if he paid for it and it was then recovered? It was hard work. An hour left me exhausted and dizzy with accomplishment. We had matched wits with the sharpest minds the study of Torah had produced. Rava! Rav Hiyya! "Rav Huna says, 'Even if he offers to pay for it, first make him swear he doesn't have it.'" Why? Why make him swear? You couldn't tend to God's house unless you could follow His instructions.

It was springtime; my father's study window was open. "At a time when the stars are aglitter/And the grasses whisper and the wind tells its tales,/A plangent voice may reach your ears,/And your eyes may spy a distant light/In a window, and through it/A shadow like a ghost's,/Swaying, moving, moving, rocking back and forth,/Its soft croon coming to you/ Across pathways of silence:/ It is a Talmud student,/ Up late in his prison cell." We had studied this Hebrew poem by Hayim Nahman Bialik in school. Now I swayed, moved, in its lines.

And so if I thought at all of changing schools, it wasn't for the Bronx High School of Science. It was for a yeshiva where I could be a real Talmud student—and where my parents would never permit me to go.

I would stay at Ramaz then. When I was notified that I had passed the test for Bronx Science and had a month in which to register, I felt proud of my success and put it out of my mind.

But there was another boy in my class, Stanley Nussbaum, who had gotten into Science too. Not only that, he had announced his intention of going there. Now, sitting in class and looking at him—he occupied the front seat in the row nearest the door—I felt a combination of admiration and resentment that I knew well enough to identify as envy.

This envy made no sense. What was it to me if Stanley Nussbaum went to the Bronx High School of Science? It was the voice of the *yetzer ha-ra*, the evil inclination that, like everyone, I had inside me. The *yetzer ha-ra* would be happy if I dropped my Jewish education entirely. It would gladly lure me to a place where I couldn't behave like a Jew.

It stood no chance. And yet there I was, staring day after day at Stanley Nussbaum and thinking, "A few months from now he'll be in the *world*." It had never occurred to me until then that the world was a place I was not already living in.

Ah, but he was making a great mistake! If the evil inclination meets you on your way, drag it with you to the study house, the rabbis said. Yet the envy only grew worse. The door was open to me, too. I had only to walk through it.

And so, gradually, the idea of going to a public high school crept into my mind. The more it did, the harder I fought it, and the harder I fought it, the more it fought back. "He'll soon be free," the *yetzer ha-ra* said, pointing at Stanley Nussbaum. "And you'll still be in your prison cell."

I was in a state of inner turmoil. Never in my life had I had to make such a momentous decision. And I had to make it on my own, because my parents refused to express an opinion on the matter. To this day, I don't know whether they had one.

It went right down to the last day. I sat at the breakfast table with my parents and prayed that they would tell me what to do. But they didn't. And so I made up my mind: I would be a good Jew and stay at Ramaz. I rose from the table with a sense of relief and went off to school.

And yet all morning I could only stare at Stanley Nussbaum. "You're a coward," the *yetzer ha-ra* whispered. "Go ahead, then, be one. The world is full of cowards. But admit you're only staying at Ramaz because you don't have the courage to leave."

Sometime in the course of that morning, I broke down and admitted it. I went home and told my parents that I was going to Bronx Science. And Stanley Nussbaum, as fate would have it, broke down too. At the last minute, like me, he changed his mind and decided to stay at Ramaz.

—⟋⟋⟍—

My freshman year at Bronx Science was a miserable one. Instead of spending all day with the same small group of students who sat in one classroom while the teachers came and went, it was now I who went from room to room and was surrounded by different faces in each. I made no friends. I missed my old ones from Ramaz. I lived in terror of a class called "Shop" in which we were taught by an intimidating southerner with a cracker drawl to work with drills and power saws that I was inept at. (In my home on West End Avenue, my parents called the super for anything more than changing a light bulb.) And I was becoming increasingly entrenched in a faith that I felt increasingly unfaithful toward.

Covering my head in school was unthinkable. "Jewish beanies," as yarmulkes were sometimes mockingly called in those days, were not the common sight in the streets of New York that they were to become. My *arba kanfos*, too, was abandoned after our first gym class, when I realized that I would have to change clothes in the locker room in front of everyone. I managed to yank it off and stuff it away without drawing laughter, but I never wore it to school again.

I had not been brave as a lion.

Had I thought about it more deeply, I might have wondered about the nature of a faith that is so easily embarrassed. It might have occurred to me that one does not fear ridicule so greatly unless one identifies with it in some part of one; that, just as the smallest crack in a wall portends its eventual collapse, being the first sign that the ground has begun to sink beneath it, so my faith was already doomed. But I was too stung by my perfidy to be any more aware of this than is a wall.

Today, after reading some of the reunion-year autobiographies in which my high school classmates have brought one another up to date on their lives, I realize that I was not the only Orthodox Jew in concealment at Bronx Science. There were other boys from observant homes like mine who were "passing" and who may have suffered the same pangs of guilt. But we were well camouflaged, and I can't recall a single case of mutual disclosure. The irony of it was that Science in those days was probably 80 percent Jewish, even 90 percent when it came to the top students. (Today, the prize-winners listed in the alumni news bulletin all seem to be Asian.) Yet the Jews I met there were like none I had met before. Many were as bookish as I was, but there were also tough Jewish kids, wild Jewish kids, and Jewish kids who, by the second month of school, were cutting class to go to the neighborhood pool room. If I had wanted the world, I had gotten a chunky first bite of it to chew on.

But now, every morning at prayer in my room, I strapped the leather thongs of my tefillin so tightly to my arm that it hurt, as if to bind myself, like Odysseus to the mast, against the world's siren song. I envied Stanley Nussbaum once more—this time for having stayed at Ramaz. I thought of returning there. I would have done it if not for my pride. No one would have the satisfaction of seeing me come back in defeat.

And so that freshman year of high school went by, and I felt more and more lost. And then, toward the end of it, I hit on an idea: I would leave Bronx Science not to return to Ramaz but to enroll in Talmudical Academy. That way, not only would I not lose face, I would be a real yeshiva student at last.

My parents, however, would never agree to it. It was one thing to humor me through what they hoped was an adolescent phase, another to deliver me to the portals of obscurantism. This time they would not leave the decision to me.

It was then that I did something utterly outlandish. I cut school one day, took the subway to Talmudical Academy in upper Manhattan, asked for registration papers for the sophomore year of high school, filled them out, forged my father's signature, and returned them. I didn't tell anyone about this. At the end of that summer, when the first day of school came around, I got up in the morning, dressed, had breakfast, and set out—not for the IND line and the Bronx as my parents thought I was doing, but for the IRT and Washington Heights.

Today, I find it hard to believe that I actually did this. What did I think I was doing? Did I plan to hide where I was studying for the next three years? Who would pay my tuition? These are not questions that I remember the answers to. There are times in one's younger years when, though possessing not a shred of the confidence one later acquires, one does things whose audacity stuns the future self. But this is only because that self, being calmer and more self-assured, can no longer conceive of the desperation that drove one to do what one did.

From the moment I passed through the doors of Talmudical Academy until I fled several hours later, I hated every second of it. The place had a seedy, shabby air. It smelled bad. The only teacher I recall, a Talmud instructor, had forgotten to zip his fly and stood with it open before a smirking, all-boys class. I felt far more constricted than I had ever felt at Ramaz. I wanted only to get away.

Fortunately, I had never bothered to inform Bronx Science that I was leaving. I walked out of the Talmud class, took the IRT back down to 59th Street, changed for the IND, rode it up to 183rd Street and Creston Avenue, and arrived at Science in time to finish the first day of my sophomore year. To the best of my recollection, I never breathed a word of the whole episode to my parents.

—⟋⟋⟍—

A good if not outstanding athlete, I was always fast on my feet. At the beginning of my second year at Science, I tried out for track. I turned out to be a better-than-average middle-distance runner and second leg on our mile relay team, which came in fifth one year, out of sixty or seventy schools, in the New York City championships.

I now had my first group of high school friends, all from the track team and all West Siders like myself. After school we walked to the Jerome

Avenue El and rode the subway together to Van Cortlandt Park, where we trained. We ran sprints for speed and laps for wind, and joked in a locker room pungent with liniment and shower steam, and stopped on our way home at a little place that sold Italian ices in all the colors of an artist's palette. On weekends we hung out together, too, playing handball or basketball, or bowling at an alley on Broadway, or gambling away our modest allowances at poker. There were no more thoughts of leaving Bronx Science.

The one problem with track was that many of the meets were on Saturdays. In winter this wasn't so bad. The competitions were held in an old armory on 167th Street; I only had to walk three miles to get to them, and, the days being short, I could take the subway home when they were over. But in autumn we ran cross-country up in Van Cortlandt, and the days were longer. I had to walk seven miles to get there, run a two-and-a-half mile race, and walk back again. By the time I arrived home, my legs were too heavy to lift over the rim of the bathtub.

There was an obvious solution. "Take the train," said the evil inclination. "The Torah doesn't say you can't travel on Saturday. It says you should let your donkey rest. You don't own a donkey."

This was not a serious argument. You could score the same points against practically all of Judaism. Kosher slaughtering, praying at regular times—none of it was in the Bible. It was part of the Oral Law codified by the rabbis of the Talmud.

"Indeed," came the answer. "And next you'll tell me the Oral Law was given with the Written Law at Mount Sinai. That's why Moses spent so much time up there. He was memorizing the Talmud."

No, he wasn't, I replied. But God had wanted mankind to be His partner. The Written Law was His constitution. It had to be interpreted by human courts.

"And what makes you so sure," the next question was, "that the Written Law was given at Mount Sinai? Because the Bible says it was? That's brilliant. The proof that God gave the Torah is that the Torah says so! If you used logic like that in your geometry class, you'd flunk."

But surely, I reasoned, God needed to educate mankind. Why not from a mountaintop?

"Because," the voice said, "God is everywhere. He can't be more in one place than in another. And why educate only the Jews?"

Perhaps so that they could serve as a model for the rest of the human race that God had created.

"God didn't create anyone. For goodness' sake, you go to the Bronx High School of *Science*. I don't have to tell you about evolution."

But evolution was a form of creation too. Why couldn't God have created man step by step? Why not the whole universe that way?

"You've heard of Spinoza? Then listen: *Since God is Being absolutely infinite, of whom no attribute can be denied which expresses the essence of substance, there cannot be any substances except God, and consequently none other can be conceived.* God didn't create the universe. He is the universe. How could God create Himself?"

These exchanges didn't take place in a single conversation, or in a single day or month. They were part of an extended battle. And I was losing it. I was a country at war in which the fighting was moving steadily closer to the center: first the outlying districts were taken, then the provincial towns, then the roads leading to the capital. Each time another position was overrun I fell back and threw up new defenses; each time, they were overrun again.

This was all perfectly ordinary. The same battle had been fought since the time of the Haskalah, the nineteenth-century Jewish Enlightenment in Eastern Europe, in the minds of vast numbers of young Jews—almost always with the same outcome. No theme is more widespread in the Jewish literature of the nineteenth and early twentieth centuries than the loss of faith resulting from the collision of religion with modernity.

And yet I was on the verge of becoming an anachronism. By the time I was a student at the Bronx High School of Science in the 1950s, an understanding between Judaism and modernity was being reached. Religious faith had ceased to be an issue in Jewish literary and even religious life. Orthodoxy, which had been in headlong retreat for over a century, had rallied and was holding the line. Today, fifty years later, a large percentage of my own classmates at Ramaz are still observant.

Perhaps this is because the understanding was not really with modernity. Rather, it may have marked the moment at which Judaism, precociously ahead of its times, slipped through the gates of postmodernism. No longer, it seemed, was there a need to decide between the rabbis and Spinoza, God and Nature, Genesis and *The Origin of Species*. Now there were alternate systems, multiple perspectives, equally legitimate takes on reality, mutually compatible contradictions. One could be Orthodox and heterodox, a Talmudist and a physicist, a believer in relativism and in revelation, all at the same time—or one could simply bypass questions of ultimate reality entirely by regarding them as stale epistemological and metaphysical conundrums. Did God exist? He did and He didn't, like Schrödinger's cat, and it all depended on which box you opened.

Had I left Ramaz and gone to Bronx Science a few years later, I might have become a Schrödingerian myself. But we were not taught quantum mechanics at Science in the mid-1950s, or even relativity theory. The physics we learned was Galileo's and Newton's. We were told to think in terms of "either/or," not of "both/and." I don't recall who it was who once said that what you haven't learned by the age of twenty you'll never internalize if you live to be a hundred, but he was an astute psychologist.

Born two months before the outbreak of World War II, I fought the battles of a nineteenth-century Jew. My faith in the Jewish God was like a soldier tragically killed, for no good reason, in the last hours of combat before an armistice is signed.

In my junior year at Science, I fell in with a literary crowd. It started with a creative writing class. Our teacher, Mrs. Applebaum, sat on the front of her desk, with her legs, her best feature, draped over it. She had us keep journals that she collected and read every month. If anything was considered too personal, we were allowed to Scotch tape the pages together. There were rumors of Scotch tape being removed and replaced.

We wrote sketches and stories and poems and read them aloud and discussed them. Dorothy Applebaum may have peeked at our inmost thoughts, but she taught me what writing was about. It wasn't about the thoughts themselves. It was more like shop. You had your tools—nouns and verbs and adjectives and punctuation marks—and each had its use, and you used them to make anything you wanted: phrases and sentences and paragraphs and pages. The difference was that these were tools I knew what to do with. I was handier with a comma or a semicolon than with a jigsaw or a drill. I wrote a story that took place on Martha's Vineyard, where I had spent part of the previous summer with my parents. It began, "The ocean lay before him as gray as a gull and sifted the wind with its spray." The words came to me in an ecstasy while walking down Broadway in a thunderstorm, the rain streaming down my face, and the story was published in the high school literary magazine.

The students who clustered in the magazine's office were a new type of friend. We sat around arguing about Dylan Thomas and Dostoevsky and went to cafés on MacDougal Street and saw plays in tiny off-Broadway theaters and sat on floors at parties singing folk songs to the plunk of a guitar. Spanish Civil War songs were popular:

> *Los cuatro generales!*
> *Los cuatro generales!*
> *Los cuatro generales,*
> *Mamita mia, mamita mia!*

So were songs of the American Left:

> I dreamed I saw Joe Hill last night,
> Alive as you and me.
> Says I, "But Joe, you're ten years dead."
> "I never died," says he.

Joe Hill was a Wobbly. The word gave me the shivers. There were hobos in it, and railroad tracks, and great American distances I had never seen.

That year I read Thomas Wolfe's *Look Homeward, Angel*. I was floored by it. For three days I read without stopping, staying home from school. It was a huge book. Its emotions were huge. I recognized them as mine, only vaster, magnified a hundredfold, flung far into the world like the starry sky of a planetarium that comes from a small box of light. All the immense hunger for life, the terrible loneliness of having to be oneself, the nagging question, "When will it begin?" were in this story of a childhood and adolescence in rural North Carolina utterly different from my own. It expressed a yearning so great that only America was big enough to hold it. It was, this America, a great, restless, dreaming giant of a land. I pictured it as a Gulliver, its head propped against the skyscrapers of New York, its feet dipped in the Pacific, tossing in bed at night, tossing and turning as I did, aflame with desire. A whole, vast, restless, yearning continent! And the farthest I had ventured into it were six years of a Hebrew-speaking summer camp in the Poconos and the house my parents had rented on Martha's Vineyard.

I spent that summer in southern Tennessee. I could thank my mother for that. Browsing in the back pages of the Sunday *New York Times Magazine*, she had come across a small ad placed by a Jewish organization seeking high school volunteers for a summer work camp at an adult education institute in the mountains near Chattanooga. I didn't want to spend another summer on Martha's Vineyard, and I signed up for it.

There were nine of us, four of whom drove down with our counselor from New York in a red Chevrolet convertible. It was my first car trip through America. There were no thruways or interstates then. We drove through small and big towns on one-lane roads with stop lights and junctions, and slow-moving trucks, and country diners with pinball machines that buzzed and flashed while you ate, and four-dollar-a-night motels in one of which we slept. It took two whole days to get there. Somewhere in Virginia I had my first encounter with segregation. I was walking on a sidewalk when an elderly black man coming toward me stepped into the gutter to let me pass.

The Highlander Folk School was a unique place in the American South, one that flouted Jim Crow laws to hold racially mixed workshops on social and political issues. (That summer, one of them was attended by

Rosa Parks, who would soon afterward launch the civil rights movement by refusing to move to the back of a segregated bus in Montgomery, Alabama.) Highlander had left-wing connections and could survive only because it was located high up in hillbilly country. The local inhabitants, whose Southern speech had a rapid, high-pitched twang, disliked government regulations and snooty city folk far more than they did black people, and they got along well with the Highlander staff and protected it. Once, the story went, back in the 1940s, when the Ku Klux Klan drove up from Chattanooga in order to burn the place down, they ambushed its cavalcade and sent it fleeing back down the mountain.

Highlander was located on a working farm, and when we weren't on duty in the kitchen, we were kept busy baling hay, building fences, and painting barns. It was my first experience at hard physical labor, and I loved it. To lean into a bale of hay with a pitchfork, the sweat running down my bare back, probing for the center of the unformed mass I was about to lift—to hoist it clean in one movement and toss it into a wagon hitched to a tractor, pulling back at the last second to send the hay flying free—and again and again until the wagon was full—there was in this an exhausting, devotional pleasure not unlike a page of Talmud or the relentless pace of a quarter-mile.

There were other new things that summer. I heard my first rock and roll, sung by Bo Diddley and Little Richard from jukeboxes in roadside cafés. I fired my first gun, a .30-caliber Winchester rifle. I necked with my first girl in the back of a car in my first drive-in movie. I got drunk for the first time on the moonshine bourbon made by the locals, who joked that it acquired its taste from the dead flies floating on the surface.

They were a resourceful lot, those Tennessee mountain men. When they ran out of money, they looked for a job. When they had enough money, they quit their job. If their car broke down or their roof leaked, they fixed it themselves. If the larder was empty, they shot some squirrels or caught some trout. A social scientist might have described them as a marginal and vanishing class, living on the fringes of an American economy that would soon swallow them. They were men of few words. Their only strong creed, as far as I could tell, was not to be messed with. They had an instinctive sense of fairness and of competence that were really one and the same thing, for they judged a man by what he did or was able to do, and no amount of bluster could sway those judgments. They smelled of gasoline and tobacco, and they were the real America that until now I had only sung about at high school parties.

Who but a city-born-and-bred Jewish boy falls romantically in love with his native country at the age of sixteen? This, too, had happened many times before me in modern Jewish history, to young Jews in Warsaw and in Minsk and in Berlin and in Budapest—in all of whom the same battle had been joined, since they found no way of integrating the Jew they were brought up as with the Russian, Pole, or Hungarian they had become. There were the well-known cases, like that of the Yiddish novelist and dramatist S. Ansky, a yeshiva boy who spent nearly twenty years of his life in the 1880s and '90s "going to the people" as a Russian *narodnik* and social revolutionary before returning to the Jewish fold.

And there were the unknown ones. Once, leafing through an album in the home of a cousin, I was startled by a photograph of my grandfather, a religious Jew who, wispy-bearded and bespectacled, always wore, in every picture I had seen of him, a black gabardine and skullcap. Yet here—the photograph must have been taken in the '80s when he was still an unmarried young man—he had a bare head full of wild curls and a Russian peasant tunic, looking for all the world like a revolutionary himself. What secret chapter of his life had I stumbled on? My cousin had no idea; there was no longer anyone in the family to ask.

I myself was now to lead not one secret life but two, each with its own set of friends. In them, I didn't speak to my "Jewish" friends about my American side, and I didn't speak to my "American" friends about my Jewish side, and the Jew and the American within me did not speak much to each other, though they fought fiercely enough when, like moles whose tunnels have crossed, they sometimes met.

But in this, too, was I not a throwback to another age? I was struggling with nineteenth-century ideas of nationalism and identity just when they were being swept away for good. These ideas presupposed both a people and an individual striving for a wholeness that was now about to be exposed as delusory. Nations and selves were arbitrary constructions, and the more of them one belonged to, or that belonged to one, the better. Why indeed only two? Long after the period in question I was to meet a writer, a man considerably younger than myself, who took pride in thinking of himself as an American, a Mexican, a Hispanic, a Jew, and a Sephardi; if he could have acquired a few more identities on the cheap, he would have done so. Told how I had felt torn for years between being an American and being a Jew—for although I could easily conceive of myself as one or the other, I was not prepared to submit to the compromise of being both—he looked at me as astonished as if I had confided that much of my life had been spent debating which of my two legs to walk on.

That summer marked the end of my religious observance. In early July I was still putting on my tefillin, which I had brought to Tennessee in their velvet pouch. By the end of August I was eating pork. Viewed from the outside, this was a bewilderingly abrupt transition. Yet it was only the surrender of the final citadel after all other resistance had laid down its arms. Who, the last defenders dead or captive, was left to go on fighting?

Still, I continued to put on my tefillin. Throughout my last year at the Bronx High School of Science, I used them to deceive my father, who had no idea how I had changed. Every weekday morning I closeted myself in my room with Milton's *Paradise Lost*, whose proud, fallen Lucifer I understood. When a half hour, the normal time for the morning prayer, had gone by, I shut the book, took my tefillin from their pouch, strapped them hard enough to my arm to leave visible welts, and emerged for breakfast before leaving for school. It had been easier to be a mutineer at Ramaz than it was to be one with my father, who only years later confessed to me that he had not the slightest belief in the Supreme Being to whom he poured his heart out every day in mournful prayer.

2006

The Great Jewish Language War

Man *trakht un got lakht*: man thinks and God laughs, the Yiddish saying goes. I grew up thinking of Yiddish as an enemy and am now, among other things, a translator of Yiddish literature. It was a hidden enemy, I should add, because as a boy in New York in the 1950s, I could not have said what the precise menace was of a language that arrived harmlessly at the front door every morning in the form of the *Morgn Zhurnal*, the daily Yiddish newspaper that my father subscribed to along with *The New York Times*. In fact, it was with the help of them both that I learned to read Yiddish. Since the *Morgn Zhurnal* copied all its non-Jewish news from the *Times* of the day before (the joke in those days was that no one understood how the *Times* knew on Tuesday what the *Morgn Zurnal* would publish on Wednesday), my Hebrew education, the German I was studying in high school, and a copy of yesterday's *Times* were all I needed to acquire the rudiments of the language.

Yet Yiddish, the mother tongue of both my parents and a language used by them matter-of-factly when there was a need for it, was one of the few things that could get my father, an even-tempered man, visibly angry. My one childhood memory of him in a rage is of his shouting at Yiddish—or rather, at a friend of his named Ben Dworkin whose wife was the daughter of the Yiddish poet Solomon Bloomgarden, better known by the pen name of Yehoash. I cannot remember exactly what Dworkin and my father were talking about, or what made my father lose his temper and begin to shout, but it was clear to me from their argument that Ben Dworkin and Yiddish were on one side of a great divide, and my father was on the other.

In time, I came to understand that I had witnessed a minor clash in a great war—a war that for all practical purposes was over by the time this scene took place. This was the language war between Hebrew and Yiddish, itself part of the great cultural and political conflict between Zionism and Diasporism that sundered the Jewish world in the first decades of the twentieth century, and that ended only when an even greater conflict left the European Diaspora in ruins beside a newborn state of Israel. My father, his subscription to the *Morgn Zhurnal* notwithstanding, was a Hebraist and a Zionist. Ben Dworkin was a Yiddishist. And long before I knew the meaning of that word, the shouting that night in a living room in which I had never heard shouting before told me that Yiddish, the enemy of my father, though admitted to our home every morning with the milk bottles like a servant given the run of the house, was my enemy, too.

This attitude lasted long past these years—so much so that, until the mid-1980s, I had hardly opened a Yiddish book. I, who had studied English literature at great universities, had read everything by Jewish authors like Kafka and Babel and Bellow, and was a lover and professional translator of Hebrew literature, had never read a Yiddish line by Sholem Aleichem, a Yiddish story by I. L. Peretz, or a Yiddish poem by Ya'akov Glatshtein, Moyshe-Leyb Halpern, or Avraham Sutzkever. And not only had I never explored Yiddish literature, much less realized that it constituted one of the most glorious chapters in the history of Jewish creativity, I had instinctively shrunk from it as I never shrank from the *Morgn Zhurnal*. One might consort with the enemy's servants. One did not consort with the enemy himself.

The conflict between the supporters of Hebrew and of Yiddish that lasted roughly from 1900 to 1940 was one of the great Kulturkämpfe, the nonviolent civil wars, of Jewish history. At its most intense, it rivaled in bitterness the ninth-century schism between Karaites and Rabbanites, or the late-eighteenth-century rift between Hasidim and Misnagdim. Unlike these, however, it did not pit something new in the Jewish world against something old. Yiddish and Hebrew had coexisted symbiotically for nearly a millennium, ever since Yiddish first developed in parts of German-speaking Europe as a Jewish dialect rich in Hebrew vocabulary. The two languages had achieved this coexistence by dividing Jewish life between them, with Hebrew serving for liturgy, religious ritual, sacred text, rabbinic discourse, and formal literature, and Yiddish for speech and for written communication, simple prayer, and edifying homilies among the less educated, particularly women. As the two languages fully complemented each other, there was no cause for friction between them.

In this respect, the bonding of Yiddish with Hebrew was like that of other languages spoken by large numbers of Jews after Hebrew lost its vernacular status in antiquity. Though each of these partnerships had distinctive features—Hebrew and Aramaic, Hebrew and Greek, Hebrew and Arabic, Hebrew and Judeo-Spanish—a similar pattern prevailed in all. In each case, Hebrew retained its position of *leshon ha-kodesh*, a sacred but colloquially defunct language of revelation and high culture, while its partner was *la'az*, an originally foreign but now domesticated vulgate used for all ordinary purposes and generally containing a suffi- cient proportion of Hebrew words to set it off from the speech of one's non-Jewish neighbors.

The traditional relations between Hebrew and its vernacular coun- terpart could be characterized—and were—by different metaphors. The two languages could indeed be compared to a master and a servant, the vernacular performing life's daily chores under the supervision of the superior tongue that assigned them. Or they could be likened to two social castes, one upper, priestly, and brahmin, the other lower, laic, and plebeian. Or they could be imagined as a husband and wife, the former following the pursuits of the mind while the latter ran the household. Or as *s'fat avot*, the "language of the fathers" and of stern masculine duty, and *mamaloshn*, the maternal tongue of love and warmth.

Such comparisons were more than mere metaphors. The structure of Jewish life was such that, although everyone prayed in *leshon ha-kodesh* and spoke *la'az*, the adepts and main users of Hebrew were the rabbis, the wealthy, the educated, and the menfolk, while those whose lives were largely restricted to the vernacular were the poor, the unschooled, and the women.

To be sure, the lines were never rigidly drawn. The servants were always sneaking, as it were, into the master's bedroom, the masters poking into the pots in the kitchen when the servants were not around. Already in the Bible we find the erotic love poetry of the Song of Songs in Hebrew and the apocalyptic prophecy of the book of Daniel in Aramaic, while alongside the many post-biblical Jewish religious texts of the Hellenistic period written in Greek is a Hebrew volume called *Sefer ha-Razim*, "The Book of Secrets," in which you will find all the black magic needed for success at everything from love to playing the ponies. There are numerous such examples throughout Jewish history, many of them fascinating and all of them exceptions proving the rule.

Yet only in the case of Hebrew and Yiddish did these border crossings, at first minor, lead to hostile raids, then to massive incursions, and finally to all-out hostilities. Like two peoples who have lived together peacefully for centuries under imperial control only to turn on each other in a spirit of combative nationalism with the empire's collapse, Hebrew and Yiddish ultimately went to war.

This, too, is more than a mere metaphor—for if the "empire" to which Hebrew and Yiddish owed allegiance is but a figure of speech for the rabbinic culture that regulated traditional Jewish bilingualism, the nationalism that disrupted this empire was literal. It was part of a great wave that swept Europe in the nineteenth century as real empires began to crumble—the Napoleonic, the Hapsburg, the Ottoman, the Czarist—and the Jews joined the universal struggle for recognition and self-determination.

There was no room for bilingualism in this struggle. European nationalism was an offspring of European romanticism, and like its parent, radically monistic. "One people, one language, one land" was the rallying cry of every national movement in Europe, a collectivized version of the romantic vision of autarkic selfhood. For late nineteenth- and early twentieth-century Jewish nationalism, this meant living in Hebrew or in Yiddish, not in both. Either the people who spoke Yiddish would create a literature and a high culture in it, or the people whose high culture and literature were in Hebrew would learn to speak it again. In either case, the old order had to go.

—⁓—

It is beside the point to look for the historical aggressor or aggressed-against in this war. Although it is common, and perhaps natural, to think of Yiddish as the revolutionary challenger and Hebrew as the ancien régime under attack, this is to take a simplistic view. Both languages, each in its way, were enlisted in support of revolution *and* tradition. If Yiddish was championed as a live vernacular overthrowing the oppression of a mummified holy tongue, or as the voice of the Jewish worker and woman demanding access to privileges long denied them by a Hebraic ruling class, it was also the flag of those who wished to stay safely put in a familiar Diaspora rather than make a bold new start in Zion as Hebrew-speaking pioneers. Its fiercest proponents included the most conservative rabbis and religious factions alongside radical secularists dreaming of Jewish cultural autonomy in a multi-ethnic Eastern Europe.

The two languages' conflict, which began casually and escalated, took place with great symmetry. The first modern Yiddish invasion of the Hebraic domain of belles lettres, the sentimental novels of the Vilna author Isaac Meir Dik, commenced in the 1850s; the first Hebrew-speaking society in Eastern Europe was founded in 1862 in the Galician city of Brod. In 1864 there appeared Yiddish literature's first aesthetically accomplished work of fiction, S. Y. Abramovitch's *Dos Kleyne Mentshele*; in 1879 came the earliest serious proposal, put forth in an essay by Eliezer Ben-Yehuda, to reinstitute Hebrew as a spoken language in the land of Israel. In August 1897 the first Zionist Congress, most of its delegates ardent Hebraists, convened in Basel; a month later, the socialist and anti-Zionist Yiddisher Arbiter Bund, henceforth Yiddishism's main political arm, was founded in Vilna. By the first decade of the twentieth century, a serious Yiddish literature was flourishing in Eastern Europe; in the same decade, Jewish children were talking Hebrew to each other on a daily basis in the agricultural colonies of Palestine. In 1907, Poale Zion, the less militantly Hebraistic of the two major Palestinian Jewish workers' parties, declared Hebrew the exclusive language of the Yishuv; in 1908, at a much-celebrated conference in Czernowitz, Yiddish authors like Sholem Asch, Chaim Zhitlovsky, and Hersh-Dovid Nomberg fought for a narrowly defeated resolution proclaiming Yiddish the sole national language of the Jewish people.

Czernowitz and the debate it engendered, though their importance was more symbolic than practical, have been taken to have signaled the formal outbreak of hostilities between the two languages. True, of the great Yiddish literary triumvirate of Abramovitch (or Mendele Mokher Sefarim, Mendele the Bookseller, to use his pen name), Sholem Aleichem, and I. L. Peretz, only Peretz was in attendance at the conference, but for him it indeed marked a watershed. Until then he had been a fully bilingual writer, publishing many of his stories first in Yiddish and then, rewritten, in Hebrew, and many others in the opposite order. Now, he declared in an address to the conference, "The Jews are one people—their language is Yiddish." Moreover, Peretz told the delegates, if Yiddish was to replace Hebrew as the national language of the Jews, it would first have to appropriate the Hebraic heritage—to accomplish which, he continued, "I propose the translation into Yiddish of all the cultural assets of our golden past, above all those of the Bible—*iberhoypt fun der bibl.*"

A century later, Peretz's choice of words still lacerates. Not the *tanakh*, not *kisvey ha-koydesh*, not any of the other Hebrew or Hebrew-derived words by which Yiddish speakers, including Peretz himself, traditionally referred to Jewish Scripture, but the *bibl*, a thoroughly Christian term that no Yiddish speaker ever used. Whether or not he consciously intended to stab Hebrew, a language he loved, in the heart, Peretz could not have found a more cruelly pointed stiletto.

In point of fact, the Hebrew Bible had already been translated into old Yiddish in the sixteenth and seventeenth centuries. Nor was Yiddish the first *la'az* language into which it was put by Jews, having been preceded by Greek, Aramaic, and Arabic. The rabbis, while making their peace with such translations, well understood their dangers, one being that Hebrew would be rendered supererogatory. And yet none had ever been part of a program to supplant Hebrew in the name of the Jewish people. None was deliberately patricidal. None aspired not only to push back Hebrew's frontiers, but to sack its Holy of Holies, to which every previous *la'az* translation had been but an approach, by turning it into an abandoned ruin, a purely archeological site: a *bibl* that would be read in Yiddish from now on.

In the years between Czernowitz and his death in 1915, Peretz personally began his project of Bible translation with the five scrolls of Esther, Lamentations, Ecclesiastes, Ruth, and the Song of Songs, leaving it to others to carry out the bulk of the work. The task was taken up by Yehoash, the father-in-law of my father's friend Ben Dworkin. Yehoash was a lyric poet with a religiously devotional bent who did not mean to offend Jews such as my father by carrying out Peretz's program. But my father was a *ba'al korei*, a reader of the Torah in the synagogue, and a man who knew the Hebrew Bible practically by heart. Although it hurt his intellectual pride to admit it, he, too, had a devotional soul, and it sometimes poured out absentmindedly.

One of these times was late Saturday afternoons, when he would sit in the darkening living room, watching the Sabbath ebb away and singing the twenty-third Psalm to a melancholy melody he knew from childhood. "A Psalm of David: The Lord is my shepherd, I shall not want. He maketh me to lie down in green pastures; he leadeth me beside the still waters." That is the King James Version, and it sounds pretty good to me. The Hebrew sounds better. Recently I came across Yehoash's Yiddish translation of this psalm. *Af grozike fiterpletser makht er mikh hoyern, bay ruike vasern tut er mikh firn*: the fat Germanic syllables made me think of a Lutheran pastor. "We don't need your damn *bibl*!" something shouted in me, just as my father had shouted at Ben Dworkin. How I take his side even now.

There is no need to linger on the great language war that was officially declared at Czernowitz or on its worst years, in which it became brutally politicized and reached an extreme that saw the partisans of Yiddish and Hebrew turn the tools of power against each other. History has pronounced its judgment. The Hebrew revival triumphed in Israel, where well into the 1950s the public use of Yiddish was excoriated. Yiddishism, which presided over the persecution and jailing of countless writers, teachers, and even readers of Hebrew in the Soviet Union, breathed its tortured last—quite literally shot to death—at the 1952 trial of Yiddish writers in Moscow. To read the minutes of this trial, made available in English last year, is to weep once for the fate of the fine writers condemned by it and a second time for the groveling betrayers of themselves and their comrades that they were reduced to being. And it is to weep a third time, and most copiously of all, for the gullibility of the large part of the Jewish people taken in for so many years by the fraud of the Great October Revolution and its deceitful promises of Jewish cultural independence, with Yiddish as its medium, in the Soviet Union. That Yiddishism became tragically identified with this revolution can be explained not only by its ideologically leftward drift in the years after Czernowitz but by the steady demographic and economic erosion of Yiddish life in Eastern Europe and the United States in the period between the two world wars, to the point that only a totalitarian state supporting and enforcing Yiddish culture seemed, to many Yiddish writers and intellectuals, capable of stemming the tide.

Let us rather return to the pre-Czernowitz Peretz. There is a short story of his, called "A Happy Family," that was published in both Yiddish and Hebrew in 1901. It is the same story in each, one in which a simple Jew, a water carrier, is hurt to the quick when told by his rabbi that, in the World to Come, the wife he loves and is contentedly married to will be his "footstool." Yet its two endings differ significantly because of the different nuances of this single word in each language.

The rabbi has meant no disrespect. On the contrary: knowing that he is talking to an uneducated Jew, he has used the Yiddish word *fisbenkele* for the biblical term *hadom-raglayim,* which occurs in the Bible in such verses as Isaiah's "Thus saith the Lord: the heaven is My throne, and the earth is My footstool," and the Psalmist's "Exalt ye the Lord our God and worship at His footstool." A *hadom-raglayim* is no lowly *fisbenkele*. It is the resting place of God, His earthly dwelling, the nether half of his Creation. Although the rabbi may be placing the water carrier's wife in a position of subservience to her husband, it is nonetheless an elevated one. The simple water carrier, however, unaware of the word's biblical resonance, takes *fisbenekele* literally to designate a lowly object to put one's feet on and returns home to protest to his wife that he will never agree to live in paradise in an arrangement so demeaning to them both.

These two ways of looking at it, moreover, are not just the rabbi's and the water carrier's. They are those of the two different versions of the story themselves. For whereas the Yiddish version has only the word *fisbenkele* and not *hadom-raglayim*, the Hebrew has the reverse. The Hebrew story thus reflects the point of view of the rabbi, who is not to blame for an ignorant Jew's comical misunderstanding of a well-intentioned remark. The Yiddish story is told from the water carrier's perspective, in which the rabbi is cruelly disdainful of the woman he loves. You have to read both to get the whole point.

Although a particularly salient example, "A Happy Family" is typical of the ways in which, when it came to prose fiction, Yiddish and Hebrew had different dispositions. The former was more suited to representing ordinary life, the latter to conveying the consciousness of the Jew steeped in the associative wealth of tradition. The two languages appealed to different audiences. Hebrew readers, like Hebrew writers, were themselves products of a rabbinic education, which alone enabled a Jew to acquire a literary knowledge of the language. Although secular Hebrew literature existed independently of the rabbinic world and often in rebellion against it, it retained some of its values and was heavily preoccupied with elitist issues of religious faith, Jewish identity, and cultural authority and authenticity. Yiddish writers and readers were more concerned with everyday existence. As a result, in the years before World War I, when both Hebrew and Yiddish literature were still largely confined to Eastern Europe and its life, the two languages continued, despite their intense rivalry, to observe something of the old division of labor. Though they were now in direct competition and were describing the same Jewish world, it was not a world described from the same vantage point.

—⟋⟋⟍—

Take, for example, the character known to Hebrew literary criticism as the *talush*, the "lost soul." This is characteristically a young Jew who has had a rigorously religious upbringing; experienced heights of adolescent piety; been sent, in recognition of his intellectual talents, to study at a yeshiva, the traditional institute of Jewish higher learning; lost his faith in God in a crisis of intellectual maturation that eventually leads to the abandonment of his religious studies and observance; retained, however, amid the emptiness of loss, a fierce sense of Jewish allegiance; and now drifts, a proud and lonely figure, on the margins of Jewish society, unable either to reconnect with the tradition he has broken with or to assimilate into the non-Jewish world.

"I write," writes Yirmiyah Feuerman, a typical *talush* and the narrator of Yosef Hayim Brenner's 1901 autobiographical Hebrew novel *In Winter*, "for myself and in secret"—and indeed Yirmiyah lives largely in silence, having almost no one to talk to. And yet while such figures are so common in pre-World War I Hebrew fiction that there is a generic name for them, they are extremely rare in the Yiddish literature of the period.

On the contrary: the Yiddish literature of this period talks obsessively. It talks, quite literally, most of the time, a high proportion of its pages consisting of dialogue or monologue—sometimes, as Mendele the Bookseller says of himself in the late Ted Gorelik's marvelous translation of Abramovitch's *Fishke the Lame*, until "the gab is sure to come running out at my mouth apace, like meal out the bottom of a tore bushel sack of feed." It talks because this is what ordinary Jews do when they get together, and because it is bursting with the liberating realization that this talk—this servant talk—is, at last, fit matter for the printed page.

Here, in Gorelik's translation, is Mendele introducing Fishke to us—or rather to the friend to whom he is telling the tale:

At the brick bathhouse in Glupsk, a young feller I know has been earning his keep for the longest time now, from ever since he was little. Name of Fishke, Fishke the lame, to be more precise, on account of him being crippled, you see. Ever hear of him? No; thought not.... So, who's this Fishke feller anyway? You're maybe asking, I mean, where'd the feller come from? How'd he come to be there, in such a place? Well, sir, somehow it just never occurred to anybody, nor to me, to even ask. So that part of it's a blank, pretty much. Though what else you expect? For here you have this poor article of humanity knocking about the place; and maybe he's even got a name—say, Fishke, or whatever—but, well, after all, he's no different from any of the rest of the wretched cast-offs in our midst which are his equal, and which are forever cropping up among us; and seemingly overnight, as well, and fully formed, like so many mushrooms after a rain, with all their features and parts already pricked out, and in place.... See, there are all these poorfolk amongst us have taken to nesting in every sort of odd out-of-the-way hovel and hole-in-the-wall cubby, where they quietly breed away unseen, bringing babies into the world in dark squalor. And, well, whyever shouldn't they?

And now listen to what happens when this same passage is translated into Hebrew by Abramovitch himself twenty years later and then retranslated into English by me:

In the bathhouse in Kislon [Mendele's Hebrew name for Glupsk] there was a lame fellow named Fishke, a fixture from the time he was young. Just who and whence was he? That's a question neither I nor anyone asked. What did it matter? So God's world also had in it a Fishke, one more wretched soul no different from all the others who sprout like so many shiny toadstools or mushrooms, so that, though each has a form, a complexion, and even thoughts of his own, you hardly notice him or how he's grown. Our beggars are begotten and betake themselves to their dark corners to beget more beggars on the sly, and who even knows they're there? Let them spawn to their hearts' content!

Abramovitch's Hebrew was as innovative as his Yiddish and was greatly admired by his contemporaries for its easy, richly-layered flow. And yet even when he is talking out loud, the Hebrew Mendele is being essayistic. He had to be, because the vernacular Hebrew then starting to develop in Palestine was still in its swaddling clothes. Mendele's Hebrew Fishke is less verbally impetuous than his Yiddish counterpart, less comically entangled in his own words, more concisely calibrated and judiciously balanced. Like Peretz but more so, Abramovitch—who began writing in Hebrew, then shifted to Yiddish to compose all his major works, and then rewrote these works in Hebrew—is the same and yet a different author in each language. It was this difference, in part, that impelled him to go back and forth between the two languages, because he could not be his full self in only one of them.

—〰—

He was not alone in this. Apart from Peretz and Mendele, the number of bilingual Hebrew/Yiddish authors around the turn of the twentieth century is staggering. Not all were equally committed to both languages. Many experimented briefly with one before settling permanently on the other because they felt it better expressed their deeper selves. In some cases, this had to do with their being Zionists or Diasporists; in others, with the depth of their identification with Jewish tradition, or with their politics; in still others with whether they were living in a Hebrew or Yiddish environment. Indeed, in the years right before and especially after World War I, as Yiddish and Hebrew began losing their stylistic complementarity, they took on a geographical one, Hebrew literature coming to convey the experience of Jewish Palestine, and Yiddish literature that of Eastern Europe and the United States.

Still, there was no end of exceptions, zigzags, more complex loyalties. Sholem Aleichem, who stopped writing in Hebrew after briefly flirting with it at the outset of his career, was a Zionist; Peretz, who wrote in it continually up to Czernowitz, was not. Uri Nisan Gnessin traveled to Palestine in 1907, wrote from there to his father, "The Jewish soul is in the Diaspora, not here," and returned to Russia to author his great Hebrew novellas. The essayist Hillel Zeitlin vigorously defended rabbinic Judaism—in Yiddish. In 1919 the Hebrew fiction writer Eliezer Steinman published a Hebrew manifesto entitled "The Hebrew Communist" and calling for "a red Hebrew culture." Avraham Sutzkever has lived in Israel for the past fifty-five years while writing poetry in Yiddish alone. Gabriel Preil, a shy and secluded New Yorker, was still publishing wonderful verse in both languages in the 1980s, long after the Hebrew and Yiddish literary scenes alike had vanished from the city. The young Uri Tsvi Greenberg wrote expressionist Yiddish poetry in Warsaw after World War I and was prominent in Yiddish literary circles. In 1923, he said goodbye to all that in a poem entitled "In the Kingdom of the Cross" and soon left for Palestine, where he joined the ultra- nationalist Zionist Right— which in those days led, sometimes violently, the fight against Yiddish. Most of his verse was henceforth in Hebrew, but he never stopped writing Yiddish poems, and in 1939 he was briefly back in Poland editing a Yiddish newspaper.

Such inconsistencies were legion. They point to the fact that, although the Hebrew-Yiddish language war was real, it was rarely fought by the real writers. It was fought by the ideologues, the politicians, the organizers, the theoreticians, the literary hacks. It is no accident that every one of the important Soviet Yiddish writers, many of whom— in the early years, at least—were true believers in the revolution, kept away from the anti-Hebrew campaign conducted by the Yevsektsia, the Yiddish-oriented "Jewish section" of the Communist party; no accident that when, in 1927, the faculty of the Hebrew University in Jerusalem was fractiously split by a proposal to establish a chair in Yiddish studies,

Hayim Nahman Bialik, the "Hebrew national poet," as he was sometimes referred to, came out in favor of it.

Whatever their politics, the Jewish writers of Eastern Europe did all they could to avoid being torn apart by Yiddish and Hebrew's bitterly contested divorce. Many refused to choose between them. Many who did choose chose heavy-heartedly; their selection of Yiddish was not a rejection of Hebrew or vice versa. How does a writer reject a father tongue or a mother tongue?

The most tragic thing about the language war was that it pitted one form of Jewish nationalism against another, the most Jewish Jews against the most Jewish Jews. Yet it was not a war between two literatures. The truth of the matter is that there never were two literatures. In the words of a 1918 essay by Ba'al Makhshoves, the pen name of the Yiddish literary critic Isidor Elyashev:

> [We] have two languages and a dozen echoes from other foreign languages, but... we have only one literature. And therefore, the reader who seeks to become acquainted with the currents of Jewish life, to comprehend the spirit of the Jewish individual and multitude and how they find expression in Jewish literature, that reader does not separate Hebrew writers from Yiddish ones.... All are representatives of our literature, all embody a piece of Jewish life in their writings; all of them are Jewish artists.

I would like to second the motion. The great language war between Hebrew and Yiddish is over, but against the counsel of Ba'al Makhshoves, it has left behind it a map with a partition line. On one side we have the Jewish Commonwealth of Hebrew Letters; on the other, the Jewish People's Republic of Yiddish Literature. Although the borders between the two are open and travelers can and do cross them, each country retains its own government, its own customs officials, and its own police force—or, to step out from behind the metaphor, its own departments of literature, curricula, scholars, and critics. Sholem Aleichem? Down the hall and to the left. Agnon? That's at the other end of the campus.

I do not make light of the need for institutional frameworks and academic specialization. Nor does teaching Sholem Aleichem and Agnon in different survey courses necessarily mean erecting an iron curtain between them. But what do we do with Peretz? Teach the Yiddish and Hebrew versions of "A Happy Family" in different buildings? Create the fiction, more fictional than anything Peretz ever wrote, that these are stories written by two different authors and that a *fisbenkele* and a *hadom-raglayim* never meet? Or the even greater fiction, widely accepted today, that there is only one Peretz, a Yiddish one, of whom the Hebrew Peretz was a mere shadow?

Of course, Peretz is a special case; he turned his back on Hebrew at Czernowitz, and the institutions of Hebrew literature have retaliated by neglecting him to this day. But the institutions of Hebrew literature have also been, to this day, antagonistic toward Yiddish literature as a whole. They have viewed it—as I, too, did for many years—as a Hebrew literature manqué, a literature that would have been written in Hebrew had only its writers understood their Jewish duty. Much of it has never been adequately translated into Hebrew; little of it has been absorbed by the Israeli literary consciousness; almost none of it is taught in Israeli schools. Great Jewish novelists and poets like Sholem Asch, Moyshe Kulbak, and Katya Molodovsky are not thought of as being "ours" by Israel's intellectuals in the way that Agnon, Brenner, or Leah Goldberg are.

And yet not only are they "ours," they grew up in one home with Agnon, Brenner, and Goldberg and had the same parents, brothers, and sisters. The very differences between Hebrew and Yiddish writing—what I have called their complementarity—only demonstrate that they are two halves of one whole. Of what other two literatures can this be said? You do not need to be familiar with Dickens's London in order to know Balzac's Paris, but you are not fully acquainted with Sholem Aleichem's Kasrilevke unless you have also been to Agnon's Szybusz.

Nevertheless, the Jewish language war had to be fought. It had a right side and a wrong side. It was a conflict between two political and cultural conceptions of the Jewish future, of which one represented a catastrophic misjudgment.

At bottom, Yiddishism was a radical amputation of Jewish peoplehood and Jewish history. In place of Hebrew, the only language common to Jews in all times and places, it proposed a Judeo-German that most parts of the Jewish world did not speak. From the demographic mosaic of that world, with its Sephardic Jews, Middle-Eastern Jews, Central Asian Jews, Italian Jews, French Jews, Dutch Jews, Middle-European Jews, and English- speaking Jews, it crowned as the "real" Jews the Yiddish-speaking population of Russia, Poland, Romania, and the Baltic states alone. Eastern Europe, a region first settled by Jews in the Middle Ages, was now the true Jewish homeland. Of a Jewish past of 3,000 years, the first two-thirds, in which Yiddish did not exist as a language, was to be effectively discarded.

Peretz's, "The Jews are one people—their language is Yiddish," was an absurd self-contradiction. The Hebraists were right. Hebrew alone was the eternal language of the Jews. In the best of circumstances—which, alas, did not prevail—Yiddish was doomed in modern times to go the way of all the *la'az* languages of the past. Those who, failing to understand this, acted as the political and intellectual accomplices of the liquidation of Jewish culture in Russia, and of the worldwide Communist campaign against Zionism and Israel, did become the enemies of their people. And the attitudes of Yiddishism live on, not only in the voguish sentimentality of much of the current revival of interest in the Yiddish language but in Jewish intellectual circles as well. In this sense, Yiddishism can be said to have survived the disappearance, in all but the ultra-Orthodox circles in which the language is still spoken, of Yiddish itself.

These attitudes can be enumerated. They include the belief that Zionism was a mistaken political strategy for the Jewish people; that an identification with Israel need not be a central feature of Diaspora Jewish life; that minority status in the Diaspora is the optimal Jewish cultural and spiritual condition; that the political interests of Diaspora Jews lie in the forging of alliances with as many "progressive" and Left-wing causes as possible; that solidarity with non-Jewish victims of capitalism, colonialism, racism, and other injustices is more important than solidarity with other Jews; and that the very notion of other Jews, of that *klal yisra'el* or collectivity of the Jewish people that all Jews traditionally felt responsible to, can be trimmed at will to suit one's ideological proclivities.

Few serious Yiddish writers would have shared such an outlook. The distinction between Yiddish culture and literature, on the one hand, and Yiddishism or the neo-Yiddishism that has succeeded it, on the other, is elementary. If I myself needed many years to realize this, that is perhaps only because, as a boy in my family's living room, I heard the shots of a small skirmish at the end of a long war and mistook the nature of the foe.

2002

Holy Land

Not long ago, several years after settling in Israel with my wife, we moved with our nine-month-old daughter into a house we had built on nearly an acre of land in the hilltop village of Zichron Ya'akov. "What will you do with so much land?" my Israeli friends asked me concernedly, whereas I was worried about how to get along with so little: at the very least I wanted flower beds, a rock garden, a vegetable garden, fruit trees, a chicken run, room for a donkey, and space enough left over for a nature reserve. I had been land hungry ever since I could remember, even as a small city boy whose practical knowledge of the green world beyond Manhattan was limited to the ability to recognize poison ivy, and it grieved me to have to sell the one hundred fifty acres that I owned in the state of Maine in order to help pay for our acre in Zichron—all the more so because they didn't even cover the full cost of it. Proportionally, I might not have struck a bad bargain, since by exchanging one twelve-millionth of the land area of the United States for one five-millionth of that of Israel I was trading fewer shares for more. But I found such statistics cold comfort. *I* had remained the same size; so had the world; and the world was less mine than before.

I bought the land in Maine in the summer of 1966 when I borrowed a car and headed northeast from New York City armed with an Esso map of New England, a Strout Realty catalogue, and fifteen hundred dollars, with which I intended to purchase as much territory as I could.

I had crossed the Maine line from New Hampshire and gotten as far as Waldo County, midway between Bangor and the state capital of Augusta, when I found what I was looking for: a tract of abandoned farmland and woodland with a small brook flowing through it, selling at ten dollars an acre, a cut rate attributable to its being backed by only a quitclaim deed, which attested to its seller, but no one else, having relinquished his right to it. There was no house on it, just the cellar hole of one burned down for the insurance by its owner before quitting it during the Depression, and I planned to build a log cabin and live as a hermit. For this, the property was admirably suited, being located half a mile in from the nearest paved road and many times that distance from the closest town.

Not long after that I married and had to revise my plans. As a gesture to them, my wife agreed to spend the summer camping on the land in a tent. I had promised her Arcadia; there was a bit of that, but there were also mosquitos and steady rain, and mornings when I left her to go roaming by myself in the woods. I needed to be alone in them. One could dedicate a lifetime, I thought—I *would* dedicate part of mine—to getting to know their every tree, bush, and rock. One day I chased a fox through the broad meadow on which we had pitched our tent, following at top speed the brown sightings of its tail in the high grass. I had no illusions about catching it, and before long it was lost to sight, but I didn't stop running until, exuberant and out of breath, I had reached our property line. It wasn't the fox I'd been chasing—it was the physical sensation of what belonged to me.

There are no foxes on our near-acre in Israel, though mongooses do slink across it, and while we can see for tens of miles from our hilltop, I can throw a stone from our house to any of our borders. Still, it's clear that my work is cut out for me. You can devote as much time to a thousand square meters as to a square mile of woods. You have to, because the woods can take care of themselves while a garden can't. I was taught that lesson quickly. Bring in some topsoil and you had better plant on it fast,

HILLEL HALKIN

or the winter rains will wash it away and cut gullies in the old soil beneath it, leaving you worse off than before. Inherit half a dozen trees that bore tangerines as big as oranges, and they're now the size of cherries because you haven't watered or pruned them. Let the spring wildflowers grow high, and you'll have snakes when the dry weather starts, one of which, *vipera xanthina*, the Palestinian viper, you wouldn't want to be bitten by. Several townsmen have warned me that it's time I took a sickle to the bright yellow clumps of wild chrysanthemum and mustard growing around our house, but they're so pretty that I haven't had the heart to.

I haven't yet run into a viper, but I did once find the skin of one, discarded under a bush like a burdensome sweatshirt on a hot, dusty day. We have other tenants, too, of whom I know only by inference, such as the porcupine who leaves his gray-white quill by our house as a calling card, or the mole-rat who periodically puts out a pile of fresh dirt by the entrance to his tunnel as though for the dustman to collect. I *have* seen snails, spiders, scorpions, earthworms, tortoises, ants, butterflies, field mice, and over a dozen species of birds, including two brilliantly blue-winged kingfishers who are currently nesting in an earthen embankment at the lower end of our property, in an abandoned condominium of holes that formerly belonged to some geckos. These lizards are curious beasts who like to run up and down, and sometimes upside down, over the walls of human dwellings on their suction-padded feet; the rough stucco of ours is perfect terrain for them, and I suspect that they moved to new quarters to be closer to it. In speed and agility, they are the opposite of tortoises. Once I came upon a pair of these copulating behind a rock, the male precariously atilt the female, who kept advancing beneath him as though determined to be about her business, their shells clicking and clacking like billiard balls. I modestly looked away, and when I turned back, they were gone—into thin air, it must be, for it's common knowledge that a tortoise can't run.

To a tortoise our hilltop acre *is* a woods, big enough for all its needs. For us, it's three-quarters of an easily surveyable rectangle. Below it is a dirt road, beyond which stretches a vista of olive groves, vineyards, the gentle hills of the Carmel, and the distant lights of Haifa at night, all occasionally disfigured by a carelessly smoking lime works located behind the first ridge. Across an empty lot to our left is a cottage inhabited by the Traubs, a middle-aged, vegetarian, Scotch-drinking couple, both artists by trade. They are splendid artists, splendid gardeners, splendid people; beneath their somewhat proper and colonial South African exterior, they are as merry as larks. Uphill from us, in a house that fronts on one of the town's main streets, lives toothless old Betsalel Ashkenazi. Both Betsalel and the house have been sold to a couple from Haifa, which he hasn't been told about because he's stone deaf. The younger brother who sold him did so on the condition that he be allowed to remain in the house for as long as he lives: it's a kind of insurance policy in reverse, whereby the insured benefits in his lifetime, and the company wins by his death. The couple from Haifa occasionally comes to inspect its property and let its children romp on their future lawn. Betsalel does not hear them or show a sign of life, which raises false hopes.

The land to our right belongs to Ezra Goldstein, who cut down the plum trees.

Goldstein, from whom we bought part of our property, kept an adjacent strip for himself. The land had been in his family, he told me, since the town's founding by early Zionist pioneers nearly a hundred years ago; only because he was hard-pressed for cash was he selling some of it now. In town, where he had a reputation for being a miser, he was unpopular. "He's a crafty old peasant," we were warned by the Traubs. "You'd better watch out for him." We did; yet we had no cause for complaint until discovering, while having the land surveyed prior to building, that the border between us ran directly through the trunks of two plum trees that had won my admiration by their profusion of blossoms and promise of sumptuous fruit. Since Goldstein lived in a house some distance away, I suggested he might agree to move the border a few feet to his side in return for fitting compensation

I was unprepared for the vehemence of his response. The trees, he declared, had been planted by his father when he himself was a child; he had watered and tended them ever since; he could not possibly part with them now. Instead, he proposed, he would pay us to move the border the other way.

Now it was I who refused. I had no intention of surrendering our claim. If the plum trees couldn't be all ours, we would at least keep our half. Let the border stay where it was.

And there the matter rested—or so I thought until, returning a week later, I had the sensation of looking at a picture from which a detail—but what?—was missing. The plum trees! I ran with a sinking stomach to where they had stood; all that was left were two pathetic stumps that barely came up to my knees. They had been mangled with an axe, not even cut cleanly, their still green branches scattered about like clothing after an orgy, hacked and splintered to pieces with a maniacal fury. Goldstein! Though he was no longer young and hardly seemed capable of such a crime of passion, it couldn't have been anyone else. I ran to his house—he was out. That evening I got him on the phone.

"Goldstein!"

"Halkin?"

"Goldstein! How could you have done it?"

"Halkin! I had to. You made me." His voice was touchy, aggrieved, as though he were the injured party. "They were my trees. I helped my father plant them. I watered them as a boy. I offered to pay you for them."

"For God's sake," I said. It was as though the true mother in the biblical story of Solomon had torn her baby into shreds and accused the false mother of murder. "I would have let you have them if I knew you would chop them down. Why didn't you tell me first?"

"It wouldn't have made any difference. I wanted us to be good neighbors."

"You wanted us to be *what*?"

"Good neighbors. Believe me, I'm a farmer. I know about land. Sooner or later we'd have quarreled. I did it for both our sakes."

And perhaps he did, though if so his intentions misfired, because we avoid each other now when we meet in the streets of the town. You dreamed of land, it seemed, until you owned it. Then you fought over it and wanted more.

Still, an acre isn't so little when it comes with a coefficient of time. Poking around one day in an overgrown area toward the bottom of our land, I lost my footing and fell several feet through the tangled branches of a wild pistachio tree to land on my knees in a hidden depression that sloped counter to the grade of the hill. Directly in front of me was a small opening leading into a cave, the stone above which had been crudely but unmistakably worked into a rough lintel. After clearing away the dirt at the entrance, I crawled inside. A subterranean must filled the space I was in, a rectangular chamber that measured some ten feet by fifteen and had barely enough clearance at the center to enable me to stand straight. Niches had been carved in the walls, two in the shorter rear wall, three in each of the side ones. Black beetles scurried at my feet, roused from their graveyard vigil, for it was clear that I was in a burial cave.

But whose? The country is full of such caves: Byzantine, Roman, Hellenistic, Jewish, Canaanite, prehistoric, antediluvian. An archaeologist could have told me at one glance; a Talmudist told me at none. Without waiting for me to finish my description, he pulled a volume off his shelf, opened it to the sixth chapter of the Mishnah of *Bava Batra*, and read aloud:

> "He who sells a burial place to another, or who comes to possess one, shall make the interior of the cave four *amoth* by six, and shall hollow out eight niches, three in one side, three in the other, and two in the remaining one…. Rabbi Shim'on ben Gamliel says, it depends on the rock."

An *amah* was about a foot-and-a-half, the distance from a grown man's fingertips to his elbow. The cave was a Jewish one, then, and since a Jewish family was unlikely to have lived and buried its dead in such a fashion in the hills of the Carmel before the Hasmonean expansion of the second and first centuries B.C.E., or later than the eve of the Islamic conquest, it was possible to date the cave's use to fifteen hundred to two thousand years ago.

I nursed no dreams of buried treasure, since to judge by the cave's crudeness its owners were not well-to-do; besides, it had clearly been ransacked by grave robbers, and in all likelihood by the department of antiquities. Nevertheless, I returned to it one day with several companions, equipped with a lantern and spades, to see what we could unearth. The results were unremarkable: little fragments of red pottery, the bones of a sheep or goat that had probably been roasted by shepherds, the inexplicable ostracon of a phonograph record with the partial inscription UMBA TUMBA on the obverse side and the letters RAEL on the reverse. "Middle Ben-Gurion dynasty," grumbled the companion who found it and went on digging. It was he who later came up with the one real discovery of the day: half a human jawbone, yellowed like old parchment but otherwise in good condition, with two of its rear molars intact in their sockets. The rest of its body had vanished, leaving it behind like the grin of the Cheshire Cat.

I took the jawbone home and put it in the drawer of my desk, from which I occasionally took it out for a *tête-à-tête*. I wondered about it. Had it belonged to someone who lived on our property, or had the cave been purchased the way one nowadays buys a plot in a cemetery? There is a record of such a transaction in the Book of Genesis:

> And Sarah died in Kiriatharba—the same is Hebron— in the land of Canaan; and Abraham came to mourn for Sarah, and to weep for her. And Abraham rose up from before his dead, and spoke unto the children of Heth, saying: "I am a stranger and a sojourner with you; give me possession of a burying-place with you, that I may bury my dead out of my sight..." So the field of Ephron, which was in Machpelah, which was before Mamre, the field, and the cave which was therein, and all the trees that were in the field, that were in all the border thereof

round about, were made sure unto Abraham for a possession in the presence of the children of Heth."

What might the owner of the jawbone have recognized of our property today? Not the foundations of our house being churned out by a cement mixer; but the wild almonds and figs, the wild olives and pomegranates, the wild mustard and garlic that shoot up every spring in a reckless green rush as though aware that life were but a brief season—"all the trees that were in the field"—these he would surely remember. He? But it probably wasn't a man's jaw at all, for it was so petite that it barely came halfway to my ear when I tried it on for size. Was it a woman's? A small child's? This question was answered one evening while dining at the house of friends in Haifa. Midway through the soup, the guest opposite me revealed that he was a dentist. Could he tell me, I asked, something about a jaw? He imagined he could. The rented apartment in which we were living was not far away; I was there and back again with the jaw before the main course was served. There was a hush at the table while the dentist examined it by candlelight, turning it this way and that like a bridge prepared for a fitting before passing judgment. "She was a middle-aged woman, I'd say. About forty years old. The molars are ground flat; she must have chewed a lot of bread. No cavities, though. I can't tell you much more. Oh, yes: she had gum trouble. Here, look at these irregularities in the alveolar ridge." There was a definite sag in the set of the bone where it had met the membrane around it.

Since the discovery of the cave, our property has seemed larger to me. Surely an acre times fifteen-hundred years comes close to equaling one-hundred-fifty acres multiplied by the time gone by since the Depression. How many of those years, I wondered, was the cave guarded by the descendants of those buried in it before being abandoned to the shepherds and the grave robbers? The dead may bind us to places even more than the living, whom we can at least correspond with. I once knew a widow in New York who refused to go away on vacation because she did not want to leave her husband alone in the cemetery, and even Abraham called himself "a stranger and a sojourner" in the Land until he buried Sarah in it. Traditionally, one of the first things a newly formed Jewish community did anywhere was to dedicate a graveyard, and the pious Jews over the centuries who came to the Land of Israel to die and be buried in it did so in part, I suspect, so that their mortal remains would not embog their children any deeper in the grime of exile. Here, though, there was another consideration, too, it being held that on Judgment Day the resurrection would take place only in the Holy Land, which would have to be reached by those not buried in it by the ordeal of *gilgul mehilot*, the arduous trek of their bones through underground passages in the earth.

There is nothing overtly holy about the soil of our property, a yellowish-brown loam of stubborn though not intractable character, beneath which the limestone bedrock juts closer to the surface in places than a gardener might wish. Yet a pickaxe can crumble this rock easily enough, whereupon it breaks into numerous pebbles of a chalk so pure that one could write with them on a blackboard. When rolled between the fingers, they become a white powder; when licked, they taste somewhat sweet. They are best savored with a brush of the lips, a pilgrim's kiss—a mode of contact with the earth that is not much in fashion these days, both because tourism has replaced pilgrimage as a mode of travel and because the expanse of concrete by which the modern traveler is surrounded upon arrival at his destination is unconducive to the custom.

And yet to the true pilgrim this difficulty is surmountable, as my wife and I had occasion to witness when, on our way to beginning our new lives in Israel, we sailed from Venice on a Greek ship that anchored in Limassol to pick up a consignment of Cypriot Christians bound for Easter week in Jerusalem. These gnarled little men and women in black, so short and stumpy of stature that they seemed to belong to another, pygmified race, passed the night on deck eating and praying beneath the stars and were in a state of rare excitement when we docked in Haifa Bay in the morning. For a while they were content to point their fingers anticipatorily landward; but growing impatient as the disembarkation proceedings dragged on, they soon flung themselves on the deck of the ship and began to kiss it as if it had been transformed into sacred ground by being moored to the wharf extending from the shore. The rest of the passengers, mostly vacationers on an organized tour, looked on with discomfort, regaining their composure only when, as though on a signal from their guide, they pulled out their cameras to record the event.

Already at the start of their trip, in effect, both the vacationers and the Cypriots were getting what they had paid for. The tourist travels to see something different, the pilgrim to see differently—and for this the deck of a ship is as good a place as any to begin. Jewish sources have wrestled with the question of what sort of vision ascending to the Holy Land involves. If the Baal Shem Tov, as is known, put off an intended voyage there time and again and died without ever having made it, this was not, we may conjecture, because he doubted the Land's holiness but because he doubted his ability to perceive it; while that most enigmatic of all *tsaddikim*, the riddlesome Rabbi Nahman of Bratslav, was ready to depart from the Land of Israel the day after his arrival, for he had, so he told a traveling companion, seen all he needed to see. Whether this was that the Land was indeed more holy than the Ukrainian country-side around Bratslav or, on the contrary, that it was not, is something he never revealed.

For of course all land is holy to those with the eyes to see it, which makes it seem foolish of the Jews to have insisted that their land was holier than others. As far back as Greek and Roman antiquity, such implausible hierarchies of holiness, the bread and butter of Judaism, infuriated the Gentiles, who resented absurdities like the claim that God loved all His creatures but loved the Jews more, or that He valued the seventh day of His week above the preceding six. Christianity subsequently took up the banner of equality; and there was a time of my life in which it seemed to me not only the more rigorously logical, but also the more humanly profound, of the two religions. Everything is holy! I cried out with Blake, with that youthful passion that is as determined to level differences in the realm of ontology as in that of social relations or economics. As I've grown older, I've become less of a spiritual sans-culotte, having seen that it is but a short step from believing that everything is holy to living as though nothing were, the totality being a slippery category to embrace; yet I still do not believe that our one hundred fifty acres in Maine were any further from divinity than our hilltop in Zichron because the weeds they produced were not mentioned in the Bible. Both smell equally good after a rain, and the mosquitoes in summer are as annoying when encountered on either.

Not *the* holy land then, just one of many that I have chosen for my own, and I confess to the occasional wish as a Jew that the rest of the world would take its shrines elsewhere and leave us to putter around here by ourselves. Not that I think we can do a better job with this tiny patch of the globe than anyone else would; on the contrary, I am reasonably convinced that we will make a mess of it, thereby confirming the rule about what is bred by familiarity, that dulling condition of the spirit from which tourists and pilgrims are in flight. We Jews returned to Palestine in order to get back to the land but now seem more interested in what we can get out of it. Those lime works over there, for example, smoking up the vineyards when the wind blows the wrong way, blotting out the landscape in which Elijah smote the priests of the Baal, disemboweling the hidden part of the hill facing our house until one day there will be nothing left but a paper-thin carapace, as brittle as an empty snail shell: are they not a profanation? To be sure, there must be lime, which is an ingredient in the house we built, but I refuse to concede that it must be gotten so messily. The great white storks who fly overhead every autumn on their way to changing hemispheres and make the return trip again in the spring must look down and wonder what benighted species of gardener would put such a stinking gray hole in the middle of his greenery.

So we are back to gardens again. "And He shall make her wasteland an Eden and her wilderness a garden of God," says Isaiah, who did not conceive of wilderness as does the Audubon Society. In part this has to do with the Palestinian environment, in which untamed nature means not cool and verdant forests with their brooks, fish, and berries on which a woodsman can survive for months but harsh and ungenerous surroundings, if not desert then thistly *maquis* lacking permanent water sources and difficult to penetrate, exposed to fierce wind and rain for half the year and to even fiercer sun for the other half. Equally, however, Isaiah was speaking in the name of a biblical tradition that did not believe in keeping man out of nature's hair. "Be fruitful, and multiply, and fill the earth, and subdue it," says God in His maiden speech to humanity, which has been interpreted in some circles as an incitement to population explosion and mass zoocide. Actually, it is a plea for good gardening.

For what is the ideal garden? It is a state of interdependence between nature and man, the outcome of a contract by which one side agrees to be pliant and domestic, and the other, benevolent, responsible, and just. It is not a forest or jungle in which nature runs free; but neither is it a farm on which nature is enslaved or obliterated. It may be used to raise food, and so be planned for utility; but variety is no less its goal, and it must have flowers, and shrubs, and trees that bear only green leaves, and places to walk in and play, and wild areas that blend into the cultivated ones, corners of self-expression in which nature is left to improvise on its own. Since it is not a purely economic enterprise, it cannot be judged in purely economic terms; yet it must not be wasteful and should strive for self-sufficiency, using the resources closest to hand. In size, it may vary from a backyard to a country; if it encounters an obstacle, like an anthill, lime works, or city, it may not be able to eliminate it, but neither can it just go around it, and it must incorporate it into its structure as artfully as it can. For above all, a garden is an art and must concentrate on the relations of things as much as on the things themselves.

To the wilderness lover all this is tame stuff, about as exciting as a pet lamb to a hunter. And yet with every year it is more apparent that if wildernesses are to survive at all in our world, they will do so only as parts of a larger system of gardens to which they belong. We *have* multiplied and filled the earth, quite without the help of the Bible, and the real choice is no longer the wilderness or the garden; it is the garden or the garbage dump, Isaiah or the rusty tin can. If we were presently to divide up the habitable globe among all its inhabitants, even an acre apiece is more than could go around; one hundred fifty is a dizzying extravagance, and while

I could have lived on mine had I wished with no worse harassment than marauding snowmobiles and the sounds of my neighbors' chain saws, my children or grandchildren might have seen them broken into smaller holdings by the state. I did well then to sell them—though to be honest, something in me wishes that I hadn't. I never did get to know a woods very well the summer we were in Maine, and it's useless to pretend now that I ever shall. In elegiac moments, I regret that I didn't build my cabin there after all, so that I might be chasing foxes today instead of growing geraniums. Not that it's so easy to grow a geranium. Although it's indeed hard to kill one, it's just as hard to get one to flourish. There are some on our front terrace that are moping right now, and I'd better find out why.

1974

Driving Toward Jerusalem

1.

1.
Haifa to Jenin: One hour.

> From Samaria northward two routes of great interest and beauty lie before us. The one leads westward through a line of valleys of extraordinary fertility, where in spite of the sparse population and the depredations of the Bedouin, large crops of wheat and barley meet the eye... The town of Jenin, which lies at the juncture of several valleys and roads, is a place of considerable importance. Its Scripture name (En-Gannim), the fountain of the gardens, seems to be derived from a magnificent fountain of water which rises in the hills just behind the town, and irrigating the rich alluvial soil, turns it into a garden.
>
> —The Reverend Samuel Manning,
> *Those Holy Fields*, 1874

I head out from Haifa along the bay toward Acre rather than south on the road to Tel Aviv, turning inland at Nesher by the great four-chimneyed cement works. It's an unpromising beginning for a scenic route, a dismal industrial sink of smokestacks and foul tarns that could pass for New Jersey were it not for the occasional fronds of an asthmatic palm tree.

Soon, though, I'm out of it, past suburban Tiv'on and skirting the western edge of the Valley of Jezreel. To one side is the well-watered valley, heroically green after six months of rainless summer, dotted with kibbutzim and moshavim, whose little red-roofed houses look requisitioned from a Monopoly board. Purple bougainvillea athletically scales their white walls. A combine is harvesting cotton in a field, dragging a large cage covered with white burrs. Sprinklers whir and jerk, their jets forming Gothic arches in the air. Visible in the distance are the gray mountains of Samaria, the heart of Arab Palestine, whose curving spine runs southward from Jenin, untouched by Jewish settlement to this day. It's a long-cut to Jerusalem, adding half an hour to the trip, but if you're not in a hurry, the empty roads and mountain views redeem lost time.

Being in a hurry, though, isn't why I haven't driven this way since the Yom Kippur War. "I know," nodded an acquaintance sympathetically a while after the war, "I feel the same way. The less Arabs I see, the better." I shrugged: it wasn't an outrageous sentiment at the time, it just didn't happen to be mine. Fear, then? If the criteria were actuarial, I'd rather take my chances with the infrequent grenade thrown at Israeli cars on the occupied West Bank than on the murderous traffic on Israel's coastal roads. A conqueror's qualms? But the war has shaken Israel's grip on the territories taken in 1967; I should feel less like their conqueror, not more. It's not that either, then—and yet it is, too, only the opposite: a feeling more like relinquishment, that retrenchment of emotional interest that takes place when you know or fear that you are about to lose something precious, to ease the final wrench of which you begin to let go in advance. You do it in little ways, without really paying attention. Like driving to Jerusalem the old way, along the coast and up from the west. After all, it *is* quicker.

The road passes Megiddo, site of the once strategic pass where young King Josiah was killed by the Egyptians, trying vainly to stem the advance on Assyria of Pharaoh Necho, the pointless victim of his own foolish courage and the power politics of the day. It crosses the Hadera-Afula highway soon after, and several kilometers beyond that, the pre-1967 Israeli-Jordanian border, the "green line," as it is known in Israel today.

What a simple, complicated little phrase, half cartographic, half iconographic in its referents. An allusion to the color used on Israeli maps to denote the country's borders prior to the Six-Day War, it is at the same time a description, a metaphor, a challenge, a boast, a vindication, a tourist guide's cheap witticism, a fundraising slogan, a title claim to a country. "Look!" it says. "The border is gone now, see the difference. We, not they, have drained the swamps. We, not they, have reforested the mountainsides, irrigated the fields, raised the yields per dunam five- and tenfold. We, not they, have made the desert bloom. Our side is green—and so it is our land, not theirs. Let the land speak!"

All that still marks the old border is the remains of a smashed Jordanian tank barrier along the sides of the road, already weathered to look like something far older, part of the ruins of a Turkish aqueduct perhaps. Farther on a sign informs you that you have entered the occupied territories, and another, that the road has soft shoulders. The houses are built of stone now, flat-roofed, hiding behind dusty stone walls. A woman in a long cotton dress draws water from a well. Black Bedouin tents. Two barefoot boys on a donkey. The dun-colored fields are empty, abandoned. It is the dry, the dead time of year, in which the harvest is in and autumn planting has not yet begun, well past the season in which a shocked Ezekiel saw the women in the Temple mourning for the lovely Tammuz, whose willowy body perished with nature each summer. A peasant in the stubbly distance plows slowly behind a mule, turning up the dry earth to await the first autumn rains, after which he will sow. A field of beheaded sunflowers stands blindly in the morning heat, its pale stalks the color of raffia. A lone flowerhead, missed by the reapers, bows in final homage to the sun.

—⟋⟋⟍—

The traffic coming against me is light: an old truck with its hood flaps removed in lieu of a cooling system, a shiny Mercedes taxi full of passengers from Jenin. A donkey trudges by with a load of firewood, its master nowhere in sight. A farmer stands barefoot in his yard, shoveling the last ears of a mound of yellow grain into a large gunnysack. Puddles of chaff still lie scattered about where the wind let them drop. I think of a day a few years ago when I saw grain being harvested at the other end of the West Bank. It was the holiday of Shavuot, the Feast of Weeks, and my wife and I had driven that morning with friends to visit the excavated old synagogue at biblical Eshtemoa, the Arab village of Sammu'a, which sits on a hilltop east of the Hebron-Beersheba road. *"Knees al-yahud, knees al-yahud!"*—"The church of the Jews, the church of the Jews!"—shouted the band of boys who led us to the site, past the shells of several buildings that had been razed by an Israeli task force in a 1966 raid that helped set the stage for the Six-Day War. What was left of the structure, whose fine, squared building blocks, with their raised Herodian borders reminiscent of the stones of the Wailing Wall, had been mostly carted away over the centuries for the cornerstones and lintels of houses, stood at the high point of the village across a narrow lane from the mosque. Over the remains of its northern wall, in which it was still possible to trace the outlines of the Ark that had been placed there to face the razed Temple Mount in Jerusalem, there was a fine view of the mountains of Judea, already turned the dull tawn of the early Palestinian summer. *Judea capta*; yet here, hundreds of years after Titus's legions gutted the Sanctuary, Jews had still worshipped freely on the heights.

We were heading home along a back road when our car dipped down into a small, bowl-shaped valley in which our eyes were met by such a carnival of activity that we could not take it in all at once. A whole village seemed to have turned out from somewhere in the hills to stage a Brueghelian tableau. At the turn of the road was a field of ripe wheat in which a row of women in peasant embroidery were reaping, bending low to cut the high grain: bending, cutting, and moving ahead, bending, cutting, and moving ahead, in a dancelike, repetitive two-step. After every few strokes they paused to gather the fallen wheat, binding it into sheaves with one of its stalks. A round threshing floor had been laid out behind them to which these were removed. Tied to a pole, two yoked oxen orbited in a circle, crushing the grain beneath mindless, lumbering hooves. Windward of them the village men were winnowing, tossing the crushed wheat into the air with spread wooden fans. The winnowed grain fell to the ground while, caught by the breeze, the chaff streamed away like confetti to where sheep were being shorn at the other end of the valley. Two men pinned each squealing animal to the ground by its legs, its fat rump marked red with henna, while a third dodged expertly in and out with a pair of shears. Each stunned lamb lay unmoving for a while when released, then wandered off to eat back its pride in the fading grass. Peasant women were carding the fresh wool on the rocks. Where the road wound out of the valley an old crone, an ancient Lorelei, sat on a rock spinning, rolling a little wooden distaff back and forth on her thigh. She giggled like a girl when we stopped the car to look....

The road narrows, grows rutted, forcing my car to slow down. I pass more houses, poorer ones, parts of them built of unplastered concrete blocks. Assorted bundles of things are drying on the roofs: wood, figs, almonds, dung, indistinct grasses and herbs. Two women walk wide-hipped down the road, one balancing a wicker basket on her head, the other a plastic jerry can. A boy explores a hedge of ripe prickly pears with a tin can to seize the fruit and a torn rubber glove to protect his hand from its piercing filaments.

The land is rolling now. The mountains of Samaria loom closer, gray and bare. A flock of goats grazes by the roadside. They have picked the groundcover clean and are working on the scattered shrubs and small trees, standing on their hind legs in strangely humanoid postures to strip the leaves and bark. The goatherd sits on a rock, staff between his legs, un-shaven, a dirty white rag wrapped turban-like around his head. Suddenly he bends to pick up a stone, hand scraping the ground in one motion, eyes fixed on a point on the road. One hand automatically comes off the driver's wheel to shield my face. He flings the stone ahead of me, at a goat that has strayed too near the road and now scrambles hurriedly back. No, I don't feel like a conqueror—but would my hand have come up just as fast, its own impulsive agent, if I weren't? It flutters awkwardly for a moment before the windshield, then transmutes itself into a wave. The goatherd waves back.

HILLEL HALKIN

I think again of the unassuming pageantry of that morning near Sammu'a. "And you shall count from the morrow after the Sabbath, from the day you brought the sheaf of the wave offering, seven full weeks shall they be.... Then you shall present a cereal offering of new grain to the Lord." So biblical! In all the nightmarish blood feud between Arab and Jew, is there anything quite so ironic, so absurd, as this? The Jew goes into exile long ago, taking with him his books, his rituals, and his ancient way of life, which he struggles to preserve in more or less the same order, that is, to the extent that they are detachable from the context of the everyday. He copies his books and recopies them, surrounding them with more and more books. He codifies his rituals, embellishes them, adapts them to meet the changing times. But his Palestinian life is inexorably shattered. It survives only in bits, in isolated fragments encapsulated within the overlapping layers of the sacred that continue to accumulate around it like hardening stone around fossil footprints. The flat, round, simple bread he ate with every meal, dipping it in oil or vinegar when there was nothing else, is now eaten once a year, dry and yeastless, in the form of the Passover *shemurah* matzah. His head covering, worn out-of-doors to protect himself from the blazing Palestinian sun, blackens, shrivels into the little *yarmulke* of the synagogue; his flowing, toga-like robe becomes a fringed *tallit*, a prayer shawl. On annual holidays like Rosh Hashanah and Tu B'shvat, he spends extravagant sums to buy the exotic fruits of the Holy Land, dates and pomegranates, almonds and figs, which were staples of his diet long ago. When the winter snows come in Europe he prays for rain, and when the summer rains come, he prays for dew, for such are the demands of his ancestral soil. The Jew changes, yet remembers, turning his whole life into a mnemonic for a lost golden age, one more intricate than the original. He remembers; yet when long generations later he returns to his native land, inspired equally by the promises of his books and the ideologies of modern Europe, whose despised, problematic, yet thoroughly authentic stepson he has become, he finds, lo and behold, the Arab, the usurper, living there in his place, eating round, flat bread with every meal, covering his head with an elegant *kaffia* against the sun, wearing a long, flowing robe that ripples when he walks, eating figs and pomegranates, almonds and dates, for his daily fare, and living the agricultural rhythms, the seedtimes and the harvests, of the Bible, Talmud, and prayer book. An upside down world!

The usurper? Or perhaps the lost brother, descendant of the descendants of the worshippers at Eshtemoa, who rather than stay a Jew and go into exile, chose with no less stubbornness to become a Christian or Muslim and stay where he was, taking on the beliefs of his rulers as naturally as the Jews in exile took on the food and clothing of theirs, mixing with his neighbors like the peasantry of Judea after the first, Babylonian exile, as we hear from that troubled Zionist, Ezra the Scribe ("Now when these things were done, the princes came to me, saying, the people of Israel, and the priests, and the Levites, have not separated themselves from the peoples of the lands, doing according to their abominations, even of the Canaanites, the Hittites, the Perizzites, the Jebusites, the Ammonites, the Moabites, the Egyptians, and the Amorites.... And when I heard this thing, I rent my garment and my mantle, and plucked off the hair of my head and my beard, and sat down astonished."); keeping faith with Mother Earth instead of Father God, the other half, as it were, of the tragically torn lottery ticket that fate dealt the Jews, illiterate, primitive, benighted, barely recognizable, yet still flesh of one's flesh, one's own kin. Could it be?

It would have been surprising had at least a few Zionist romantics in modern Palestine not thought that it could. One hears it asserted that Jews came to Palestine not knowing that the Arabs existed, and looked down on them when it was discovered that they did; yet the first part of this proposition is sheer nonsense, and the second at best a half-truth. What can be said of the attitude of early Zionist settlers toward the country's Arab inhabitants, of whose existence they were well aware in advance, is that it was an intensely ambivalent one, characterized not only by that confused complex of attraction and repulsion, admiration, fear, and disdain that has often been found in modern times when a colonizing, culturally "advanced" people has come in contact with a more "backward" one, but by a clear consciousness of the unique historical paradoxes involved. One has only to read the fiction of an early Palestinian Hebrew writer like Smilansky, or consider the Arabizing manners of the *shomrim*, the first Palestinian Jewish self-defense forces, to see what conflicting emotions the Arab brought out in the Jew. On the one hand, he was unwashed, ignorant, untrustworthy, treacherous, emotional, violent, temperamental; he stole Jewish crops and animals, waylaid Jewish travelers, harassed Jewish settlements when he could. On the other hand, he was bold, brave, graceful, spontaneous, and lived close to nature and the earth; he was the embodiment of that physicality, that proximity to the natural passions, that the Jew had lost in his exilic life; he was, in however fallen and degraded a state, a precious missing link with the Jews' own past, a living gloss on the imagery of the Bible, the stories of the Patriarchs, the books of Judges and Ruth. Was not the blood that flowed through his veins, informing his dark eyes and olive skin, more "Jewish" than that of many Jews? Was not he the true son of the lost tribes of Israel, to be sought not, as legend had it, beyond the mountains of darkness or at the far ends of the earth, but right where they had vanished, beneath the returning Jew's very nose? Was not this an ample basis for Jew and Arab to live together, sharing, if not one identity, then still a blood brotherhood, each giving to and taking from the other, the Jew bringing the Arab the secrets of modern civilization, the Arab teaching the Jew to live on and with the land?

Clearly, it was not. We all live in some sense imagined identities, but we do not want them to be imagined for us by others. Why should it have mattered to a Palestinian Arab to be told that he was a lost Jew any more than it should have mattered, let us say, to a Jewish Zionist to be told that he was a descendant of Asian Khazars whose ancestors never set foot in Palestine? What is true is not always relevant, and what is relevant is not always true.... And yet, I reflect, swerving to avoid a pothole on the road, if I share an oblique destiny with these people through whose fields I am driving, it is not just this outward one, this having been thrown together by history or blind chance to quarrel and kill each other over the same piece of land. It is all so terribly complicated. Something in me answers to the peasant certainties of their lives—yet across such a distance that I cannot possibly tell them what I know. They hate me for my alien power over them, mock the democratic barbarism of my manners—yet envy the freedom and wealth that accompany these. I covet their lands because they are promised me, biblical—but it is above all their presence that reminds me that this is so, informing a landscape so stripped to its barest essentials that every cloud throws a shadow with a tone that is stark and peremptory, like that of my ancestral book. Let the land speak! But once the land has spoken, what has it said?

Jenin. I pass in front of the open labor exchange outside of town where Arab workers board buses to be taken to their daily jobs in Israel, across the green line, where they work in factories or the building trade. On the outskirts of town stands a British-built police station, flying a blue and white flag. Jewish troops briefly held this building in 1948 too, attacking from the direction of Afula, before being driven back by an Arab counter-attack. I was nine years old at the time and remember hearing the news on the radio in New York. "We've taken Jenin," I ran to tell my father, whose eyes promptly filled with tears. But it was soon taken back. En-Gannim, city of fountains and gardens. It is a dingy-looking place. The main street is lined with little stalls, workshops, garages, from which comes that steady sound of pounding that seems to give the beat to Arab life: of iron, of stone, of wood, of human hands. A fat green mosque points its erectile minaret at a cloudless sky. A month ago an Israeli shopper was shot to death here in the marketplace by a terrorist, who escaped. None of the local merchants reported hearing the shot, apparently, the police conjectured, because a silencer was used.

2.
Jenin to Nablus: Thirty minutes.

Elsewhere in Palestine we are struck by the contrast between the grandeur of the history, and the unimpressive character of the scenery; but these noble and massive mountains form a fitting theater for the grandest events. They are Ebal and Gerizim. In the narrow valley between them was Shechem, where Abraham pitched his tent, and built his first altar, on his entrance into the Promised Land.

—Ibid.

Once out of Jenin the road begins to climb, twist. I change gears frequently, like a musical scale: fourth, third, second, back up to third. The earth is a rusty red now, the *terra rossa* of the Palestinian highlands. Forests of olive trees cover the terraced hillsides, split-trunked, looking as old as the stones. A row of dusty cypresses grasps the embankment above the road, roots clutching at its drop-off. A falcon sits motionless in the blue sky, its talons wrapped around an invisible branch. A woman on a donkey. A taxi coming from Nablus. A village schoolmaster, dressed like a wedding guest in a trim gray suit, moves to the pavement as I pass to keep his shined shoes out of the dust my car kicks up. The villages are perched high on the mountaintops, dull outcrops of stone, reached by steep paths that look like ladders. When the road winds through one of them I am escorted in and out of it by knots of crop-headed boys who pop up from around curves, from under trees, like targets at a carnival booth, waving little straw baskets of ripe figs, the year's last, like a distress signal. "*Teen, teen!*" they shout, each undaunted by the failure of the boy before him, each screwing his face into an expression of defiant hope that his figs— soft, purple, pulpy, tasting too much to me like sugared water—will bring me screeching to a halt. "*Teen, teen!*"—but the car speeds away, leaving the words like dead leaves on the wind.

These worn, stoop-shouldered mountains, rising between the Jordan and the sea; used and re-used: in the endless struggle for Palestine they have always been the bastion of the technologically weaker side. In Joshua's time the conquering Israelites could not break out of them onto the flat land below, where the Canaanites had "chariots of iron," the tanks of ancient warfare that were at their deadliest on open terrain. Next the Philistines, Greeks, and Romans spilled forth from the sea onto the coastal plain, founding their port cities of Ascalon and Gaza, Apollonia and Caesaria, whose encroachments on their highland kingdom the Jews struggled to prevent with sometimes more, sometimes less success, before finally, slowly, going under. Centuries later the Crusaders held this same coastal beachhead, where their heavily armored horsemen reigned supreme; inland, in the hills, where the light Arab bowmen could punish them brutally, their grip was never better than tenuous. And finally, in our own times, the Jews too, completing their arduous circumnavigation of the globe, have returned from the west, from the sea, by which they have clustered like the Philistines of old, building their ramshackle new cities on the beaches, the mountains to the east of them a gray line against the sky. Once again technology determined demography, though this time the plow's before the sword's. On the one hand, the modern agriculture that the Zionists brought from Europe could best be practiced in the coastal lowlands and inland valleys; on the other hand, it was precisely these areas, once the bread-baskets of Palestine, that a primitive Arab agriculture had been unable to prevent from degenerating into sparsely settled dunes and swamps, which absentee Arab landlords were glad to put up for sale. The more heavily settled highlands, except for Jerusalem, remained solidly Arab, falling only to Jewish military might, first in 1948, with the capture of the Galilee, and then in 1967, with that of the West Bank, the biblical Judea and Samaria.

Thus again we have the paradox, the strange reversal of roles. The Arab sits in the mountains where once the Jew sat, insular, conservative, while the Jew resides in the lowlands, the bearer of the culture of the West. No national movement of our times has been so ambiguous in its attitude toward history as Zionism—and history has repaid it in kind.

What other nationalism has been so committed to history as to see in it its main moral legitimation, taking as its models events that occurred millennia ago and seeking to reenact them on their original geographical stage? Yet what other nationalism has been at the same time so defiant of history and the irreversible processes by which it works, insisting on breaking all rules of how nations are constituted, countries possessed, states established? And history? Look at the broad view, and it has rewarded the fealty paid it with a generous sweep of its hand. Examine the details and it has gotten them fiendishly wrong.

—∞—

The air is hot and dusty; my throat aches for something to drink. I stop at a roadside cafe with faded posters that advertise Coca-Cola and Syrian Arab Airlines and sit on a patio overlooking the mountains. The only customer is a striped tiger cat sleeping on one of the white tables. A passion flower vine profuses over a trellis overhead, its starry flowers too gaudy to be real. A retouched color photograph of Nasser, his lips rouged, his cheeks green, adorns the wall. Near it hangs a map of the world in Arabic from which, I notice, the State of Israel has been omitted. The proprietor appears in a starched white shirt and black suspenders. "Yes?" he declares in so-far excellent English.

"*Kafé shakhor, b'vakasha.*" Stubbornly. Illogically.

"I'm sorry," he says in English. "I don't understand Hebrew." But the tone is more in anger than in sorrow. He's lying, of course. What café owner on the West Bank doesn't know what *kafé shakhor* means after seven years of Israeli rule?

"I'd like some Turkish coffee, please."

He brings it on a copper tray with a glass of water by its side, and joins the sleeping cat at the table. We sit there, the occupier and the occupied, and stare gloomily out at the mountains. The cat opens a glowing eye to regard a waistcoated bumblebee that is busily courting a passion flower. The sweet grinds on my tongue are a sign that I have drunk my coffee too far. I empty the glass of water, ask for the bill in English, pay it, and leave.

Back on the road I stop to pick up a hitchhiking soldier who falls asleep before he has settled into his seat. Ahead of me rises Mount Ebal, a white quarried wound in its flank, the biblical mount of the curse on which Moses bade the Children of Israel to listen patiently to the imprecations of their God in a Hebrew so blunt that any schoolboy can understand it today. "Cursed be he who removes his neighbor's landmark, and all the people shall say: Amen. Cursed is he who misleads a blind man on the road, and all the people shall say: "Amen." Opposite it is the mount of the blessing, Mount Gerizim, the sacred site of the dwindled sect of Samaritans, once Jews themselves, whose temple was sacked by the Jewish king Alexander Janneus in 125 B.C.E. and never rebuilt. There are about five hundred of them left today, and their identity is precariously linked to this peak, which is, their scriptures assert, God's true chosen dwelling place, for wherever the Pentateuch refers to Nablus, the Jews have cunningly convinced the world that it means Jerusalem instead.

Nablus, the Greek Neopolis, the biblical Shechem, still lies in the narrow valley between these twin peaks, the grand stone villas of the rich rising high on the mountainsides, the business and poorer sections down below. The main street runs the axis of the valley from north to south. Workshops. A restaurant. A grocery. Garages. Sounds of pounding. Furtive Hebrew signs advise the conqueror that his business is welcome even if his presence is not. The old stone Turkish railway station stands abandoned in the maze of its tracks, which today lead nowhere though once they wound down to Tulkarm near the coast, and from there to Alexandria, Beirut, Damascus, and the Hejaz. An Arab policeman and an Israeli soldier stand chatting with each other against a Jordanian military monument in the main traffic circle at the center of town. Signs point to Joseph's tomb, to Jacob's well, modest relics for the pilgrimage trade, but all Nablus has been left, as a poor relation might be bequeathed an impractical heirloom of dubious value.

On my way out of town I pass a refugee camp, a sprawling tin shantytown such as is found outside every city on the West Bank. Children throw stones at one another in an alleyway. Stones lie scattered on the tin roofs of the dwellings, some no bigger than pebbles, others the size of human heads. They have been put there to keep the roofs from blowing away in the wind, but at first glance they seem to have rained down from above in a fit of absentminded wrath. The Palestinians have their refugees, their exile, and their diaspora; they contest every bit of Jewish ground; they are the Samaritans of our day. The soldier next to me stirs uneasily in his seat, then heaves himself back to sleep.

—ɯ—

3.
Nablus to Ramallah: One hour.

The valley leading from Nablus…is one of great beauty. Dr. Porter says, with slight exaggeration, "It is the finest in Palestine—in fact, it is the only really beautiful site from Dan to Beersheba." Without the grandeur of the snow-crowned peaks of Switzerland, it yet reminded me of the Swiss-Italian valleys in its bright color and rich vegetation.

—*Ibid.*

"You're unusually sentimental today," I remark to myself when we are a few kilometers out of Nablus.

"I tell you, it's these mountains. They speak to me. Just look at that fig tree over there, growing almost horizontally out of bare rock. What powers of tenacity! As a traveler, I'm sure I'd prefer the Alps. But this happens to be mine."

"Unfortunately, the Palestinian thinks it's his."

"It is. There ought to be some way of sharing it."

"Just how do you propose to accomplish that?"

"I wish I knew. I've already told you that's why I've stopped driving this way. I can't bear the thought of losing all this."

"At least you've become more realistic. Several years ago, I remember you saying that the solution lay in us becoming one people. The Jews should ride about on donkeys and the Arabs should be converted to Judaism at sword point, as the Edomites were by John Hyrcanus in Hasmonean times."

"You're misquoting me. I actually said that there was no need to convert the Palestinians like the Edomites—who, by the way, became the most fanatical of Jews within a few generations. My proposal was to have the Israeli ministry of the interior declare the Palestinians Jews by virtue of the Law of Return, which is based on Jewish ancestry, and give them all the tax breaks and benefits that Jewish immigrants get."

"I hope you were joking even then."

"Of course. Even had the Palestine Liberation Organization agreed, the Rabbinate would have fought it tooth and nail."

"Where does that leave us?"

"Still with two peoples. And still in one land."

"Then why not divide the land up again?"

"You're referring, I suppose, to a Palestinian state."

"What better alternative is there?"

"With that enlightened humanist Mr. Arafat as its first president?"

"You needn't take that tone with me. I didn't choose him. It's partly because of biblical sentimentalists like you that we're stuck with him now. If we had been willing to trade the West Bank for a peace treaty with King Hussein right after the 1967 war, we wouldn't be where we are today. You can't deny that the Palestinians have a case. We have a state and so should they."

"One from which the very heartland of Jewish historical experience in this country would be excluded?"

"You *are* beginning to sound like one of our scriptural hawks who can't understand why it isn't clear to everyone that if we have a right to Tel Aviv and Haifa, we have one to Nablus and Jenin too."

"Let's say that if we don't have one to Nablus and Jenin, I'm not sure what ours is to Tel Aviv and Haifa either."

"But we live in Tel Aviv and Haifa, and not in Nablus and Jenin. Isn't that enough?"

"French Algerians lived in Algiers, and overseas Portuguese live in Angola."

"You're the last person I'd have expected to hear that comparison from. Surely the whole justification of Zionist settlement in Palestine lies in its having been different in its behavior from European colonialisms—in its nonexploitation of native labor, for example, or its legal purchase of the lands it acquired, or its basic willingness to reach a political compromise with the other side. The very fact that the Jews were a persecuted people with nowhere else to go...."

"Excuse me, but Jews generally have had quite a few places to go—and have gone to them. There were periods of Jewish settlement in Palestine in which cheap Arab labor was widely employed, as it is today; most of the land owned by Jews in Israel is former Arab property abandoned by its owners without compensation during the 1948–49 war, and the Jewish side has not always been so reasonable in its demands. If we Jews have a right to this country only by virtue of our good behavior, then every time we behave badly our right to be here diminishes."

"Then that right is..."

"...the same as the unconditional right of any people to its homeland—in this case one that was taken from us by force and never ceased to play a central role in our national consciousness."

"Which is how the Palestinians define their right to be here, too."

"Justly so."

"Then isn't the only way out of the impasse to conclude that our right to Haifa is stronger than theirs, and that their right to Nablus is stronger than ours, and partition the land accordingly?"

"I can't speak for the Palestinians. Speaking as a Jew, though, how do I partition a right that is grounded in the historical consciousness of a people of which I—of which all the Jews who are alive today—constitute only a fraction?"

"Good lord! When did the historical consciousness of the Jewish people, whatever *that* might be, ever agree on where the Land of Israel lies? Abraham was promised the Euphrates, and Ezra and Nehemiah were content with a few square miles around Jerusalem. You yourself just said that the areas of Israel most heavily populated by Jews before the Six-Day War were traditionally not highly Jewish at all—which didn't prevent their borders from being considered final until the war whetted appetites for more."

"Centuries of Jewish law and literature define rather precisely where the Land of Israel lies—and it isn't on the Euphrates and does include Judea and Samaria."

"Then you support the recent attempts at illegal settlement on the West Bank whose aim is to force the Israeli government to let Jews settle freely there?"

"I support the position that any Jew who wishes to settle there, and can legally and without coercion acquire the land or property to do so, should be allowed to. I find it scandalous that a Jewish government should take for granted the right of Jews to live in Paris or New York but not in parts of the one country they have always thought of as their own."

"Would it not be scandalous for such a government to give in to the pressures of religious and nationalist extremists by annexing Palestinian territories and making peace in the Middle East impossible?"

"Who said anything about annexing territories?"

"What difference does it make what you call it? You just said a Jewish government had an unconditional right to rule in all of Palestine."

"I said that the Jewish *people* had an unconditional right to *live* in all of Palestine. I didn't say anything about ruling there."

"Now you're confusing me. You mean that Jews should live in the West Bank as part of..."

"...a Palestinian state? Why not? There are hundreds of thousands of Palestinian Arabs living in a Jewish state today and we accept it as a matter of course."

"With the enlightened Mr. Arafat as their President? It seems to me we've changed sides."

"I'd prefer someone smoother-shaven myself. But if he or any other Palestinian leader would be willing to recognize the sovereignty of Israel within its pre-1967 borders, and the right of all Jews to live in areas of Palestine that lie outside of those borders, the answer is yes."

"What Jew would be willing to live in a PLO state?"

"If Jews living in a Palestinian state could remain Israeli nationals, as an American living in Canada can remain a national of the U.S., and have their welfare guaranteed by reliable safeguards, some certainly would. It's a blind spot that we find it impossible to conceive of a Jewish presence anywhere in this country apart from Jewish sovereignty. It's the common denominator of the annexationist Right, which insists on both sovereignty and presence, and the anti-annexationist Left, which wants neither."

"But can you conceive of either a Palestinian or an Israeli leadership agreeing to such a thing?"

"In their present form, hardly. But in their present form each doesn't recognize the existence of the other at all. Should the PLO eventually come around to accepting a pre-1967 Israel in return for the right to establish a Palestinian state, Israel will have to respond. Why not with such a proposal?"

"Which would be….?"

"That just as any Jew would have the right to travel, work, buy property, and reside in Nablus or Jenin, but not to vote or have a Jewish government there, so any Palestinian would have the same right and limitation in Haifa or Tel Aviv."

"So we're back to the old bi-national state idea of the 1930s!"

"Not at all. The idea of a binational state was unworkable because it was based on the utopian expectation that Jews and Arabs could share one sovereignty and one set of political institutions. Now we're talking about two peoples in two states…"

"…but still one land?"

"Precisely."

"And you think it could work?"

The soldier beside me awakes with a prescient sixth sense and asks to be let off at his army base. An Arab taxi coming from Nablus honks screamingly at him as he crosses the road. A minute later it overtakes me: the white *kaffias* of the men inside make them look from behind like a party of hefty nuns. A scarecrow stands in an empty field beneath the noonday sun: it is wearing sun glasses, a trench coat with the collar turned up, and an old gray fedora with the brim turned down. One empty sleeve is stuck into the pocket of its coat as though holding a hidden gun. "Welcome To Ramallah, City On The Move," says a sign. A dog lies comfortably curled on the road, the red froth beneath its nose the only indication that it is dead.

"Don't be silly," I say to myself. "It's far too sensible for that."

—⟋⟍—

4.
Ramallah to Jerusalem: Fifteen minutes.

> For some miles along the road, or from the eminences which skirt it, Jerusalem is visible. Age after age, invading armies, or bands of pilgrims, approaching from the north, as they turned the crest of Scopus, have gained their first view of the city...Here the first Crusaders halted at break of day, and as Jerusalem burst upon their view, they knelt, and with tears of gladness, kissed the sacred soil. Richard Coeur de Lion, leaving his camp at Ajalon, pressed forward alone, and as he ascended one of these hills, buried his face in his mailed hands, and exclaimed: "Oh! Lord God, I pray Thee that I may never look upon Thy Holy city, if so be that I rescue it not from Thine enemies."
>
> —*Ibid.*

Soon out of Ramallah one enters the long northern finger of the ex-Jordanian municipality of Jerusalem, which was annexed in its entirety by Israel after the Six-Day War. The Bible slams shut. Bulldozers are carving out a road heading off into nowhere, trimming and slicing the stony earth. Another road, showing no point of connection with the first, is being covered with a sleek new coat of asphalt. A small airplane takes off from the old Jordanian airport at Kalandia, which is being lengthened to accommodate big jets. New housing projects sit on hilltops that wince beneath them, unaccustomed to their weight. A sign pointing to a plateau of rocks proclaims that the Jerusalem Industrial Park is to rise here. There is something intensely aimless- seeming about all this activity; one has the sense of a giant jigsaw puzzle to which each player has brought his own pieces. Presumably, it will all fit together in the end, and if it doesn't, no matter. You can't argue with the facts.

The newly-widened road passes through Shu'afat, the wealthy Arab suburb of Jerusalem in which King Hussein was building his summer hideaway, complete with swimming pool and heliport, when the 1967 war broke out. Obvious fortunes have gone into these pink stone houses with their porticoes, their archways, their paneled windows, their balconies and balustrades—yet something there is that gives the whole less the appearance of a wealthy residential quarter than of a peculiarly ornate slum. One gropes for it for a moment…the television aerials! They jostle one another for room, rising here with an even more frantic density than in Israel itself. Some have the shape of Eiffel Towers, others of rapiers or broken umbrella frames; some stick out of the houses at odd angles, like darts in a gaming board or matador's lances in a bull. Some are double the height of the roofs that they stand on, as if the house underneath them were merely a platform for their launching into space. Higher is further. Two meters will fetch Amman; five, Beirut or Damascus; ten, Cairo; twenty, perhaps Baghdad. What is playing this month in Shu'afat? Kissinger in Moscow. Hussein in London. Arafat in New York. Sadat in Rabat. About whom are they talking so much? They are talking about the people of Shu'afat, who fish for their faces and voices in Jerusalem's skies.

Ah, Jerusalem! If ever a city has huckstered the world for a living with its mosques, churches, synagogues, crypts, caves, walls, tombs, stones, bones, and souvenirs, it is you. And the world will not admit it has been taken and will not leave you alone. French Hill. Mount Scopus. Sheikh Jarrah. Outside The American Colony Hotel a party of tourists is boarding a waiting bus. They are pink-faced, innocent of passion, and if the postcards they send home are to be believed, they are having a good time. For a moment it almost seems to me that I hate them. Or is that warm flash of feeling rather an unreasonable burst of affection, call it love, for the little Arab boy, a hole in the knee of his pants and no laces in his shoes, who is trying to sell them some worthless wooden trinket? He badgers them; they retreat into the shadow of the bus. We are accomplices in this land, he and I, and will be here when they are gone. I stop at a red light, the first I've encountered since leaving Haifa, across from the Old City wall. A throng of shoppers heading home for lunch struggles through the Damascus Gate. For a moment it hangs there, as though held together by its own viscosity, then scatters quickly like smoke.

1975

My Pocket Bible

A t the time, it seemed so striking an exegesis that I thought of basing something fictional on it, perhaps even a biblical novel. In the end, nothing came of it. The other night, though, I found myself reading the *parshah* of *Vayera*. That's the fourth Torah reading of Genesis, the one that tells of the binding of Isaac. Although I rarely go to synagogue, there have been times when I regularly kept up with the weekly Torah readings at home: on Saturday mornings I would sit down with my edition of *Mikra'ot G'dolot* and go through the week's *parshah* with the Aramaic translation of Onkelos and the medieval commentaries of Rashi, Ibn Ezra, and Nahmanides, alias the Ramban. In recent years the habit has lapsed, but I still keep a little Bible by my bed that I sometimes open before falling asleep.

It's the same Bible I was given at a ceremony that ended two months of basic training for new immigrants after my induction into the Israeli army in 1974. The ceremony was held at the Western Wall with floodlights, flags, and full pageantry, but the part I remember best was the soldier standing next to me. He was a Russian who spoke little Hebrew, and when, asked to swear to defend the state of Israel, we raised our Bibles and exclaimed, *"Ani nishba, ani nishba, ani nishba"*—"I swear, I swear, I swear"—he shouted earnestly, *"Anyi nyishbar, anyi nyishbar, anyi nyishbar"*—"I can't take it anymore, I can't take it anymore, I can't take it anymore."

This Bible fit comfortably into the pocket of my army fatigue pants and had the insignia of the Israel Defense Force's chaplaincy corps on its dark blue cover. At its back were maps of Palestine and the ancient Middle East, including one of the Promised Land from the Nile to the Euphrates and two or three of Joshua's conquest of Canaan. I liked my little Bible that I had sworn allegiance to a Jewish state on and took it with me when I traveled as a good luck charm. Once, it almost brought me bad luck.

This happened on an Air France flight from Djibouti to Jedda. I hadn't planned to be in Djibouti. I was sailing from Muscat, the capital of Oman, to Eilat on a yacht owned by a Dutch shipping magnate whose autobiography I was ghostwriting. This Dutchman was an elderly madman who liked to swim with sharks, and as we approached the Red Sea from the Gulf of Aden he let me know that he intended to do some illegal coral reef diving off the coast of Sudan. A stay in a Sudanese jail was nothing to look forward to and I told him I wanted to get off.

He dumped me in Djibouti with the advice to stray no more than three city blocks from my hotel in Place Rimbaud, an area patrolled by French sailors from their nearby naval base; a deckhand from one of his ships had ventured further, he said, and returned with only one ear. Djibouti was a hellish place. Place Rimbaud cringed beneath a malignant sun, the blackened branches of its dead shade trees roosted on by sinister crows. I was desperate to get out, and told by a travel agent that the only available seat in the days ahead was on an Air France flight to Jedda, from which I could get a connection to Istanbul and from there to Tel Aviv, I took it.

Now, however, as we began our descent, I was given a Saudi Arabian landing card to fill out. It had a line asking for my religion. I flagged a stewardess, explained that I was Jewish and traveling on a U.S. passport issued in Tel Aviv, and asked what I should do. She went to talk to the captain, came back, and told me to leave the line blank.

The passenger next to me, a Lebanese who did business with the Saudis, overheard the conversation. "Don't worry," he said. "The worst they'll do is search your bags and ask a few questions. You'll make your flight to Istanbul."

It was only as we were touching down that I remembered my little Bible with its IDF insignia and maps of conquest. It was in my suitcase in the baggage hold. I told the Lebanese businessman about it. He said: "Don't get off the plane."

I called the stewardess again. Fortunately, the flight was continuing to Paris; unfortunately, it was full. After some hurried consultations, a purser came aboard, bumped a boarding passenger, and issued me a new ticket. It was for "Jedda-Paris-Tel Aviv," which made it one of a kind in the history of aviation, and it was among my prized curios until I accidentally threw it out one day while cleaning my desk.

The reserve unit I was assigned to after finishing basic training was a ninety-millimeter antitank gun company. Towed by a command car, the ninety-millimeter was a World War II American weapon. It made a huge bang and had a savage kick, and since it wasn't very accurate at over six or seven hundred meters, the idea was to camouflage your position well and let the enemy's tanks come as close as possible before firing. The conventional wisdom was that if your first round missed it would be best not to stay around for a second since against an Egyptian or Syrian Soviet-made T-72, there wasn't likely to be one.

Although the ninety-millimeter was being phased out of the IDF, to be replaced by TOW missiles, the process was still incomplete. The gun was truly ripe for decommissioning. Once, on a visit to New York, I came across a shop that sold antique toy soldiers and stepped in to look for a present for a friend in Jerusalem who collected them. Amid the display of Greek hoplites, Roman legionnaires, Persian archers, Crusader knights, Turkish janissaries, Russian hussars, and Napoleonic grenadiers, I spied a familiar sight: four helmeted GI's, a gunner, loader, server, and crew captain, crouched behind my IDF gun. My expertise in identifying it so impressed the owner that he kept me in his shop for half an hour for a connoisseur-to-connoisseur talk.

My company trained on its antique cannon one week a year, firing at metal barrels in the Negev. The rest of our annual month of reserve duty was spent in the occupied territories or manning a line on the border. We belonged to the 300th Infantry Brigade, whose headquarters were in the north, as were the borders we were sent to.

My first long stint in the reserves came a year after the Yom Kippur War. It was on the border with Lebanon, the other side of which was controlled by the Palestine Liberation Organization. Our company was responsible for a ten-kilometer stretch, and I was in a platoon stationed in a hilltop outpost facing a sleepy Lebanese village called Maroun-e-Ras, whose residents shared its streets with donkeys and beat-up old cars. I could once have told you the numbers of the cars' license plates, since one of our jobs was to peer at the village through a small telescope, report on anything that might have military bearing, and record it in a log. The only things that were of any interest never made it into the log. *The young man living in the house next to the Maronite priest's was flirting again today with the girl from the grocery store. This morning the owner of the vintage Chevrolet slapped his son as the boy left for school.* It was like bird watching, except that you were always looking at the same species.

The nights were often lit by flares. Beyond the electrified fence that marked the border was a jungle teeming with nocturnal life: Israeli ambushes for PLO infiltrators, PLO ambushes for the ambushers, Lebanese informers rendezvousing with their handlers, drug smugglers who tossed bags of cocaine or heroin over the fence for pickup by accomplices. Now and then, the headlights of a patrol swept the macadam road that paralleled the dirt security path running along the fence. The path was checked every morning for footprints by Bedouin trackers and smoothed out again for the next night.

Several nights a week, I had guard duty. The outpost consisted of a concrete bunker in which we slept, washed, cooked, ate, and sat around watching TV or playing cards; a double perimeter fence of barbed concertina wire; connecting trenches; and a watchtower equipped with a .50-caliber heavy machine gun at either end. For four hours you made the rounds with a partner. The worst shift was the twelve-to-four. By the time you fell asleep before midnight, it was almost time to get up, and by the time you fell asleep again before dawn, it was almost time to get up again.

—⁘—

One night I drew the twelve-to-four shift with someone I hardly knew. He didn't belong to our company and had been assigned to it temporarily. My only contact with him, if you could call it that, had come a day or two earlier. I was reading the week's *parshah* in my little Bible when he passed behind my chair, paused for a moment, and moved on. I didn't look up. I'm that way myself. If someone is reading something, I like to know what it is.

October nights are cold in the Upper Galilee. We both wore our army windbreakers, bulky beneath our M16 rifles and our battle harnesses with their magazines and grenades. The sky was bright with stars. Cassiopeia, Perseus, Cygnus the Swan—I got to know them all in the army.

He had on a stocking cap pulled down over his ears in place of the skullcap I had seen him wear in the bunker. He was the only soldier in the outpost who went around with one; there weren't many religiously observant men in our company. This was one of the few things you could tell at a glance about someone in uniform. The rest—who was a spiffy dresser and who wore jeans and sandals, who liked loud colors and who preferred quiet ones—had to wait for the day of your discharge. That's what uniforms are for, of course: to suppress differences. But the consequence is that you talk more than you might otherwise. In ordinary life, one look at most people is enough to know that you have nothing to say to them or they to you. In the army, it took a while to find that out.

I don't remember his name and won't bother making one up. His Hebrew had a French accent. He and his wife, he told me as we walked between watchtowers, had come to Israel from Strasbourg soon after their marriage. He had fought in the 1967 war as the driver of a halftrack on the Golan Heights and was wounded when it hit a mine, after which the two of them went back to France; they had a baby there and then split up. His wife was now living with their son in the countryside—in Quercy,

I think it was. I gathered that she was with another man. She wanted a divorce, and he didn't want to give her one.

He took out his wallet and showed me a frayed photograph. Beneath the beam of a pocket flashlight, the woman was pretty, with large, dark eyes. The boy on whose shoulder her bare arm rested looked just like her. Behind them was the mossy stone wall of an old house or chateau.

He'd returned to Israel by himself after the Yom Kippur War. His old unit no longer needed him, and the army hadn't decided where to place him. Meanwhile, he was doing his reserve duty with us.

We had made several rounds of the outpost and were standing by the entrance to the bunker. "I'll make us coffee," I said.

He wanted his strong and unsweetened. When I brought it we gulped it quickly before the cold air could drain its heat.

"So what made him do it?" he asked.

"Who?" I had been looking up at the sky and must have missed something.

"Abraham."

"Avi Rahat?" That was the only Abraham in our outpost.

"Avi in the *parshah* of *Vayera*. You were reading it."

So I was. "I suppose he was desperate," I said. I assumed he was asking about the near sacrifice of Isaac. It's a difficult story. As I saw it, God was desperate, too.

"Too desperate to care who screwed his wife?"

I gave him a sideways glance. "That's not quite what the Bible says," I said.

"It isn't?"

"Not in *Vayera*. It says that Avimelech didn't touch her."

"I'll bet he didn't. And Pharaoh?"

"That's ambiguous."

"Ambiguous, my eye! What do you think they were doing while he was giving Abraham all those he-asses and she-asses?"

You had to grant he knew his Bible. The story about Pharaoh wasn't in *Vayera*. It was in the chapter before it, the *parshah* of *Lekh-Lekha*, the one that begins with God's telling Abraham to "get thee out of thy land."

He's called Abram then, and he leaves Ur of the Chaldees with his wife Sarai, eventually making it to Canaan, from which he heads for Egypt when famine breaks out. As they near it, he says to her, "Behold now, I know that thou art a fair woman to look upon. Therefore, it shall come to pass, when the Egyptians shall see thee, that they shall say, 'This is his wife,' and they will kill me, but they will save thee alive. Say, I pray thee, thou art my sister; that it may be well with me for thy sake; and my soul shall live because of thee."

It turns out as Abraham feared. "And it came to pass that, when Abram was come into Egypt, the Egyptians beheld the woman that she was very fair. The princes also of Pharaoh saw her, and commended her before Pharaoh, and the woman was taken into Pharaoh's house." Pharaoh treats Abraham well and showers him with gifts, sheep and oxen and he-asses and she-asses and camels, until "the Lord plagued Pharaoh and his house with great plagues because of Sarai, Abram's wife. And Pharaoh called Abram and said, 'What is this that thou hast done unto me? Why didst thou not tell me that she was thy wife? Why saidst thou, "She is my sister?" I might have taken her to me to wife. And now behold thy wife, and take her, and go thy way.'"

The story in *Vayera* is similar. Now Abraham and his wife are back in Canaan. He decides to try his luck in "the south country," in the little kingdom of Gerar. Its king is Avimelech. Again, Abraham tells everyone that Sarah is his sister and again the king takes her to his palace. This time, though, "God came to Avimelech in a dream by night and said to him, 'Behold thou art as good as dead for the woman which thou hast taken, for she is a man's wife.' But Avimelech had not come near her. Then Avimelech called Abraham and said unto him, 'What hast thou done unto us? And what have I offended thee, that thou hast brought on me and on my kingdom a great sin? Thou hast done deeds unto me that ought not to be done.'"

You had to wonder. *Twice?* Once should have been more than enough. The Ramban certainly thought so. To excuse Abraham's behavior, he turned the biblical sequence of events around and proposed that, on both occasions, Sarah was first snatched on royal command because of her beauty. Only then, when she was already a prisoner in Pharaoh or Avimelech's palace, did Abraham claim she was his sister.

"The Ramban," said my partner, "is full of it."

"He tried."

"He shouldn't have bothered. You still haven't answered my question."

"What made him do it? The Bible says he was afraid to be killed."

"By whom? As soon as they find out who she is, they apologize and hand her back. And besides, he's no coward."

"You think sacrificing his son makes him brave?"

"Forget about Isaac. Think of the four kings."

That was in *Lekh-Lekha*, too.

"He's got three hundred and eighteen men against four armies, and he chases them to Damascus! Does that sound like a man who would be afraid to protect his own wife?"

"You tell me, then," I said. "What made him do it?"

"No, you tell me. Where did she get the clap?"

"What?"

"The plagues Pharaoh caught from her. They weren't the chicken pox."

A mortar whumped in the distance. We fell silent, waiting for the flare. It ignited beyond Maroun-e-Ras, out toward Bint Jbeil, a midnight sun drifting slowly earthward beneath its invisible parachute. It vanished before hitting the ground, leaving behind a briefly struggling spark, like the tip of a candle wick before it goes out.

"She didn't get it from Abraham either."

He was a very angry religious Jew. But I was beginning to get the picture. "All right," I said. "For the sake of argument, let's say you're right. Our mother Sarah was not who we've been taught she was. She slept around. Abraham doesn't know what to do. He can't control her. He's brave, but he's no wife-beater. And so he says, 'Look, just do me one favor. Don't tell anyone we're married. At least spare me that. Wherever we go, you're my sister.' Do I follow you?"

"So far."

"But why does he stay with her? Why not leave her?"

"He can't."

"Why not?"

"He's been promised her son."

He was right about that, too. "And God said unto Abraham, "As for Sarai thy wife, thou shalt not call her name Sarai, but Sarah shall her name be. And I will bless her, and give thee a son also of her. Yea, I will bless her, and she shall be a mother of nations.""

"And maybe he's dumb enough to still love her," he added.

"So he's stuck with her." The woman in the photograph wore what looked like an expensive watch on the wrist that rested on her son's shoulder.

"Forever," he said bitterly. I was touched by him.

"You know," I said, "you should try seeing Sarah's side of it."

He said nothing.

"After all, she's just a girl from Ur of the Chaldees. She marries Abraham. He's ten years older than her. The Bible says he's a hundred and she's ninety when Isaac is born."

"If he's a hundred, so am I."

"I agree. Their ages in the story don't make sense. They would, though, if they were divided in half."

I had a theory about that. Jewish tradition tells us there were once two New Year's Days, one in autumn and one in spring. Count every year in the story of Abraham, as in the other stories in Genesis, as half of a year, from autumn to spring or spring to autumn, and it worked out perfectly.

"She's seventeen, say, and he's twenty-two. She's young and pretty, and she comes from a good home, and she loves her handsome new husband who has wonderful thoughts that he talks about in words she pretends to understand, and she wants to be a good wife, and have lots of children, and go on being the darling of her family and friends.

"A year or two go by, and she's still not pregnant. And then, one day, her husband comes and tells her that they're leaving Ur and moving to somewhere called Haran. Why? Because. This time she doesn't pretend to understand. She argues. She cries. It doesn't do any good. A wife does as she's told."

I was improvising on his theme now.

"They move to Haran. It's not a big city like Ur. It's a provincial capital, a hick town. No one knows how to speak or dress. She hates it. She misses her family and friends. All the women her age have children. If she had a child, it would play with them, and she would have new friends; she wouldn't be so bored and jealous and miserable. She and Abraham quarrel all the time. *'Why did you bring me to this place?' 'But can't you see there's a purpose to it all?' 'Then tell me what it is!' 'I'll tell you when I know.'* Much of the time, he's not home; he's busy accumulating the wealth the Bible says he gathered in Haran. Perhaps it's now that she has her first affair. At first she's frightened. But she's surprised how simple it is, how easy to conceal. It fills the days, dulls the pain of an empty womb.

"And then it happens. A voice speaks to Abraham. It tells him to leave Haran for a land he will be shown. 'I will make of thee a great nation,' it says. 'I will bless thee and make thy name great.' It's what he has been waiting for. Sarah doesn't know what to think. Half of her no longer believes a word he says. Half is full of new hope.

"They set out for Canaan. Her hopes don't last long. It's worse than she could have imagined. They live in tents, they wander from place to place, here today, there tomorrow. Haran was heaven by comparison. One morning she wakes up with lice in her hair. Lice! And Abraham doesn't even notice. He's listening to his voice. *'Sarai, it said to me, "Unto thy seed will I give this land!"'* What land? What seed? She is almost forty. No seed can sprout in barren soil. When she sleeps with other men, she imagines they are tilling her not like the rocky earth of Canaan but like the deep loam of Ur. She no longer bothers to hide it from Abraham. He hears voices? Let him hear what they are saying about her.

"There is famine in Canaan. They set out again, this time for Egypt. Abraham is silent most of the way. When they are almost there, he says to her—"

"Say thou art my sister." He said it so softly that I had to strain to hear him.

"It's your turn to make the coffee," I said.

I stood outside the bunker, looking up at the sky. Orion had risen in the east, his sword glittering with diamonds. I thought of that night in Canaan:

"And Abraham said, 'Lord God, what wilt thou give me, seeing I go childless?' And He brought him forth abroad, and said, 'Look now toward heaven, and count the stars, if thou be able to number them.' And He said unto him, 'So shall thy seed be.' And he believed in the Lord, and He counted it to him for righteousness."

People have trouble with the sacrifice of Isaac. It makes Abraham a monster in their eyes. And maybe he becomes one. Who can imagine killing his own child?

But you have to imagine harder than that.

He is in his twenties when he leaves Ur. Fifty when Isaac is born. Fifty-seven or fifty-eight when he puts a knife to the boy's throat. And all those years, the voice speaks to him.

A voice of his own! He has never known anyone else who had one. For it, he has gambled away everything, caused the woman he loves to hate him. For years she has been convinced he is mad. *A mother of nations!* What nations? From whom? From his concubine Hagar's son Ishmael? But God said it would be from Sarah. He lets her drive Ishmael and his mother away.

His wife is childless. His whole life has been a delusion. He has kept faith with a voice that has lied to him.

And then the miracle takes place and Isaac is born. This doesn't win Sarah back. It's too late for that. A wary peace now reigns between them. Their son is a hostage to it. Still! Thirty-five years. Now every one of them is justified—if, that is, it is justifiable to lose a woman for a voice.

For a long while, he doesn't hear from it. It doesn't matter. He knows it will be there when he needs it. And then it speaks to him again. "Abraham!" it says. "Take now thy son, thine only son Isaac, whom thou lovest, and get thee into the land of Moriah. And offer him there for a burnt offering upon one of the mountains which I will tell thee of."

Murder the son who you were told would make you a great nation!

What should he do now? What would *you* do? Not what Abraham does, of course. But that's why he's in the Bible, and you aren't.

The coffee was good. "How many times did you boil it?" I asked.

"Twice," he said.

We laughed. There was an army superstition that you had to bring Turkish coffee to a boil an odd number of times. Some said three, some five or seven, but it couldn't be two or four.

The night was getting colder. The warmth of the coffee wore off quickly.

We resumed our rounds, walking from watchtower to watchtower. The subject of *Vayera* was exhausted. We talked about our leaves. Each of us was given forty-eight hours. There were arguments over who got which days. Most men preferred weekends, but it also might happen that someone wanted Wednesday to Friday because his business needed him on Thursday and someone else's daughter had a birthday that same day. My partner didn't care. He lived alone and had no one to go home to.

"When will you see your son?" I asked.

He shrugged. "Maybe next summer. If I go to France."

Something was still on his mind. I waited for it.

"He's not even his, you know."

"Who isn't whose?"

He looked at me as though I were a slow pupil. "How many years did you say Sarah spent trying to have a child?"

"Twenty-five," I said. "More or less."

"And after twenty-five years with Abraham she suddenly gets pregnant from him? She's not even living with him when it happens. She's with Avimelech. They've been shacked up for months."

It was in the little Bible in the pocket of my fatigue pants: "And Avimelech took sheep, and oxen, and menservants, and women servants, and gave them unto Abraham, and restored him Sarah his wife.... And the Lord remembered Sarah as he had said, and the Lord did unto Sarah as he had spoken. For Sarah conceived, and bore Abraham a son in his old age."

"He's not even his. He's Avimelech's. Sometimes he feels he could kill him."

We trudged in silence, our M16s slung over our shoulders. *Va'nehegeh bahem yomam va'layla.* That wasn't in my Bible. It was from the evening prayer. *Therefore, O Lord our God, when we lie down and when we rise, may we converse about Thy laws and rejoice in the words of Thy Torah, for we shall think of them by day and by night.*

It was only two-thirty.

2008

My Uncle Simon

In *A Tale of Love and Darkness*, his highly praised memoir of a Jerusalem childhood and adolescence in the 1940s and '50s, Amos Oz mentions my uncle, the Hebrew poet, novelist, and literary critic Simon Halkin.

My Uncle Simon was appointed in 1949 to head the department of Hebrew literature at the Hebrew University of Jerusalem, to which he moved from New York; until then, the position had been held by Oz's great-uncle Yosef Klausner, who vacated it for a chair in Second Temple studies. In his memoir, Oz records that in the late 1950s, his father Yehuda Arieh Klausner, who was Yosef Klausner's nephew and a librarian with unfulfilled academic ambitions, sought, after receiving his doctorate from London University, "to secure a foothold in the literature department in Jerusalem as an outside lecturer." The application, Oz writes, was turned down because my uncle had made "a fresh start [in the department] by eliminating the heritage, the methods, and the very smell of Klausner and certainly did not want to take on Klausner's nephew."

There are two other, briefer references to my Uncle Simon in Oz's book. One mentions him as the Hebrew translator of Walt Whitman's *Leaves of Grass*. The other lists a "Professor and Mrs. Halkin"—my uncle and my Aunt Minnie—among the condolence callers at the *shiva* for Oz's mother, whose suicide in 1951 forms the climax of *A Tale of Love and Darkness,* a book that jumps back and forth chronologically.

My aunt and uncle would not have had to walk far to the *shiva*, because they lived in Rehavia, the neighborhood of Jerusalem to which Oz's parents had moved a few years previously and in which many university faculty members—what Oz calls "the Rehavia intelligentsia"—resided. Gershom Scholem lived a few blocks away; Martin Buber, a few blocks in the other direction, across Gaza Road, in the adjacent neighborhood of Talbiya. Jerusalem was a small city, further diminished by its physical division into hermetically separated Arab and Jewish halves, and Rehavia, which is now at its center, was then at its western edge. With its quiet, tree-lined streets and small, stone-faced apartment houses, it was a pleasantly middle-class area—keeping in mind, that is, that Israel's middle class was in those years its upper class and lived in what might today be considered lower-class conditions. My Uncle Simon's apartment was dark and had four rooms plus a tiny kitchen, a little washroom, and a separate, cramped toilet that smelled of the matches lit by my aunt in place of deodorizer.

Yosef Klausner was an exception. His residence in Talpiyot, then in the far south of the city, was a private house that struck the young Amos Oz as a mansion fit for a "sultan" or a "Roman emperor." Over its front door hung a brass plate with the motto "Judaism and Humanism." Its library, with twenty-five thousand volumes in "Hebrew, Aramaic, Syriac, classical and modern Greek, Sanskrit, Latin, medieval Arabic, Russian, English, German, Spanish, Polish, French, [and] Italian," plus "languages I had never even heard of, like Ugaritic or Slovene, Maltese or Old Church Slavonic," seemed like "the antechamber of some palace of wisdom."

My Uncle Simon's library, in the back room of his apartment, was far smaller and had only seven or eight languages—none, except for the classical Greek he had taught himself, calling for explanation like Ugaritic or Maltese. Yiddish was the language of his White Russian childhood; Hebrew had been drilled into him by his father, a *heder* teacher; Aramaic came with the Talmud lessons that followed later; Russian was picked up from the Gentile neighbors; English was learned in America, to which the family emigrated on the eve of World War I; and German...but what shtetl-born Jew could not master German (which was, as Jews joked, merely badly spoken Yiddish) in a few hours by putting his mind to it?

Such polyglots were not unusual among Jewish scholars who had had the head start of an Eastern European childhood. Oz writes that his father could "cite lines of poetry in ten languages." My own father, Abraham Halkin, my uncle's younger brother, an Arabist and professor of medieval Jewish philosophy, knew languages I didn't know he knew. Although I was aware, for example, that he could read Spanish along with a dozen other European and Semitic tongues, I had never heard him speak it and had no reason to think he could. Yet a year or two before his death from Alzheimer's disease, when his mind lay in ruins, an Argentinian geriatric psychiatrist who examined him told me he had enjoyed the visit greatly because he hadn't heard such beautiful Spanish— *un castellano tan puro*—in years.

Of course, the Eastern European shtetl, which was looked back on without affection by most Jews who had left it, offered no courses in Spanish. Yet, if born elsewhere and educated differently, its products would not have become what they did. The onerous schooling that subjected them as small boys to dawn-to-dusk days in the *heder* taught them what Yiddish calls *zitzflaysh*, the ability to concentrate on a text for long hours; trained their memories to perform athletic feats; and stocked them with a wealth of Jewish knowledge that they retained after turning to secular studies. My father, who had been required by his father to read, every night before going to bed, five chapters of the Bible, which he thus went through book by book many times as a child, had the lifelong ability, as uncanny as a mind reader's, to finish any biblical verse whose first half was read aloud to him.

The accomplishments, starting with the late nineteenth century, of the Eastern European Jewish mind, honed to a fine edge by the endlessly repetitive study of the same religious books and then let loose from its confinement in the schools and universities of Europe and America, comprise one of the great intellectual stories of modernity. Important scientific discoveries and great works of literature and the other arts are only a part of it. Within the space of two generations, Jews like Yosef and

Yehuda Arieh Klausner, who studied in Odessa, Heidelberg and Vilna, and like my father and uncle, who went to high school and college in New York, passed from a Jewish cloister to the domain of universal culture, where they applied themselves to Homer and Virgil, Dante and Goethe, as assiduously as if they were sacred texts. For those among them who at the same time remained loyal to the world of their fathers, if not in outward observance then in inner identity, the synthesis of Judaism and Humanism was an existential imperative.

Many such men found this synthesis in Zionism, which they felt so strongly about because it was their way of remaining whole within themselves. "To absorb alien culture and turn it into our own national flesh and blood," Oz quotes Yosef Klausner as writing, "is the ideal I have fought for most of my life." Both Klausners were ardent supporters of another polyglot, Ze'ev Jabotinsky, the founder and leader of the right-wing Revisionist party. Uncle Yosef even ran unsuccessfully in 1948 against Chaim Weizmann as the Right's first candidate for president of the state of Israel.

The Zionism of my Uncle Simon, who had lived in Tel Aviv in the 1930s and returned to America until his invitation to Jerusalem (where my father also settled upon his retirement in 1970), was less partisan. Yet, an emotional man, he could be just as passionate about it. I once heard him say, "If I had known how all this would turn out, I'd have gone to North Dakota and lived as a Red Indian!"

—⟋⟍—

This was in the early 1980s. In those days, I sometimes accompanied my father on Saturday mornings to the Conservative synagogue on Agron Street in Jerusalem, at which he was the regular Torah reader—a task he had previously performed for decades at the Jewish Theological Seminary in New York, where he taught. On our way back from services we often stopped at my uncle's apartment, which lay on our route.

My Uncle Simon never went to synagogue, not even on the High Holy Days. He read the Torah on his own. If we were the first to arrive, we would find him, a yarmulke on his head, still bent over a Bible with its commentaries, studying the weekly portion—which this Sabbath was *B'shalach*, the installment of Exodus telling of the crossing of the Red Sea and the miracle of the manna in the desert. However, today we were not the first. While waiting in the ground floor hallway for my aunt to open the door we had knocked on, we heard voices arguing inside. One belonged to my uncle; the other, to his upstairs neighbor Ezra Fleischer, an observant Jew who taught medieval Hebrew poetry at the university.

On a coffee table in the living room my aunt, an indifferent house-keeper, had put out her usual refreshments for the regular Saturday morning guests: a plate with some disassembled squares of milk chocolate, a bowl of small, salty doughnuts, and a bottle of 777 Carmel brandy. "Nu, Avreml," my uncle greeted my father, picking up the bowl in one hand and the brandy in the other, "which of these is an *ashisha?*"

"The bottle, the bottle," Fleischer said impatiently, as if the argument should have been settled by now.

In perusing the Aramaic translation of Exodus attributed to Yonatan ben Uziel, which describes the manna in the desert as being like *zera kusbar heyvar ve-ta'amei ka-ashishin b'dvash*, "white coriander seed tasting like wafers with honey," it had occurred to my Uncle Simon that the word for "wafer," *ashisha*, which also designated a drinking vessel, might be a suitable equivalent for the Greek *krater*, a wine bowl, in a satiric dialogue of Lucian's that he happened to be translating. Fleischer disagreed. "It says in the tractate of Shabbat," he pointed out, citing a passage in the Babylonian Talmud, "that you mustn't remove a cloth plug from an *ashisha* on the Sabbath because you might perform forbidden work by squeezing liquid from it. How can you plug a bowl?"

"Ezra, Ezra!" my uncle retorted. "Think of your medieval poetry. *Ve'hashkeni yeshisha ba'ashisha*, Shmuel Hanagid says, 'Pour me some old wine in an *ashisha*'—not from it!"

"Who drinks wine from a bowl?" asked Gentilla Broyde, who was there with her husband Ephraim, the editor of the literary periodical *Me'oznayim*.

"Brush up your Shakespeare, Gentilla," Broyde told her. "Give me a bowl of wine./I have not that alacrity of spirit,/Nor cheer of mind, that I was wont to have."

"*Macbeth*?" Gentilla asked.

"*Richard the Third*," my uncle corrected her. "Greek wine was such rotgut that it had to be mixed with water in a bowl—*kratera keran-nunai*—before serving."

"Speaking of rotgut, I'll have some more *yashisha*," Fleischer said, reaching for the brandy while punning on the Hebrew word for it, *yash*.

"A clever Jew, Lucian," said my uncle.

"What Jew?" my father protested. "A Syrian."

"Oho! You too, Avreml? A Syrian who laughed at every god and religion in the Roman Empire except one?" My uncle tapped his shut Bible. "About that one, not a word. A Syrian? A clever Jewboy from Syria-Palaestina!"

These conversations could continue, while the brandy bottle emptied, for an hour or more, caroming off languages, texts, authors, and subjects, from the weekend papers to the sonnets of Petrarch and of the Hebrew poet Emmanuel of Rome, like a dizzying game of billiards. This was a period of my uncle's life when, retired from teaching and dark with grievance against old acquaintances and students for having, as he thought, abandoned him, he saw his circle of weekly Sabbath visitors dwindle. Besides Fleischer and the Broydes, the poet Dan Pagis and his wife sometimes dropped in, along with the writer Yudka Ya'ari, who entertained us with stories of working on road gangs in the Valley of Jezreel, or as a kibbutz shepherd, in his pioneering days in Palestine. A small man with a sweet, shy smile, he had a library with a large collection of Hasidic literature, and he and my uncle liked to swap Hasidic tales.

On Saturday mornings in Jerusalem, men met like this in hundreds of apartments. On their way back from synagogue, their prayer shawl bags beneath their arms, they stopped by friends and neighbors for *kiddush*, ate a cookie or a piece of honey cake, and chatted before going home to their Sabbath lunch. Amos Oz, too, remembers Sabbath gatherings at his uncle's, to which he and his parents took the long walk from one end of Jerusalem to the other. His Uncle Yosef's guests, though, arrived in the afternoon, after their Sabbath nap, and the famous scholar presided over the table like a *rebbe* at *sholosh siddes*, the Sabbath's concluding "third meal," talking, as

Oz describes it, "in his reedy, feminine voice... about the state of the nation, the status of writers and scholars, [and] the responsibilities of cultural figures" while his guests "listened in respectful silence, or expressed agreement in a few quiet words, so as not to interrupt the flow of his lecture."

The atmosphere at my Uncle Simon's was different. That particular morning, my uncle and Yudka Ya'ari became embroiled in a dispute over the relative merits of the Polish Hasidism of Kotsk and the White Russian school of Habad, in which my uncle and father had been raised. When my uncle declared that, philosophically, Habad was Hasidism at its most profound, Ya'ari remarked scornfully (the Habadniks, while not yet openly swept by messianic fever, had already taken to the streets in those days to hector Jews to hasten the Redemption by donning phylacteries):

"A corporation of tefillin salesmen!"

"Let them hire Yona Wallach," Gentilla Broyde suggested.

Wallach, a talented poet, had just caused a scandal by publishing a poem called "Tefillin" in a literary magazine. She had written there:

> Put tefillin on me
> Bind my arms with them Play them over me
> Pass them deliciously over my body
> Rub me hard with them
> Excite me everywhere
> Make me pass out from the feeling
>
> Pass them over my clitoris
> Tie them around my hips
> So I come quickly

"*Schmutz*," my uncle now declared of it.

"But what's wrong with it?" asked Ezra Fleischer sarcastically. "Isn't that what we wanted: Judaism and Humanism?" The dig was not just at Yosef Klausner.

"Where's the Judaism? Where's the humanism?"

"And when Shlonsky wrote in the 1920s, 'My land dons light like a prayer shaw./Its houses are boxes of phylacteries,' that was Judaism? That was humanism?"

"Don't compare Shlonsky to Wallach!" My uncle was getting worked up. "You might as well compare the Italian Renaissance to the French decadents. The only difference is that it took Europe five hundred years to get from one to the other, and our Jewish brain has done it in fifty. Shlonsky may have been a man of the Left, but his cultural vision was the same as Klausner's. And Klausner, my friend, was an innocent. We all were. Who knows that Kurzweil won't have the last laugh? I tell you, if I had known how all this would turn out, I'd have gone to North Dakota and lived as a Red Indian!"

—⚬⚬⚬—

I don't know whether my Uncle Simon ever reached North Dakota or saw Red Indians there. He wandered a good deal in America when he was young, taking with him, he once told me, a few books and a violin that he played badly, and he even got as far as California. There he wrote a long Hebrew poem, called "On the Beach in Santa Barbara," that ended:

God's song has fled. Only you, Earth, are left.
Consumed by you, blinded by you, I surrender.
Your mountains, molten in the noonday heat,
Your ocean, primping in its quiet bays,
Have made me drunk, decanted in me
God-forgetfulness.
Am I to die in it, inebriate and swooning,
My stunned heart no longer hearing God's high music?

The tone was Shelleyan, but the thematics came from Habad, the most dialectical of Hasidic schools of thought. Nowhere more than in Habad was Hasidism troubled by the chasm between a transcendent God and this world; nowhere more did it seek to bridge it by teaching that the Infinite is revealed in every finitude, its dazzling light, too blinding to be apprehended directly by human eyes, dimmed there to a point of perceptibility. Yet on the beach at Santa Barbara, his body offered to the semitropical sun (he had not yet been to Palestine, had never experienced such hot, bright sunlight before), my Uncle Simon had a contrarian thought: it was not the Infinite but the finite that was overwhelmingly brilliant. Our reflections on transcendence were a vain attempt to dream the shadows in which God could be made out.

He was a deeply religious poet, which lent an irony to Baruch Kurzweil's attacks on him.

Kurzweil, whose laugh my uncle had feared that Saturday morning of the portion of *B'shalach*, was a Hebrew literary critic, a German Jewish intellectual who settled in Palestine in 1939 and died in Tel Aviv, a suicide, in 1972. For much of that period, in articles and books, and above all, in his 1958 work *Our Modern Hebrew Literature: Continuity or Revolution?*, he scathingly took the Israeli literary establishment to task for living in a Zionist self-deception.

This self-deception did not begin, Kurzweil wrote, with my uncle's generation. It went back to the beginnings of secular Zionism and its seminal thinker, the Russian Jewish essayist Ahad Ha'am; was handed down by such followers of Ahad Ha'am as Yosef Klausner, his disciple in Odessa and successor as editor of *Ha-Shiloah*, the influential literary journal founded by him; and was still being taught by men like my Uncle Simon—who, far from "eliminating Klausner's heritage" in the Hebrew literature department in Jerusalem, was its devoted propagator.

It was Ahad Ha'am who, starting in the late 1880s, had first programmatically addressed the question of culture in a Jewish state. Criticizing Theodor Herzl and his "political Zionism" for simplistically assuming that, apart from having Judaism as its official religion, such a state would be no different from any other modern European country, Ahad Ha'am argued that it would be an empty shell unless its inhabitants, though not necessarily religiously observant, lived culturally Jewish lives. But how could there be a secular Jewish culture when Jews had always been defined by their religion? Ahad Ha'am answered that the secularization of Jewish life was not the abandonment of Jewish identity but the rescuing of it. The essential point, he maintained, was that Judaism, far from having created the Jews, had been their creation, a medium for expressing their "national self" in a religious stage of human development. In the post-religious age of modernity, this self would vanish—unless, like that of other modern peoples, it were to take the form of a collective "we" based on such components as unique historical memories, literary works, intellectual achievements, social mores and folkways, and so forth. The Hebrew language and the land of Israel, Ahad Ha'am held, were the formal framework that the "national self" would fill with Jewish content.

Ahad Ha'amists like Klausner did not consider themselves anti-religious. On the contrary, they harbored warm feelings for traditional Judaism and believed it to be the necessary matrix for a secular Jewish culture to grow in. The absorption of its nutrients, as it were—the literature, legends, folklore, customs, values, and attitudes of Judaism— would not take place overnight. But just as when, in a forest, more competitive trees replace older ones, doing so gradually in a soil enriched by their decay, so in Palestine the new Hebrew culture would feed off the decomposition of Jewish religious tradition until it could stand on its own. Indeed, this was happening already. Examples were everywhere, none more pithily illustrative than a short poem entitled "Toil" by a young pioneer named Avraham Shlonsky, who was to become one of modern Hebrew literature's major figures. Its first lines went:

> Dress me, good Jewish mother, in a coat
> of many-colored splendor and send me off
> to work at dawn.

> My land dons light like a prayer shawl.
> Its houses are boxes of phylacteries,
> their leather straps the blacktopped roads
> that muscled arms have paved.
> The comely city prays to its Creator.
> A creator, too, am I, your son Avraham,
> a poet-road paver in Israel.

Every word of this poem could be taken to demonstrate the secularization of Judaism that Ahad Ha'am had in mind, starting with its opening appeal to the Jewish mother of the shtetl to offer up her son, dressed like the biblical Joseph by his father Jacob in a coat of many colors, to his pioneering labors in Palestine as once he was sent every morning to the *heder*. Shlonsky could not have written "Toil" in anything but Hebrew, or anywhere but in the land of Israel. In no other language would the reader have known that *oteh or*, "dons light," comes from the verse in Psalms, "O Lord my God Thou art very great.... Who donnest Thyself with light as with a garment." In no other land could the "comely city" of Tel Aviv—*kiryah na'ah* in Shlonsky's Hebrew, echoing the Psalmist's epithet for Jerusalem, *kiryat melekh rav*, "the city of the great King"—be so audaciously yet naturally presented as the new Zion, or the "poet-builder" as its creator-god.

My Uncle Simon had good reason to be upset by Ezra Fleischer's comparison of "Toil" to Yona Wallach's "Tefillin." Citing Shlonsky's poem in his *Modern Hebrew Literature,* written a decade before Kurzweil's similarly titled book, he had said:

> Revaluating the longings of the Jewish past, and scanning the widening vistas of the new Jewish future, [contemporary] Hebrew literature cannot indeed read into the Palestinian present anything substantially different from the idea of sacredness, of continued self-perfection and self-purification which traditional literature always regarded as the bridge across which Jewry must march, over whatever turbulent gulf, toward salvation. As interpreted by this literature, the glory of *halutziut* [Zionist pioneering] is not to be gauged by its physical achievement merely. It is rather to be measured in terms of the earnestness of purpose, of the self-dedication to the ideal which must evolve a code of *mitzvot*, of innerly prescribed and voluntarily fulfilled commandments.

My uncle's optimistic appraisal of modern Hebrew literature and culture as an organic evolution of the Jewish past was thoroughly Klausnerian. Although he may have come to the university in Jerusalem determined to make a "fresh start" based on Anglo-American rather than Eastern European approaches to literary criticism, his own teaching of literature, which stressed its social more than its aesthetic aspects, was far closer to Klausner's than to I. A. Richards's or William Empson's. He was sincere when he said of Klausner, in addressing a memorial gathering for him after his death in 1958, that he was "my master and teacher from boyhood on."

Yet for Kurzweil, Klausner's Ahad-Ha'amism, of which he considered my uncle to be the leading contemporary representative, was intellectually fraudulent. The truth, Kurzweil insisted, was that secular Hebrew culture and literature were not a natural continuation of Jewish history but a radical break with it, one that Zionist literary critics had papered over for ideological reasons. Hebrew creations like "Toil" were glib works of sleight of hand, sentimental manipulations of religious symbolism. Although himself an observant Jew, Kurzweil took as his favorite early modern Hebrew writers either defiant radicals like Yosef Hayim Brenner and Micha Yosef Berdichevsky, who viewed Judaism as a millstone to be cast off ("We will either be the last Jews or the first Hebrews!" Berdichevsky had famously declared), or anguished souls unreconciled to their loss of religious faith like the poet Hayim Nahman Bialik.

Kurzweil accused my uncle of fudging things. If one could not accept Jewish tradition on its own religious terms, he argued, one should do the honest thing and reject it. To want to have one's cake and eat it like the Ahad Ha'amists, abandoning Judaism while claiming to be its heir, and using the language of the sacred while denuding it of its theological justification, was gross hypocrisy. Moreover, Ahad Ha'am was wrong, said Kurzweil: Judaism alone was the defining mark of the Jewish people, and would continue to be so. In the long run, there could be no such thing as secular Jewishness. There could be only the transient illusion of it, produced in men like Klausner and my uncle by an upbringing that had left them a fund of religious knowledge and emotions that could fungibly be spent elsewhere. Yet this was nonrenewable capital, unreplenishable by secular means. Those who possessed it had not bequeathed it to the generations after them, whose own upbringing would leave them disinherited.

In the years in which Kurzweil conducted his polemic, I do not think my uncle took it seriously. He was stung by its venom, true; but that could be put down to envy of him, the imported New Yorker, on the part of a man, Kurzweil, who, though he would ultimately land a position at Bar-Ilan University, was for many years forced to teach in a high school, denied, like Amos Oz's father, the academic job that he craved. (Until the 1950s, the Hebrew University was the sole higher institution for the liberal arts in Israel, making the academic job market extremely tight. This was the reason, too, that my father did not settle in Israel when his brother did.) In those years, Ahad Ha'amism was the regnant ideology in Israel. Although the writers and artists of the "Canaanite" movement of the 1950s had followed Berdichevsky in proclaiming the native-born *sabra* to be a new creation, a Middle-Eastern "Hebrew" distinct from the Diaspora Jew, they were little more than a bohemian coterie. Few Israeli intellectuals doubted that secular Jewish culture in Israel was a going concern.

Now, however, on a Sabbath morning in the early 1980s, my Uncle Simon declared, "Who knows that Kurzweil won't have the last laugh? If I had known how all this would turn out, I'd have gone to North Dakota and lived as a Red Indian!"

He had by then reached old age. He had not lacked recognition or honors, and his ex-students, many now prominent literary figures in their own right, almost always spoke of him highly even if he complained that they had forgotten him. Still, he was an unhappy man.

Much of this had to do with his personal life, especially with his marriage. But he also felt recognized for the wrong things. His reputation was as an educator and literary critic; his poetry, dense and difficult, was read by few. Yet he had never liked to teach—to the very end of his teaching career, he once told me, he had an attack of stage fright before every class—and he was a far better poet than a critic.

Indeed, his verse improved with age. It grew simpler, more conversational; its Shelleyan prolixity turned terse and hard. Even the yearning of his Habad soul became more rugged. There is a poem of his from this period that I often return to. It begins with a scene: a man, the poet, is watching as a winter sun sets over a rocky crag, which, "steep, ribbed, and black," makes him think of "a child's image of Sinai." The last light beckons; he hurries toward it, not wanting "to miss from close up what seemed a strange revelation,\ The main fire of which had already gone out, leaving only/A last sliver of silver to sharpen the top of the crag." Yet, nearing it,

> I could tell I was late. Only a stiff, cautious squirrel
> Still silvered intently. It climbed upward and stopped,
> > grew grayer and stopped,
> Pressing on toward a gleam that shone for its vision alone,
> As if tuned, it alone, to a gleaming I am of an echo
> That called from the top of the crag – to a signal,
> > not much higher than it was,
> That flared for its vision alone.
>
> But even this thought was denied me. The squirrel
> > froze suddenly,
> As if what it heard, too, the echo that called from
> > the cragtop,
> Was lost all at once and forever.
> Perhaps the snap of a branch in some hidden bush
> > made it freeze. Or perhaps
> It had sniffed the despair of an unhearing man
> > and had hid from that man in a cleft—
> All-hearing, all-knowing.

So there was that, too: a religious despair that was not perhaps total, for there was room in it for a creature, smaller than a man, that could still hear, if only for a moment, God's "I am."

It was during this period of his life that my uncle read me a letter in Yiddish that he had received from a cousin of his, the last pious Habadnik in the family. The cousin had written:

> "All my life I have been a Habadnik, and now I am old and I still understand nothing. What, then, has Habad done for me? What it has done is to raise me from a lower level of understanding nothing to a higher level of understanding nothing."

Fun a niderige madreyge fun gor nisht farshteyn tsu a hekhere madreyge fun gor nisht farshteyn!

Although this letter came from New York, it bore the spiritual postmark not of the messianic sect of Eastern Parkway but of the old Habad of White Russia, the Habad of the shtetl on the Dnieper in which my uncle and father grew up, with its simple innocence yet cunning irony, so gently bemused by the divine folly of things that it hardly bothered to sing and dance as other Hasidim did, preferring its own calm, sober gaze to the fevers of ecstasy.

"Believe me," my uncle said, "when it comes to understanding nothing, I'm his equal."

He had begun to be afraid that perhaps Kurzweil was right after all.

The 1970s in Israel were years in which the center fell away, splitting the country into two warring halves, a heavily secular Left and a heavily religious Right, that were no longer talking the same language. It was not just that one camp thought it crucial to keep the territories conquered in June 1967 while the other thought it crucial to give them up. It was that the justifications offered—the Bible, the land of Israel, the claims of history; democracy, human rights, the dictates of morality—came from two different realms of discourse. A particularism that jeered at universal values clashed with a universalism that scoffed at the particulars. It was as if, from the most superficial level of rhetoric to the deepest psychology of those using it, Judaism and Humanism had become unglued.

No longer did men of the Left like Shlonsky and men of the Right like Klausner share the same cultural vision. Soon there would be no such men left at all. My uncle and Ezra Fleischer, one of whom never went to synagogue and one of whom went every week, lived in the same mental world. Their children did not. They had been raised differently, educated differently; they had gone their different ways. All the time that Ahad Ha'am was winning in Rehavia, Berdichevsky was stealing the Israeli street. And the street was illiterate: it spoke a wretched Hebrew, could not recall a verse from the Bible, went to the beach or mowed its lawns on Saturday mornings. Ahad-Ha'amism was indeed an illusion, the foolish belief in one's own immortality—in the assumption that what has come naturally to us will come naturally to those who come after us, never realizing that the circumstances that made us are gone.

It depressed my uncle greatly. "*Khnyokes* and *amarotzim!*" he once raged in my presence. "We've become a country of *khnyokes* and *amarotzim!*" Religious prigs and ignoramuses! A country of sanctimonious believers and vulgarian infidels! Yona Wallach was merely the last straw. On another day, my uncle might have been the first to admit that she hadn't written a bad poem. Now, though, its taunting of the tefillin he had once donned in holiness brought out all of his grief and revulsion. He had wasted his life on a mirage. He should have gone back out west instead of taking Klausner's job in Jerusalem, vanished there with his beloved Whitman:

A California song,
A prophecy and indirection, a thought impalpable
to breathe as air,
A chorus of dryads, fading, departing, or hamadryads
departing.

A murmuring, fateful, giant voice, out of the earth
and sky,
Voice of a mighty dying tree in the redwood forest
dense!

Although I knew it was just one of his emotional outbursts, I couldn't pretend not to be shocked. His Zionism had always been a model for me.

I wanted to talk to him about it. I didn't, though, because not long afterward he had a stroke, from which he never recovered his speech. Now and then, until he died, in the years when my father's Alzheimer's was not yet severe, we still dropped in after synagogue to say hello. I would sit there wondering whether, seated blankly in the living room of his Rehavia apartment in which my aunt had placed him like a vase of flowers, my uncle heard anything of our conversation. I felt like saying:

"Nu, Reb Shimn! It's not as bad as all that. It takes a forest a long time to grow. For you it was Sinai, for Yonah Wallach it's tefillin. Isn't that the point—that as long as the God we don't believe in is the Jewish one, there's still hope?"

But my uncle seemed only to wink at me, like the dead man in a story he liked to tell, who, eulogized at his funeral for virtues he never had, signaled the rabbi that he saw through him.

"Oho!" said the wink. "Don't be a clever Jewboy. If I had known how all this would turn out, I'd have gone to North Dakota and lived as a Red Indian!"

2005

Israel & the Assassination: A Reckoning

As a voter for the Labor party and Yitzhak Rabin in the 1992 elections and a politically angry man for the past two years, I found myself growing angrier and angrier the week after Rabin's assassination. The angrier I grew, the more I argued with everyone around me, and the more I argued, the angrier it made me. Not, like everyone else, at the assassin and those said to have incited him, but at the Labor party, and at the Israeli Left, and even at the murdered man himself, who was certainly not responsible for the thick sludge of sentimentality, so far from his own personal style (though not from that of his speechwriters), in which he was being quickly shrouded. I must have seemed a very unpleasant person. I may seem one now.

A large part of the sentimentalization in the days after the Rabin assassination lay in the event's being treated as, above all, a violation of the sixth commandment. "How could such a murderer have come from our midst?" and "What Jew would kill a Jew over land?" were the two questions most often asked in Israel, while when Ted Koppel brought his *Nightline* to Jerusalem the week after the assassination, he billed the special broadcast as "Thou Shalt Not Kill."

This is sentimental because, though murder is a frightful crime, large numbers of men and women whose right to live is as great as that of the prime minister of Israel are the barely noticed victims of murder every day. In Israel alone, the police blotters show that dozens of Jews are killed annually by other Jews without *Nightline*'s paying attention. And what, if not land, has been the single greatest motive for killing in human history? What, if not the struggle for land, has caused tens of thousands of Jews and Arabs to be killed in the Middle East?

Was it not a struggle for land that made Yitzhak Rabin join the Palmach, the elite fighting force of Jewish Palestine, as a young man, and thus begin the military career that led to his becoming prime minister? Was it not for the control of land that, as prime minister, he continued a military presence in Lebanon which in 1995 alone resulted in the deaths of over twenty Israeli soldiers? If land is never a legitimate reason for killing, every soldier who fights for the defense of his country is a murderer.

What made Yitzhak Rabin's assassination exceptionally atrocious was not its being a murder but its being a cataclysmic political blunder. It was so, firstly, because—as Likud leader Benjamin Netanyahu put it—democratically chosen governments are changed by elections, not by assassinations. Break that rule once and democracy is imperiled—and an undemocratic Israel cannot prosper, no matter how much or how little land it commands.

And it was so, secondly, because what it most damaged was the public standing of the critics of the Oslo peace process, to whose extreme wing the assassin belonged. Had Yigal Amir wished to deliver a crushing blow to these critics, he could not have found a better way. That is why a friend of mine in America, a far more unequivocal opponent of the peace process than I had been, wrote me the week of the killing: "I would gladly see the bastard hang who prevented the people of Israel from voting against Rabin."

Equally sentimental was the instant mythologization of Yitzhak Rabin as a knight of peace in shining armor.

The day after the assassination I talked with a different friend, an Israeli Arab. "I'm sorry it happened," he said, "but you can't expect me to feel sad for Rabin."

"Why not?" I asked.

"Because," he said, "I happened to be in Tulkarm [a city on the West Bank] one day at the beginning of the *intifada*, when Rabin, who was then minister of defense, gave his famous order to the army to 'break the arms and legs' of Palestinians. And what I saw in Tulkarm were broken arms and legs. Children's too. That order was not meant metaphorically."

Indeed it was not, as many Israelis who carried it out can testify.

It has been said that Yitzhak Rabin had a change of heart and came out of the *intifada* a different man, convinced of the need for a reconciliation with the Palestinians. That may be. But in the summer of 1993, after his conversion supposedly took place and Israeli and PLO negotiators were meeting secretly in Oslo, Rabin, now prime minister, launched Operation Accountability, a massive retaliatory artillery bombardment that caused great civilian destruction in dozens of Lebanese villages accused of harboring Hezbollah guerrillas. He was then what he had always been and remained until his death, several days before which he green-lighted the murder of Islamic Jihad leader Fat'hi Shiqaqi in Malta—namely, a highly pragmatic soldier and politician who had no special liking for violence but no compunctions about using it when he thought it was called for.

I voted for Yitzhak Rabin in 1992 because, like many Israelis, I felt that the situation in the West Bank and Gaza had reached an intolerable point and that the Likud government was incapable of changing it. In terms of change, I was prepared to go farther than most Rabin voters. In an essay published in 1975* I had advocated, subject to certain conditions, the establishment of a Palestinian state along Israel's 1967 borders. It was not a commonly voiced view at the time, and it was still an unpopular one with Israelis in 1992.

Why, then, did I react with such anger to the Israeli-PLO agreement when it was announced in September 1993? Because it was obvious to me immediately that the Labor party had lied to the Israeli public; that it was either continuing to lie to it, or to lie to itself, or both; and that these lies were highly dangerous.

---

* See Driving Toward Jerusalem, pages 86–106

In its official 1992 campaign platform Labor had declared:

> Israel will continue and complete negotiations with authorized and agreed-on Palestinians *from the territories occupied by Israel since 1967* [emphasis added] …. There is a need for an agreement in a Jordanian-Palestinian framework… and not a separate Palestinian state west of the Jordan… Jerusalem will remain united and undivided under Israeli sovereignty…. The Jordan Valley and the western shore of the Dead Sea will be under Israeli sovereignty.

The Labor party had lied to the Israeli public because its 1992 platform clearly ruled out negotiations, let alone a comprehensive political settlement, between Israel and the PLO, which in 1992 was based not in the occupied territories but in Tunis, and which had been considered by all previous Israeli governments a terrorist organization not to be treated with. And since the PLO had stated repeatedly before Oslo, and continued to state after it, that its immediate goal was the creation of an independent Palestinian state in Gaza and the entire West Bank with East Jerusalem as its capital, there were only two explanations of Israeli thinking at Oslo. One was that Yitzhak Rabin and his government had secretly decided to acquiesce in the establishment of such a state, thereby reneging on the rest of their campaign pledges regarding the future of the territories. The other was that they believed the peace process could be brought to a successful conclusion without yielding to the PLO's main territorial and political demands.

Let us first consider the second of these possibilities. In its final-stage negotiations with the Palestinians, set to begin next May, can Israel simply declare: "Gentlemen, you are not getting a state and you are not getting Jerusalem and other areas, and you can either take or leave what we are giving you?"

In theory, of course, it can. In practice, the Palestinians, under the terms of the Oslo agreement, will by then have nearly thirty thousand armed policemen in the West Bank and Gaza, close to the number of combat soldiers in Israel's standing army. Will Israel be prepared to risk engaging this force in armed conflict if a political impasse is reached? Would Yitzhak Rabin—who, we are told, was psychologically shaken to the core by the *intifada*—have been ready to expose Israel to a prolonged period of armed violence many times greater than that of the *intifada* in order to keep his campaign pledges, a part of which he had already violated? Will his successor Shimon Peres be ready to do so should it be necessary?

But, we are told, this will not be necessary because already at Oslo the Rabin government knew that it was agreeing to the establishment of a Palestinian state in Gaza and the entire West Bank ruled from a capital in East Jerusalem, so that all its protestations to the contrary, both at the time and subsequently, were not to be taken seriously.

"Honestly," someone said to me during the week after the assassination, "you're being hopelessly naive. You yourself say that, 'subject to certain conditions,' you believe a Palestinian state is the solution. Do you really think that Labor could have been elected in 1992 had it openly said as much to a public that had been brainwashed against such an idea for years? And with whom could it have negotiated such a solution except the PLO, an organization that Israeli voters feared and abhorred? No serious person expects politicians always to tell the truth. It is a leader's duty to get elected and lead, not to get permission for every step he takes."

Despite my own reputation among my friends as a cynic, such a view, which is almost universally held today on the Israeli Left, strikes me as cynical beyond bounds. Of course politicians frequently lie to the public, although those who lie least and with the uneasiest conscience are the ones who look best in the history books. But it is one thing to lie about ordinary matters of political expediency, another to lie about a momentous decision that will profoundly affect the future of one's country for as long as it continues to exist. If the question of Israel's borders, of their location and defensibility, of who lives and rules on either side of them, and of their relationship to the claims of thousands of years of Jewish history is not something about which to consult the Israeli public within the framework of democratic politics, what is democracy for?

Nor is it the case that Labor had to fool the voters in order to carry out its present policies. There were other alternatives. Having won the elections on the platform it ran on, Labor could have begun to prepare public opinion for the new direction it wished to take. It could have asked the PLO to help change the climate in Israel by declaring a moratorium on terror, or by repealing the provisions of the Palestinian Charter which call for Israel's destruction, or by some other dramatic act. It could have begun tentative, noncommittal talks with the PLO and then revealed their content to the public. And having done any or all of these things, it could then have said, "Citizens of Israel: now that you have seen how the PLO has changed and is ready to recognize the state of Israel and live peacefully alongside it, we are calling new elections in order to ask you for a mandate to commence negotiations with it that may lead to a Palestinian state."

Would that mandate have been given? It is impossible to say. But whether it would have been or not, the people would have spoken. And if the people had been allowed to speak, Yitzhak Rabin might be alive today.

And perhaps not? His murderer was a true believer in the Land of Israel, not in democratic politics. Still, as has been frequently pointed out in the wake of the assassination, true believers tend to reach for their guns when they feel the rage of a wider public behind them—and the rage of many Israelis against Yitzhak Rabin dated to the day when, without asking or warning them, he signed an agreement with Yasser Arafat, a man regarded by them with revulsion, and shook hands with him on the White House lawn. Although those who in the next two years accused Rabin of betraying his country were speaking overheatedly, he did betray many of the voters whose ballots helped elect him prime minister by a narrow margin.

Rabin's turnabout has been compared by his defenders to that of Likud's Menachem Begin, who was elected in 1977 on a platform that never hinted he would return all of Sinai to Egypt. But there is a huge difference. When Begin submitted the accord with Egypt to the Knesset, it won overwhelming bipartisan approval, with an even higher percentage of Labor members than Likud members voting for it; had he called for new elections, he would have won them handily. By contrast, the Rabin-Arafat rapprochement split Israel in half, both in the Knesset and in the opinion polls. The Knesset's bitterly debated ratification of stage two of the Oslo agreement, a month before the assassination, passed by a vote of sixty-one to fifty-nine. Minus the five votes of two anti-Zionist Arab parties that object to the definition of Israel as a Jewish state, the results were fifty-nine to fifty-six against.

Granted, a parliamentary majority of two is as binding as one of twenty. The question in Israel was never the Rabin government's formal legitimacy; it was its political and moral judgment in pursuing a course that turned Israel ferociously against itself on a matter of the utmost historical gravity. But as Rabin followed this course, and was applauded by the same Left that in 1982 had denounced Begin's invasion of Lebanon for violating the principle that no Israeli government should go to war without a national consensus, he and his supporters scoffed at the proposition that a radically conceived peace demanded a measure of national unity, too.

Moreover, it was clear to many thinking Israelis that, even if the Rabin government had received parliamentary backing to sign the accord reached at Oslo; and even if this accord would have led in a few years' time to a "final" peace settlement with the Palestinians, there was no certainty that its finality would have been final. A Palestinian state, even one based on a complete Israeli withdrawal to the 1967 lines, would have comprised only 23 percent of the area of British Mandate Palestine. It is no secret that many and probably most Palestinians, including the leaders of the PLO, hope such a state will be the first stage in reclaiming more Palestinian land, possibly up to the 1947 partition borders and beyond.

Thus it was that, from the autumn of 1993 to the autumn of 1995, as the Oslo agreement was implemented and thousands of armed Palestinian policemen arrived in Gaza and Jericho and began moving into the West

Bank; and as some 150 Israelis died in Palestinian terror attacks which the PLO, while procrastinating about revoking the Palestinian Charter, was not particularly vigilant in preventing; and as the Rabin government continued to keep secret from its own people what its aims in the peace process were, including the borders it planned to insist on and its conception of the fate of the tens of thousands of Jewish settlers living beyond them, much of Israel felt like passengers on a ship that had been hijacked by its own captain and crew, who were now piloting it through dense fog and mined waters, with the consent of only half of those aboard, toward an unrevealed and perhaps calamitous destination.

The emotions aroused by this were fear, helplessness, bitterness, frustration, and, as I have said, rage. All of them were channeled into the antigovernment invective that mounted in volume and vituperation throughout this period and that was, so the Israeli Left now tells us, the finger that pressed the trigger that was Yigal Amir.

I would not dispute this. Although Amir was apparently unaided on the night of the shooting, he was what is known in Hebrew as a *sh'liah avera*, a messenger of sin, for a large body of Israelis who would not have dreamed of doing what he did. This public, heavily represented in what is known as the "national-religious camp" and in the settlements of Judea and Samaria that are the most threatened by the Oslo pact, owes itself and the nation a reckoning for having allowed elements in its midst to be swept away by inflammatory rhetoric and bizarre rabbinical rulings that could have encouraged a Yigal Amir to think he was acting on its behalf.

Such a reckoning, at least part of the Israeli Right is now making. The reckoning that is not being made, and of the need for which there seems to be no awareness among those who should make it, concerns the rhetoric and deeds of the Left, hardly any less inflammatory during the period in question.

Before me is the progovernment newspaper *Ha'aretz*, Israel's most respected daily, from March 26, 1995. Its front-page headline: "Rabin: Likud Is Collaborator With Hamas." The text of the lead article reports that "Prime Minister Yitzhak Rabin sharply attacked Likud yesterday [saying], 'The terror organizations are succeeding because Likud has become a collaborator with Islamic Jihad and Hamas.'" It goes on:

> In inner consultations recently held at high levels of the Labor party, it was decided to step up attacks against the Right, especially against Likud and its leader. There is concern in Labor over polls, taken in the last several months, showing Netanyahu with a large lead over Rabin.... Ranking members of Labor welcomed this changed line. One cabinet minister said he was happy that "The Prime Minister has decided to take off the gloves with Likud." A second minister, on the other hand, expressed concern that extreme language might cause the political arena to degenerate into verbal violence a year before the elections.

It would be interesting to know who the prescient second minister was. And it would be interesting to ask the first minister whether, if a left-wing assassin had killed Benjamin Netanyahu for being a Hamas collaborator, he would now be saying that Yitzhak Rabin had "blood on his hands," as Labor has been saying of Netanyahu.

As it happens, Netanyahu and Likud have been specifically charged by the Left not so much with direct incitement as with failing to disown the incendiary language and symbolism coming from extraparliamentary right-wing groups—the prime example, repeatedly cited since the assassination, being the blind eye turned by them to a poster of Rabin in an SS uniform displayed by demonstrators at a Likud rally in October. This poster, it now appears, was commissioned and disseminated by Avishai Raviv, a right-wing extremist who was, however, acting as an agent for the Israeli General Security Service, which was seeking to discredit opposition to the peace process—that is for the Rabin government itself.

This does not exonerate the failure of the Right to denounce such incitement more strongly. Yet it is worth recalling that throughout the 1980s, long before it was employed by the right wing to abuse Rabin, the word "Nazi" was often used by the far Left to describe the settlers and the Likud government that backed them. Perhaps the most egregious case was that of the late Yeshayahu Leibowitz, a well-known theologian and political polemicist, who invented the term "Judeo-Nazi" and who in 1993 was awarded the prestigious Israel Prize for intellectual achievement by Yitzhak Rabin's Minister of Culture, Shulamit Aloni. There was nothing wrong in calling Jews Nazis, it would seem, as long they were the right Jews.

Indeed, there was nothing wrong with calling the settlers many other names, too, which were routinely hurled at them by the Left in a systematic attempt to delegitimize them after they began organizing against the Oslo agreement: "enemies of peace," "religious fanatics," "dancers on the blood [of terror victims]," "Arab-haters," and "Hamasniks" were some of the more common epithets. It made no difference that these same settlers, who for years had braved the daily dangers of the *intifada*, had been, in the name of the national security of Israel, assisted and encouraged to take up residence in their homes by previous Israeli governments, including the earlier 1974–77 regime of Yitzhak Rabin. Asked about one of their demonstrations, the same Rabin declared that, for his part, "They can spin around like propellers for as long as they like."

Another example of Right-wing incitement said to have provoked the assassination were the placards and shouts of "Rabin Is a Murderer" at many anti-government demonstrations, especially after Palestinian terror attacks. These were reprehensible—but the copyright on them, too, belonged to the Left. Such slogans first surfaced in Israel in 1982, at the huge Labor party and Peace Now rally held in Tel Aviv's Kings of Israel (now Yitzhak Rabin) Square to protest the massacre of Palestinians by Lebanese Christians in the Sabra and Shatila refugee camps. There, signs proclaiming "Begin Is a Murderer" and "Sharon Is a Murderer" were held high by many demonstrators. I can vouch that no one asked for their removal because I was there holding a sign myself (although differently worded, as I recall).

But, protests the Left, there is no comparison: although we, too, may have sinned with words, nearly all the threats and incidents of political violence that Israel has witnessed in recent years have come from the Right. This is true. Right-wing extremism in Israel *has* been more violent; one reason for this is that, ideologically, the far Right tends to view conflict, rather than the resolution of it, as the inescapable fate of Israeli Jews. And yet the Machiavellian use by a secret service controlled by the Rabin government of *agents provocateurs* like Raviv is no less frightening.

In the end, perhaps, it is pointless to try to keep score in such a game of tit for tat. Indeed, although both the Right and the Left contributed generously to the acrimonious atmosphere that was created in the period after Oslo, it is on the whole remarkable, given the passions aroused by one of the most agonizingly fateful moments the Jewish people has ever lived through, that democratic forms were so well observed in Israel up to the assassination. In terms of the tone of the political debate, Dreyfusards and anti-Dreyfusards in France, or pro- and anti-Vietnam War demonstrators in the United States, were no more polite when arguing about much less. They were fighting for the soul of their country; here the struggle is over its limbs as well.

One can point to the exact historical moment when the center dropped out of Israeli politics, leaving an overwhelmingly secular Left and a heavily religious Right facing each other across a discourseless chasm. But although this happened politically in September 1993 with the signing of the Oslo agreement, culturally it was a long while in the making.

In a deep sense, the processes leading up to this moment reflect the failure of the grand cultural project of Zionism, whose root assumption, once shared by secular and religious Zionists alike, was that it was possible to build a society that would combine a commitment to the modern world and its highest ideals with an allegiance, if not to the ritual forms, at least to the great texts and memories, of Jewish tradition and their resonance in the physical landscape of Israel.

For most of this century, as reflected in its literature, arts, popular culture, and politics, this project had every appearance of success. As late as the 1960s, the same Bible which, shortly before his death, Yitzhak Rabin referred to as "an antiquated land registry," was still a living book in secular Israel. Here is Moshe Dayan, a product of the Labor movement and only seven years older than Rabin, speaking a month after the Six-Day War of 1967 placed in Jewish hands the portion of central Palestine that had been lost to Jordan in the partition of 1948:

> We have returned to the mountainland, to the cradle of our people and the legacy of our fathers, to the land of the Judges and to the bastion of the kingdom of the House of David. We have returned to Hebron, to Shechem [Nablus], to Bethlehem, to Anatot, to Jericho, and to the fords of the Jordan.

Today, when such language in the mouth of a Labor party politician would sound hopelessly archaic, it is possible to see that Dayan's generation derived its own romantic attachment to the Bible and Jewish history less (as Zionist myth had it) from the vaunted contact of the native-born *sabra* with the soil of the land of Israel than from its East European-born parents, themselves the products of religious homes; and that the apparent link binding Hebrew secularism to Jewish tradition was perhaps less a viable carrying forward of tradition than tradition's last gasp. What has happened with the final expiration of that gasp is well illustrated by the case of Dayan's daughter Ya'el, a Left-wing Labor politician whose only known public reference to the Bible, made in defense of gay rights, has been to assert that David and Jonathan were homosexual lovers, and who has declared that she will be happy to visit Hebron on a Palestinian visa.

It was the Palestinians in the occupied territories, certainly, who hastened a polarization in Israeli life that would have taken place far more slowly and less painfully without them. For as the Israeli occupation of the territories lengthened, and the Jewish settlement movement grew, and with it the increasingly organized and violent resistance of the local Palestinian population, culminating in the *intifada*, the choice became a seemingly stark one. Either Israel relinquished its title to Judea and Samaria, the geographical core of the historical Jewish homeland, and so, by freeing the people living there from its yoke, took its stand (said the

Left) with enlightened humanity; or else it pressed its claim to the areas and kept faith (said the Right) with Jewish memory.

This was a cruel dilemma. And it represented a great irony, for it meant that the Jewish state, which according to Zionism had come to heal the inner split between the human being in the Jew and the Jew in the human being, had now driven a new and terrible wedge into the breach.

Like a man in great torment who breaks psychologically in two, Israel thus went, or was dragged, to Oslo as two nations, each willing to risk what the other was not and unwilling to risk what the other was; neither able to communicate with or to understand the other but only to blame the other rancorously; thesis and antithesis, each half of the now-fractured personality of the Jewish people in its homeland.

I am not a believer in the view that tormented nations need psychiatrists rather than politicians. Only a wise politics can help to join again what a foolish politics has helped to sunder. But can one, in today's circumstances, imagine a politics wise enough?

1995

The Translator's Paradox

My first paid translation went unpaid. It was commissioned by an Israeli writer named Matti Megged, who, in 1959 or '60, toured America on a grant from a U.S. foundation and ran into me on the Columbia University campus, where I was an undergraduate. A tall, craggy-faced man, the brother of the better-known Israeli novelist Aharon Megged, he discovered I knew Hebrew and offered me twenty-five dollars to put a short story of his into English. This I did. Before paying me, however, he took a bus to New Orleans, was rolled in a bar there, returned to New York with nothing remaining of his travel grant but a Greyhound ticket left thoughtfully in his pocket, and did not contact me again.

I can't say I felt badly cheated: my translation was wooden and never appeared in print. But it was the start of a professional career, because a year or two later, when Schocken Books in New York chose to put out an anthology of Israeli fiction in English, it asked me, solely on the basis of Matti Megged's guilt-ridden recommendation, to do several stories. That was how hard it was to find Hebrew-English translators in those days. The only ones to be had were a handful of amateurs who made their livings from other things, and the quality of their work was low. In his preface to Schocken's *Israeli Stories,* the volume's editor declared with some pride that

> special care has been taken to avoid the archaisms and crudities in language which in the past have often vitiated Hebrew literature in English.... Freed of its artificial quaintness, Hebrew prose can be enjoyed and evaluated like any other modern literature.

Even in the way of the artificially quaint, moreover, the modern Hebrew literature available in English at the time would have fit on a small shelf. There was, as I recall, one other anthology of fiction, Viking Press's *The Whole Loaf; In The Heart of Seas,* a novella by S. Y. Agnon, who had not yet won the Nobel Prize; Moshe Shamir's Israeli bestseller *A King of Flesh and Blood;* a selection from the poetry of Hayim Nahman Bialik; a novel about kibbutz life by a now-forgotten author named David Malitz; and a smattering of short stories and poems in various Jewish magazines and periodicals. That was about it.

Today, professional Hebrew-English translators—some very good—abound, and the shelf has expanded to many large bookcases. To mention a part of their contents, there is the nearly complete work of Agnon; novels and novellas by nineteenth- and early twentieth-century pioneers of modern Hebrew literature like Joseph Perl, Mendele Mocher Sefarim, Mordecai Ze'ev Feierberg, Yosef Hayim Brenner, and Uri Tsvi Gnessin; volumes of fiction by post-World War I Hebrew authors, among them Hayim Hazaz, David Fogel, and Avigdor Hameiri; more fiction by such prominent Israeli novelists of the 1950s, '60s, and '70s as S. Yizhar, Hayim Gouri, Aharon Megged, Hanoch Bartov, Pinchas Sadeh, and David Shahar; a vast amount of contemporary Israeli prose, including nearly everything written by internationally known figures like Aharon Appelfeld, Amos Oz, A. B. Yehoshua, David Grossman, and Meir Shalev; and, in addition to several anthologies of Israeli poetry, one or more individual volumes of verse by Yehuda Amichai, Dan Pagis, Avot Yeshurun,

Abba Kovner, Leah Goldberg, Meir Wieseltier, Yona Wallach, Aharon Shabtai, Dahlia Ravikovitch, Zelda Shneurson, and T. Carmi, to give a partial list.

All this is quite apart from earlier periods of Hebrew and Jewish literature. At the time I began my career as a translator, the English reader had available one Jewish translation of the Bible, the 1917 Jewish Publication Society edition. Today, fifty years later, he has at his disposal half a dozen different ones. In addition, in recent years there have appeared two complete new editions of the Mishnah, two complete new editions of the Babylonian Talmud, numerous volumes of classical Midrash, many works of medieval Hebrew philosophy, a generous sampling of medieval Hebrew poetry and prose, a completely new four-volume text of the Zohar, other works of Jewish mysticism, dozens if not hundreds of rabbinic texts and commentaries, numerous volumes of Hasidic literature, and so on and so forth, much of it in scholarly editions that come with notes and commentaries. Such a library makes it possible to acquire a thorough education in the classics of Judaism entirely in English.

It is now possible to follow events in Israel entirely in English, too. Nor does this have to be done by means of the *Jerusalem Post*, an English-language daily largely written by and for Anglophone immigrants. For a native perspective on Israeli affairs, there is YNet, the English internet edition of the mass-circulation *Yedi'ot Aharonot*, and English print and internet editions of the liberal *Haaretz*, each produced by a small factory of Hebrew-English translators working around the clock. Given the seven-hour time difference between Israel and the east coast of America, the reader in New York can often know what is happening in Israel before Israelis awaken to read about it in the morning news.

Matti Megged and I were, unwittingly, at the front edge of a wave that has changed Diaspora Jewish life, preeminently in the United States. But the change has not been all for the better. It has contributed to the loss of Hebrew as the international language of the Jewish people.

True, from the time of its demise as a vernacular in antiquity to its spoken revival by modern Zionism, Hebrew was the native language of no Jew on earth. Jews spoke other tongues, and, until the early or mid-nineteenth century, there was hardly a Jewish community in the world that did not have its distinctive medium of speech. In Russia, Poland, the Baltic states, Romania, and parts of Hungary, this was East European Yiddish; in Germany and Holland, Western Yiddish; in Italy, Judeo-Italian; in the Balkans, Greece, and Turkey, Ladino; in North Africa and the Levant, various dialects of Judeo-Arabic. Although each of these developed from a non-Jewish base (e.g., medieval German in the case of Yiddish and fifteenth-century Spanish in that of Ladino), it was partially or entirely incomprehensible to non-Jews. The moment a Jew addressed another Jew in it, a communal "we" was established.

Of course, such a declaration of Jewish identity was also an admission of Jewish dispersion, since the members of one speech community could not communicate with those of another: Yiddish speakers did not know Ladino and Judeo-Arabic speakers did not know Judeo-Italian. But even when speakers of such different languages met, they were not necessarily at a loss as long as they had Hebrew in common.

History offers copious documentation of Hebrew's use as a Jewish lingua franca. The written record goes as far back as the ninth century, when a mysterious traveler known as "Eldad the Danite" turned up in North Africa. Eldad, whose true story will never be known, claimed to have come from descendants of the biblical tribe of Dan living in Ethiopia, and he talked in Hebrew—the only language, so he said, that he knew—to the Jews he met. Throughout the ages, traveling Jewish merchants and fund-raising emissaries, generally sent from Palestine, routinely spoke Hebrew wherever they went. The German-Jewish physician Jacob Pollak, who taught and practiced medicine in Persia in the 1850s, wrote of such voyagers encountered by him in Central Asia:

> It is amazing to see how far these men manage to circulate. They travel without a qualm to Samarkand, Bukhara, Kandehar, Harat, and Balk to visit their brethren, going

to regions where the ordinary European would be in great danger and getting from place to place on the strength of Hebrew alone, guided by shepherds and nomads through tribal territories infested with bandits and always reaching their destinations safe and sound.

Such men, to be sure, sometimes had difficulty making themselves understood even in Hebrew. The itinerant nineteenth-century Jerusalem fund-raiser Ya'akov Sapir reported after a visit to Yemen that its Jews had laughed at his Hebrew accent, which they found outlandish and all but incomprehensible. But even when Hebrew was an unreliable means of spoken communication, every knowledgeable Jew could read and write it. It was in Hebrew that Jews prayed; studied the Bible and other great Jewish texts; wrote and read works of commentary, philosophy, theology, hagiography, poetry, and fiction; sent each other letters and missives; requested and received legal opinions from rabbinical authorities; and read in translation books written in other languages. (Many of the great works of medieval Jewish philosophy, written in Arabic in Islamic lands, were read by non-Arabic-speaking Jews in Hebrew, in which alone they survived in the Jewish canon.) In the age of newspapers and periodicals, the Hebrew press was for long the prime medium that brought Jews news of developments in the Jewish and even the non-Jewish world. Until modern times, a Jew with a reading knowledge of Hebrew, and only such a Jew, had access to the thought and creativity of Jews everywhere.

This still seemed true at the end of the nineteenth century. As late as 1896, when the distinguished Russian Jewish thinker and essayist Ahad Ha'am founded his periodical review *Hashiloah*, which he hoped to develop into a forum for worldwide Jewish cultural and intellectual exchange, he chose to do so in Hebrew in the confidence that this was the language best suited for the task. Not only did he deem it the natural language of

Jewish discourse, but any other language, he thought, would have been parochial, understood by Jews in some countries but not in others.

Ahad Ha'am's confidence, however, was misplaced. In the thirty years (most of them under other editors) in which *Hashiloah* struggled to keep appearing, which were also the years in which the spoken Hebrew revival in Palestine turned the corner of success, Hebrew as an international language was steeply on the decline. All over the world, a younger generation of Jews no longer had the Jewish education needed to read it; nor, now fully fluent in the languages of its native countries as the generations before it were not, did it need Hebrew to be its window on the world. Even Jewishly concerned Jews now had weeklies, monthlies, and periodicals in these languages, such as the Russian *Voskhod,* the German *die Welt* and *der Jude,* and the French *Révue des études juives.* By the time Ahad Ha'am died in 1927, American Jewry, too, had its own literary review, the *Menorah Journal,* which would have embodied Ahad Ha'am's editorial agenda almost entirely were it not for the fact that it was in English. Its readers were the vanguard of a new audience of American Jews for whose benefit the great Hebrew-English translation enterprise of the last fifty years has taken place.

Here, then, is a great historical irony. As long as Hebrew was the first language of no educated Jew in the world, it was the second language of every educated Jew; now that it has become the mother tongue of millions of Jews in the state of Israel, it has largely ceased to be known by Jews elsewhere. It has in effect been demoted to a Judeo-Israeli, a new Jewish regional speech. Far more Israeli and Palestinian Arabs now have a working command of it than do American Jews.

If an Eldad the Danite were to turn up today, Hebrew would not get him very far. It is in English that Jewish travelers speak to Jews in foreign countries; in English that Jewish physicists in Russia email their Jewish colleagues in France and Jewish psychiatrists in Argentina write their Jewish counterparts in Great Britain; and in English that our contemporary Eldads—peoples in remote regions making claims to ancient Israelite roots—enter into contact with the world's Jews.

It is in English, too, that audiences are addressed at international Jewish get-togethers. Some twenty years ago, I attended a conference in Jerusalem whose subject was the Hebrew fiction of Agnon. All of its participants were Agnon scholars and critics. The language it was held in? English, of course—not only because this was the language in which the conference's organizers wished to publish its proceedings, but because the Israeli presenters were more comfortable in it than were the non-Israeli ones in Hebrew.

Indeed, the very high level of English in Israel enables the tourist there to engage Israelis from all walks of life without having to speak a word of Hebrew. Even when speaking Hebrew among themselves, if truth be told, Israelis are often subliminally thinking in English. So great is the influence of English in the world today that a great deal of Israeli speech is little more than English in Hebrew translation.

English has become the new international language of the Jews because it has become the international language of everyone. But it has been aided by Jewish assimilation, which has deprived millions of Jewish children of the Hebrew they once acquired as part of a religious upbringing. Although a functional literacy in Hebrew was very far from universal in traditional Jewish societies, it was the defining mark of an educated Jew and the aspiration of most Jews. It is no idealization to point out that in many nineteenth-century European *shtetls* there were study groups in which ordinary workingmen—coachmen, carpenters, shoemakers, tailors, water carriers, watchmakers—gathered to read basic Hebrew texts like the Mishnah.

Of how many American Jewish university professors, lawyers, doctors, scientists, financial analysts, and hedge fund managers can this be said today? Of course, there are American Jewish professionals who can and do study Hebrew texts; the growth of Jewish day school education and the retraditionalization of a part of the American Jewish community have even brought about increasing numbers of them. And yet Hebrew as a medium of communication is not greatly emphasized in American Jewish curriculums. I have yet to meet the graduate of a day school who, on the basis of his or her schooling alone, could conduct more than a rudimentary Hebrew conversation or read a contemporary Hebrew novel. Doctor, lawyer, or professor, the Hebrew of such Jews is no better than was the *shtetl* shoemaker's.

What is lacking in contemporary American Jewry is an ethos of Hebrew, the belief that without it, Jewish lives are incomplete. Although such an attitude was never prominent in America, it did once exist and even flourish in some places. It was found in elite schools where Hebrew was the medium of instruction rather than merely a subject among others; in Hebrew-speaking summer camps that attracted thousands of campers; in a small but intense American Hebrew literary scene that boasted publications like *Bitzaron* and *Hadoar* and serious novelists and poets like Hillel Bavli, Reuben Wallenrod, Isaac Silberschlag, Simon Halkin, Abraham Regelson, and Gabriel Preil; in American Jewish readers who read such writers. All this has now vanished, along with the feeling that Hebrew is a Jewish necessity.

The Hebrew-English translator has reason to wonder, then, how much of a service he has ultimately performed. Yes, he has helped to spread knowledge, to transport it across linguistic frontiers, to make it available to those without access to it in its original language—in a word, to do what translators have always done. He has made it possible for many Jews to learn about a heritage and its riches that would otherwise be barred to them. Surely, this is a noble calling.

And yet, to whomever bewails Hebrew's plight today and calls for its reestablishment as a central feature of Jewish life, the ready answer is: why? What need for it is there? Granted, there is something to be said for literary connoisseurs reading a work in the language it was written in, be it the Bible, Shakespeare, or Agnon. But why demand of ordinary American Jews that they spend years studying a difficult Semitic language when practically everything in it that might be of interest to them already exists in a language that they know?

Most Hebrew-English translators, one assumes, have a love for Hebrew; why else would they have chosen their profession? It was such a love, more than anything, that kept me attached to my Jewishness in the years in which I met Matti Megged, when I had drifted far from Jewish life in other respects. But this only makes it sadder to realize that if Hebrew is in sore straits in America today, we Hebrew-English translators bear our share of the blame for it.

———✺———

Already in ancient times, the rabbis of the Talmud understood the paradox of translation. A midrash in the tractate of Megillah has this to say about a first-century *targum*, a translation of the Hebrew prophets into Aramaic, then the spoken language of the Jews of Palestine and the Middle East:

> The *targum* of the prophets was composed by Yonatan ben Uzziel.... When he finished it, the land of Israel quaked over an area of 400 parasangs by 400 parasangs, and a divine voice went forth and exclaimed, "Who is this that has revealed My secrets to mankind?" Yonatan stood up and said, "I am he who revealed Your secrets to mortals. It is known and manifest to You that I did it not for my own honor nor for the honor of my father's house, but for Your honor, so that controversy should not abound in the land."

Yonatan argued the case for translation: if some Jews can read sacred literature in Hebrew and others cannot read it at all, there will be two classes of Jews, one educated and one ignorant. Furthermore, the translated text is the more trustworthy document, it being a characteristic of translation that it fills in gaps of meaning, irons out contradictions, and eliminates ambiguities by coming down on one side of them or the other. Every translation is also a commentary—and Yonatan's *targum*, which caused the land of Israel to quake with astonishment and perhaps dismay, was a particularly audacious act of commentary, since it systematically introduced rabbinic interpretations into the biblical text. It indeed gave away God's secrets, to Jews as well as to Gentiles. Whereas the Hebrew reader of the prophets had to struggle with each unclear passage, Yonatan clarified God's word for him—and so deprived him of the opportunity to do it for himself. No wonder God felt presumed upon, even if the rabbis gave Yonatan the last word.

Such an ambivalent attitude toward translation runs through the Talmud. On the one hand, we find there the statement: "Aquila translated the Torah into Greek in the presence of Rabbi Eliezer and Rabbi Yehoshua and they applauded him, saying, 'Through Grecian grace you have made its beauty known among men.'" On the other hand, there is the remark in the tractate of Soferim, made about the Greek Septuagint, the early Bible translation produced in second-century B.C.E. Ptolemaic Egypt, that "the day on which the elders wrote the Torah in Greek for King Ptolemy was as intolerable for Israel as the day the golden calf was made."

Translation is double edged. It is the great go-between of humanity, the international hawker of cultural wares, the oldest and most powerful of all globalizing forces. But it is also a golden calf, a false representation. It reveals and thus conceals. It clarifies and so obscures. It betrays our secrets to mankind.

Living in translation has its advantages for the Jewish people: it facilitates communication among them, disseminates Jewish culture, creates a new Jewish literacy to replace the old one that has been lost. Yet it dilutes the culture it disseminates, weakens Jewish distinctiveness, puts Jews at a remove from themselves. It makes them vulnerably transparent to the outside world. A people's language is its private domain; in it, it can pursue its own business, conduct its own quarrels, make its own jokes, let down its hair; it can be itself without fear of eavesdroppers. One can argue in a Jewish language about Judaism, about Zionism, about any aspect of Jewish life, but one argues *in* that language, not about it; the language itself belongs to all. Precisely because it is neutral, language has always been the strongest of communal bonds, the magic circle that no interloper could cross.

For the first time in their history, most Jews no longer have a language of their own. They are overheard when they speak to each other.

The salient difference between contemporary American Jewish writing and writing in a Jewish language is that the former is also read by non-Jews; it lacks the unambiguous "we" of a community. When an American Jewish author insists on being viewed as part of American rather than Jewish literature, he is merely stating the obvious. Even if he wished to write as a Jew, he lacks the privacy to do so single-mindedly.

But does even a Hebrew author in Israel enjoy such privacy today? Not when he knows—or hopes—that his novel will soon appear in translation and be reviewed in *Le Monde* or *The New York Times*. Indeed, it is not uncommon today for leading Israeli writers to sign translation contracts with American or European publishers even before they begin work on a book. In what sense are they, too, writing as Jews for Jews? The author who thinks of being translated as he writes is like a man trying to talk intimately to his family while aware all the time that someone is listening at the window. In one way or another, what he says must be affected.

This is one reason why, though I began my career with Matti Megged, the Hebrew writers I prefer to translate are long dead. Much of my career as a translator has been spent in their company.

They're easier to work with, the dead. They do not complain. They do not argue with me about how I have translated them. They do not fret about their reputations in America or blame me if these are not what they think they should be. They are not convinced that they know English better than I do. Most of them never knew it at all.

They also tend to be better writers. Not all of them, of course. But those capable of convincing a publisher that they deserve to appear in translation have to do so on the basis of their work alone. They have no literary agent to represent them, no contemporary news value or PR to trumpet their importance or relevance; they cannot be interviewed on television or radio, appear on talk shows, or give public readings from their latest work. All they have, if they are lucky, is a translator. And they cannot even defend themselves against him.

The living can choose their translator, ask to see his work while in progress, criticize it, make suggestions, demand he redo it, change it with or without his knowledge once it is out of his hands. If a poor translation of them appears, they can write another book and find a better translator for that one. The dead have none of these options. The economics of publishing are such that even if a publisher realizes that they have been mangled in translation, he will sooner publish such a disservice to them than discard it and lose his investment. Take the English version of Agnon's *A Guest for the Night,* one of the greatest Hebrew novels ever written: it is a perfect disaster, one so bad that anyone judging its author by it alone would have to conclude that his winning the Nobel Prize was pure flimflam. And yet there it is on the library shelves and everlastingly will be, since in translation, if it is not the Bible, *The Odyssey,* or some other recognized classic, a book gets only one chance.

And so one tries to make it a fair one, even if the potential audience is small. Was it that much bigger in the dead's day? One of the most impressive things about the Hebrew writers I love to translate most, men like Bialik, Feierberg, Brenner, and Gnessin, is that they wrote what they did for a handful of readers, for that limited circle of Jews who bought Hebrew books and subscribed to Hebrew journals, without even the confidence that the language they were writing in would be read at all in a hundred years' time. They wrote because they believed in the power of the Hebrew word, with no prospect of serious material reward, for they were paid, if at all, a pittance for their work. And yet being translated into other languages, it is safe to say, was the furthest thing from their minds. Indeed, the idea could only have struck them as absurd. What interest could the reader of such languages have in the world about which they wrote, that strange and tragic world of Jewish Eastern Europe that was crumbling before their eyes and that they described, preached to, and prophesied of with a passion such as is normally reserved for what has some assurance of a future?

The desire to be translated best comes as an afterthought, when it can no longer do any harm. Not long ago, the typed manuscript of a new novel by a prominent Israeli author found its way to my desk;

he had an American publisher and was eager for me to begin work on his book even before it came out in Hebrew. I don't blame him, but I doubt that the situation is a healthy one. The globalization of culture is vitiating enough on the local level without further hothousing it in this way. Perhaps books should not be translated at all until they have been allowed to age for a while. The young ones would have to be consumed locally while those mature enough to travel would, when uncorked, taste the better for having had to wait. Once, walking into a bookstore and seized by a vertigo induced by its tiers upon tiers of crammed shelves, I thought: there should be a moratorium on the writing of books for the next hundred years until we can catch up with those already written. By then, a few might be ripe for translation.

2008

Feminizing Jewish Studies

Some three decades have passed since the formal introduction of Jewish studies as an academic discipline on American campuses, and the change has been great. Whereas in the 1950s the serious Judaic scholars in the United States, most of European provenance, could have been counted on one's fingers (as the son of a professor at the Jewish Theological Seminary whose colleagues they were, I knew most of them personally), hundreds of American-born-and-trained professors and lecturers now teach Jewish religion, history, sociology, literature, rabbinics, and Bible at a large number of American universities. This has been one of the American Jewish community's most impressive cultural achievements.

And most recently, not only a new generation of Jewish scholars but a new school of them has emerged on the American campus. Heavily influenced, like all the liberal arts, by postmodernist thinking; skeptical of traditional Jewish categories of analysis; ranging from non- to anti-Zionist in its attitude toward Israel while strongly affirming Diaspora Jewish identity; and openly embracing feminism and "feminist theory," it does not yet have a name.

One is tempted to call it "the California school," since several of its leading representatives—David Biale, Chana Kronfeld, Naomi Seidman, Howard Eilberg-Schwartz, and Daniel Boyarin—teach at institutions in that state, and Boyarin, a professor of "talmudic culture" at Berkeley, is arguably the trend's brightest star. But since its proponents can be found at universities everywhere, this would be a misnomer.

Let us simply call it, then, "the new Jewish scholarship." It forms the latest chapter in the modern writing of Jewish history, which began with the *Wissenschaft des Judentums* or "science of Judaism" movement in early 19th-century Germany. Starting with Zechariah Frankel (1801–75), a historian of rabbinics, an uninterrupted chain of teacher-student relationships leads to an academic like Boyarin by way of such eminent scholars as Heinrich Graetz (1817–91), David Heinrich Mueller (1846–1912), Jacob Nahum Epstein (1878–1952), and Saul Lieberman (1898–1983), who was Boyarin's mentor in Talmud at the Seminary. And yet the new scholarship constitutes a radical break with the *Wissenschaft* tradition. Although men like Frankel, Graetz, Mueller, and Epstein had good reason to feel that those trained by them were following in their footsteps, it is safe to say Lieberman, as Boyarin himself acknowledges, would have been appalled by the latter's views.

Of course, "paradigm shifts," to use the now-fashionable term for a major change of focus in an intellectual discipline, have occurred before in Jewish historiography. Perhaps the most conspicuous took place in association with Zionism, under whose impact leading twentieth-century historians, many connected with the Hebrew University in Jerusalem, reinterpreted a wide variety of religious and cultural phenomena from the Jewish past, casting them as forms of incipient nationalism: proto-Zionist strivings in times when the circumstances were not ripe for their mature expression. Diaspora existence, generally evaluated positively by the earlier *Wissenschaft*, was seen by the Jerusalem school as a long struggle against exilic conditions that alienated Jews from their outer surroundings and inner potential.

But even as the adherents of the Jerusalem school were rewriting Jewish history, they went on sharing basic premises with their predecessors. Like them, they believed historical truth to be objective and empirically verifiable. Like them, too, they portrayed the Jewish people as an organic unity in time and space, the evolving bearer of a core identity that remained unchanged in essence despite the historical and geographical guises worn and shed by it. Although the goal to which Jewish history was seen as moving was now different—the reconstitution of a scattered people in its land rather than the original *Wissenschaft*'s notion of an ever more refined ethical monotheism spread by Israel among the nations—the Jerusalem school, too, viewed Jewish history teleologically. And, like the scholars who came before it, it emphasized Jewish uniqueness, dwelling more on the differences than on the similarities between Jews and their host nations. It was such analogies that caused Gershom Scholem, the great scholar of Kabbalah, to remark of himself and his Hebrew University colleagues, "We came to rebel and ended up by continuing."

All of these commonalities are rejected by the new Jewish scholars. In good postmodernist fashion, objective historical truth is, for them, an epistemological illusion, the past being an inevitable "reinvention" of the present by self-interested and conceptually predisposed observers. Instead of unity, they discern in it discontinuity and conflict, leading them to dismiss as an artificial construct any idea of a single "essentialist" Jewish people or religion. Ruling out the search for direction in Jewish history, they view such old-fashioned "narratives" as disguised exercises of power, attempts by dominant groups of Jews throughout the ages to assert "hegemony" over other Jews. And while not denying that Jews have been different from others, the new scholars are more interested in their resemblance to such groups as oppressed and colonized peoples, women, and homosexuals.

The preoccupation with gender has become in many ways the new scholars' major one. Just as feminism and issues of sexual identity have roiled the American campus as a whole (not to mention the consciousness of the American Jewish community), so they have riveted the attention of Jewish studies. Among the books, dealing largely or wholly with questions of Judaism and gender, and mobilizing dozens of academic authors, that have appeared recently are Regina M. Schwartz's *The Curse of Cain: The Violent Legacy of Monotheism*; Laura Levitt's *Jews and Feminism: The Ambivalent Search For Home*; Daniel Boyarin's *Unheroic Conduct: The Rise of Heterosexuality and the Invention of the Jewish Man*; and the anthologies *Feminist Perspectives on Jewish Studies, Judaism Since Gender,* and *Jews and Other Differences: The New Jewish Cultural Studies.*

Although what unites these books is far greater than what divides them, they are not cut from a single cloth. Boyarin's, the best and most radical, is closely argued; Schwartz's, the worst and most widely reviewed, is anything but. And while the essays in *Feminist Perspectives* are largely moderate in tone, those in *Judaism Since Gender* tend to the sharply polemical and those in *Jews and Other Differences* to the contemporaneously offbeat and exotic. Still, despite the new scholarship's repudiation of grand historical "narratives," all of these books subscribe to a shared outlook. A synopsis of it might go as follows.

From its beginnings, Israelite religion was both a liberating and a repressive force, offering an emancipating vision of human brother- and sisterhood based on the ethical paternity of a universal God while also invoking this God's masculine aggressiveness, sexual puritanism, and religious zealotry in order to underwrite the values of a warlike and intolerant culture. Nor was this culture hostile only toward its neighbors. Its own women and sexual deviants, too, were, like the conquered Canaanites, treated as "Others"—dehumanized and phobicized objects on which a male patriarchy, whose myths and values are recorded in the Bible, projected its unconscious fears, anger, and guilt.

Subsequently, this account continues, when biblical culture was superseded by rabbinic Judaism, the Jewish world again mixed progressive with reactionary features. Jews were now a colonized people themselves, and in many areas, including those of human sexuality and the treatment of women, rabbinic legislation was relatively liberal; yet both it and its attitudes remained male-supremacist. Men alone made the law, studied it, applied it, and participated in the rituals prescribed by it, which continued to be understood as the will of a masculinely-imaged God. Women remained the excluded Other, their existence conveyed to posterity almost entirely through the mediation of male writers.

And in modern times as well, our synopsis concludes, though sexual equality has been inscribed on the banner of more than one movement for change in Jewish life, women's exclusion has remained a fact. The best example is the state of Israel. Despite claims of egalitarianism, Zionist settlement in Palestine was sexist from the start, relegating women to the same second-class status they had left behind in the Diaspora. Moreover, not only has the Jewish state continue the "marginalization" of women, it has regressed to the exclusionary nationalism of the Bible, turning the Palestinians into the new Canaanites and atavistically reviving the male-dominated warrior society of ancient Israel.

Finally, there is an epilogue. The notion of an impartial or objective study of the past having been "deconstructed" as a myth, the new Jewish scholar knows that he or she must work from a position of commitment. If historians of previous ages have ignored the silenced voices of the Other, thereby "privileging" the masculinist, misogynist, and homophobic forces of the male world to which they belonged, the new scholar must seek out these voices and be their tongue, not only to do justice to the disempowered dead but to defend the disempowered living.

It is not difficult to detect in all this the influence, prominent in all postmodernist thought, of both Freud and Marx. To psychoanalysis the new Jewish scholarship owes the perception that groups of people, like individuals, may react to one another out of unconscious considerations linked more to what others symbolize than to who they are. From Marxism it derives the belief that intellectual and religious superstructures are tools of domination, scripts for organizing society in ways that further class and sectarian interests. For the new scholars, Jewish history is a text to be read between the lines. Nothing in it is what it seems; everything must be "demystified"; everything conceals a hidden agenda for the exercise of power and control.

To which—at least in one case—must be added a third influence: the liberal wing of the American Jewish Sunday school. Of it, Regina Schwartz writes in *The Curse of Cain*:

> What Reform Judaism gave me in my childhood was less the understanding of Judaism as a separated identity than its strong stress on ethics; shedding traditional rituals and the trappings of group identity was accompanied

by a renewed emphasis on being "a good person." While I know that distinction will not hold under close examination, it is this anti-ritualistic strain of Judaism that I inherited, a latter-day version of Jeremiah inveighing against the hypocrisy of worshipers at the temple who were guilty of social abuses.

Jeremiah's, however, was a voice of moderation compared with Schwartz's; for whereas the prophet of Anatot merely blamed ancient Israel for bringing disaster on itself, Schwartz thinks it has brought disaster on the world. For this she holds responsible the Bible—or rather, *a* Bible, since she believes there are two of them. The first is a Bible of "scarcity," which portrays the world as a cruel place of rigid national, personal, and sexual identities. In this world there is not enough to go around. Life is a zero-sum game with right sides and wrong sides, in-groups and out-groups, elect and rejected; the rules have been dictated by an authoritarian God who assures His followers that, as members of the winning team, they have the right and even the obligation to dispossess the losers. And inherited from this Bible is "the monotheistic commitment to nationalism," which "reduces all other gods to idols and all other worshipers to abominations." It is this commitment that explains today "such seeming conundrums as the violence stemming from Islamic fundamentalism, the wars in South [sic] Africa and in Bosnia, and the proliferation of other violent clashes over identity commitments throughout the globe"—including, needless to say, Israeli oppression of the Palestinians.

But opposed to this, Schwartz also believes, there is a second Bible, by whose light we must learn to walk. This is a femininely loving book of fluid boundaries in which there is sufficient bounty for all and Isaiah's lion can lie down with the lamb: "an alternative Bible that subverts the dominant vision of violence and scarcity with an ideal of plenitude and its corollary ethical imperative of generosity... a Bible embracing multiplicity instead of monotheism." True, such a Bible exists more as possibility than as a text, since apart from a few verses or chapters in the Pentateuch and the Prophets (which do not exactly forsake monotheism for "multi-plicity," either), there is not much to base it on. But never mind. Let the new scholar write a new Bible—by which, Schwartz explains,

> I do not mean some partial commentary of sanctified unalterable authoritative texts, but a genuine rewriting of traditions: new creation stories, new exoduses, new losses, and new recoveries of what is lost.... The old "monotheistic" Bible must be closed so that the new books may be fruitful and multiply. After all, that was the first commandment.

From whom have we heard all this before? Well, from early Christianity, for one. It did exactly what Schwartz calls for—replacing, as Paul puts it in his Epistle to the Romans, the "law of sin and death" of the Hebrew Bible with the "spirit of life" of the New Testament. And, of course, from Christian writers down through the centuries. And from anti-Christian Enlightenment writers like Gibbon and Voltaire, who accused the Jews of introducing group hatred and bigotry into a tolerant pagan world. For a new Jewish scholar, Schwartz is in some very old company.

One would like to think that, at this late date, there is little need to comment on the absurdity of her charge that mankind's long chronicle of bloody warfare, ethnic and racial prejudice, and religious and ideological intolerance results from attitudes acquired from the Bible. It is as if she had never heard of the sack of Troy, the Indian caste system, the persecution of Buddhism under the Tang dynasty, the mass human sacrifices of their enemies practiced by the Aztecs, the savagery of Genghis Khan, Japanese barbarism in World War II, the horrors of the Pol Pot regime, or innumerable other cases of wholesale violence and exclusion practiced in the name of the "identity commitments" of pre- or non-monotheistic peoples.

And perhaps she has not, for, a professor of English at Northwestern University, she does not appear to have read much history—which could also have told her that, far from a biblical invention, "scarcity" has been the perennial fate of most of mankind. Faced with a rocky soil, undependable rainfall, inadequate water for irrigation, warlike neighbors, high royal taxes, and frequent raids by nomadic plunderers, the peasants and herders who were the ancient Israelites did not merely imagine that they lacked the conditions of plenitude.

Schwartz's is, admittedly, an extreme case. Most of the new Jewish scholars are less cavalier about flying in the face of reality. Yet the historical and sociological evidence is not generally approached by them (as it would be by a traditional scholar) as material to be investigated in depth, augmented by further research, and rigorously weighed before appropriate conclusions are drawn from it. With exceptions—such as David Biale's *Eros and the Jews*, a book that applies postmodernist insights in a serious, open-minded manner—the conclusions of the new Jewish scholars all too often come first, with the data trailing selectively behind.

A typical example is Laura Levitt, assistant professor of religion at Temple University, who proposes in *Jews and Feminism* to carry out a "close rhetorical" reading of the *ketubah*, the traditional Jewish marriage contract. Although the wording of this document would impress any casual reader with the considerable obligations it imposes on the husband, who alone of the newlywed couple is made responsible for his partner's financial, emotional, and "conjugal" (i.e., sexual) needs, Levitt feels deep "disappointment" both with the *ketubah*'s "ideological agenda" and with the "legacy…of being a Jewish woman." As an example of the *ketubah*'s sexism, she notes its stipulation of the bride's virginity as one of its contractual demands. By giving the husband "sole access to his wife's body," Levitt writes, the *ketubah* "presents an asymmetrical heterosexual relationship as the one and only sanctioned version of marriage. There are clearly two unequal parties involved, a man and his wife."

The trouble with Levitt's "close rhetorical" reading is not only that it is totally ahistorical, treating the *ketubah* as a display of twentieth-century *machismo* instead of the remarkably advanced legislation that it was for its time. It is also that, on the subject of the bride's virginity, Levitt, while seeking to buttress her case with passages from the ancient rabbis, simply ignores the most clearly relevant one. This is in the Mishnaic tractate of Ketubot, which dates roughly to the third century C.E. In it we read:

> If a man takes a wife and finds [after the wedding] that she is not a virgin, and she says to him, "I was raped after I was betrothed to you," and he says, "No, it happened before I betrothed you and I was deceived"—Rabbi Gamliel and Rabbi Eliezer say: she is to be believed. Rabbi Yehoshua says: we cannot go by what she says until she brings proof.

The key to this scenario is that the rabbis deliberately phrased it to make the bride appear to be lying—for what, really, are the chances of her having been raped, unbeknownst to anyone, in the period between her betrothal and her wedding? In this light, Gamliel and Eliezer's ruling—which, the Talmud makes clear, is the legally binding one, Rabbi Yehoshua's being rejected—is astounding. Even if, they assert, the woman has engaged in premarital sex of her own free will, her marital rights are to be defended by taking her word over her husband's. Exactly who, one must ask oneself, is the less equal party here?

This does not mean that rabbinic Judaism is sexually egalitarian, or that it is necessarily carping to observe that the *ketubah* does not formally require virginity of the male partner (though, being unverifiable, male virginity is not a useful legal concept). The point is, rather, that once objective evidentiary truth is discarded as a theoretical possibility, let alone as a practical goal, historical writing slides easily into agitprop.

So widespread is this tendency among the new Jewish scholars, and so little troubled do most of them seem by it, that it is exceptional to come across Judith Hauptman, a professor of Talmud at the Jewish Theological Seminary, pleading with her colleagues in *Feminist Perspectives on Jewish Studies*, "Rather than evaluate individual rabbinic texts by contemporary feminist standards, it is essential that each rabbinic work…be considered on its own terms and evaluated from the perspective of what its framers set out to accomplish in their own day." Far more prevalent than this voice in the wilderness is that of the historian Beth Wenger, who writes in *Judaism Since Gender*: "If feminist theory has taught us anything, it is that the political dimensions of scholarship are inextricably intertwined with the production of knowledge."

Not that Wenger and others needed feminist theory to teach them this; dialectical materialism could have done it just as well. Indeed, if one substitutes "women" for "workers" and "patriarchy" for "ruling class," it is hard to see in what major respects the new feminism and the old Marxism differ. Both allegedly speak for an oppressed underclass that has been a historical constant; both attribute all the world's injustices to this oppression, whether because war, racism, violence, and exploitation are unavoidable accompaniments of the concentration of wealth or because they are always associated with male dominance; both strive for the abolition of these ills through a revolution that will do away with all human inequality, replacing the old values of harsh competitiveness and possessiveness with new ones of gentle sharing and compassion.

One wonders, then, whether the appearance and spread of feminist theory at a time of Marxism's political decline and passing is not a form of intellectual reincarnation. And one wonders, too, what sort of favor feminist theory is ultimately doing women by upholding a belief in, as the Yale historian Paula Hyman approvingly puts it in *Feminist Perspectives on Jewish Studies*, "the universal subordination of women in recorded history." After all, if women have always, everywhere and without exception, been downtrodden by men, it would seem a matter of simple inductive reasoning to conclude, as some men indeed do, that it is the female's nature to be trodden on and the male's to do the treading.

It is precisely here that feminist theory, which insists on the culturally-conditioned "constructedness" of all human identities, finds itself in serious trouble; for if sexual identity too is freely "constructed" independently of biological constraints, how are we to explain the odd fact that nearly all known cultures just happen to have constructed it inimically (as feminists would have it) to women? And the new Jewish scholarship only underlines this question still further when it rejects "apologetic" Jewish claims (made by *Wissenschaft* scholars, among others) that the historical position of Jewish women was often markedly better than that of non-Jewish ones.

That gender roles often *do* seem to have been construed differently by Jews is widely accepted. Especially in times and places where rabbinic authority was strong, Jewish ideals of masculinity, at least as transmitted to us by written sources, appear to have departed significantly from Gentile ones, placing a high value on traits like studiousness, forbearance, and reactive patterns of passive endurance, and a low or negative one on physical prowess and courage, self-assertiveness, and sexual libido. Similarly, Jewish ideals of womanhood also diverged from Gentile norms, valorizing worldly practicality and economic initiative more than sexual attractiveness, feminine charm, docility, or a trusting reliance on men.

One could imagine these differences being celebrated by the new Jewish scholarship: here at last, it would seem, is historical proof both of the mutability of sexual roles and of their positive transformation in a feminist direction. And yet, as with Laura Levitt's reading of the *ketubah*, this is not the light in which they have generally been regarded. The dominant judgment is expressed by Naomi Seidman—who, in discussing the "feminization of Jewish men" in 19th-century Eastern Europe, writes in *Judaism Since Gender* that this phenomenon was nevertheless "thoroughly dependent on a patriarchal system whose hierarchies and misogyny it encode[d] and even enforce[d]."

One can see Seidman's logic: since the male world of study and ritual was held, even by women, in higher esteem than female pursuits, and was more generative of social power, female exclusion from it could be considered "misogynist." Moreover, the "economic woman" of the *shtetl* rarely engaged in much more than shopkeeping or the home production of simple goods. Though less arduous, her life was hardly more independent than that of a Russian peasant woman who might also be expected to do "men's work" in the fields.

But was her husband better off? As is the case with many feminists, who, overlooking the power often wielded by women in the home, refuse to grant the slightest dignity or satisfaction to traditional female lives while wildly glamorizing the lives of working men, the new Jewish scholars tend to ignore what life was like even for those males who successfully made it into the rabbinical world of study and authority. Their deprivation began when they were boys, robbed of their childhood by having to spend long daylight hours in a dreary *heder*, absorbing rote knowledge from an often frustrated and irascible teacher. It continued when they were adolescents, sent far from home to study in distant yeshivas, frequently penniless and compelled to cadge meals from reluctant hosts while closeted day in and day out with the same endless volumes of the Talmud. And it did not necessarily end in adulthood, when most worked as small-town rabbis who earned a living by inspecting the innards of chickens and giving lessons to the children of the rich on whom their meager salaries depended. Lucky was the girl, one might say, who was spared all this.

Few Jewish men in the *shtetl*, moreover, became rabbis or religious functionaries. Most worked as tailors, shoemakers, petty artisans, petty tradesmen, wagon drivers, peddlers, tavern keepers, porters, small entrepreneurs. They labored hard, long, and more often than not in poverty, and if they had the comforts of public rituals that were often off-limits to women, these included such misogynist pleasures as rising in the middle of the night for penitential prayers during the month of Elul or giving up the only morning of the week on which they could rest their tired bodies in order to trudge to synagogue on icy winter Sabbaths.

The paradoxical thing about the new Jewish scholars is that, although they presume to speak for the disempowered, their writing of history is elitist to the core. From their theorizing heights, they look down on the past through a thick fog of abstraction that hides the common Jew. They honestly seem to have no idea of what it is like to rise in a freezing house, to put food on the table for hungry children when there is not enough of it, to work all day with a needle or an awl, to struggle, suffer, fall ill, die, see others die—and to do all this in the company of a wife or a husband with whom, even if there was no love felt (though often, literary sources tell us, there was), one had to pull together in order to survive. Under a mantle of sympathy for the everyday experience that "conventional" history ignores, the new scholars exhibit no little contempt for it.

This elitism has another consequence. When speaking of their own society, Jews in Eastern Europe used to divide it into a majority of *proste yidn* or "plain Jews" and a minority of *sheyne yidn* or "fine Jews"—that is, into the ordinary people and the better educated and more refined. Although most of the new scholars have little feel for, or empathy with, the actual texture of the lives of either group, they are in the position of siding theoretically with the "plain Jews" while actually and almost instinctively identifying with the "fine." This is why someone like Daniel Boyarin can, in his *Unheroic Conduct*, treat the figure of the "feminized Jewish man," sociologically far more *sheyn* than *prost*, and by no means the representative East European Jewish male, as a universal type, and then proceed to offer him up as a role model.

And yet Boyarin is the most interesting of the new scholars. In his thinking, he executes the intellectual equivalent of a balletic split, which ends with one leg pointing toward religious Orthodoxy (of which he is an avowed practitioner) and the other toward a militant identification with radical feminism and "gay, lesbian, and bisexual Jews (and the Queer Nation as a whole)." Outflanking the majority of his colleagues in both directions, he is both allied with them and one of a kind.

His project in *Unheroic Conduct* is fourfold. In the first place, it is to establish, through a close reading of rabbinic texts, that the "feminized Jewish male" (and to a lesser extent, the "masculinized Jewish woman") has been not just a late East European development but a normative model for Jewish men throughout the entire post-biblical period. Secondly, Boyarin argues that, although this product of a culture "within which 'real men' were sissies" marked a great step forward in male sexual attitudes, it did not go far enough. Since it stopped short of actually admitting women into the male "locker room" of the synagogue and the study house, it remained, just as scholars like Naomi Seidman charge, male chauvinist.

Thirdly, according to Boyarin, much of nineteenth- and twentieth-century Jewish social history can be understood as a reaction to these anomalous Jewish "engenderments." Such disparate phenomena as the rise of the bourgeois Jewish family in Central and Western Europe and the spread of Zionism were attempts at cultural assimilation, whose central thrust was to remasculinize the "Jewish male femme" by recreating him in the image of European manhood. Here Boyarin particularly singles out Zionism for disapprobation; through its idealization of the "muscle Jew," it represented a flight from the effeminate stereotype that a "homophobic" European culture had affixed on Jewish men emerging from the ghetto.

Lastly, while conceding that Orthodox Judaism has itself remained homophobic and misogynist—like most feminists, he thinks these two attitudes go together of necessity—Boyarin still believes that, thanks to its long history of unconventional thinking about gender, Orthodoxy offers promising ground for revolutionary feminist reform. He sums up, "Two forms of critical work need to be engaged at the same time. One is directed at a critique of traditional Jewish culture and gender practice.... the other argues that traditional [Jewish] culture has something to offer in the effort to produce radical change within the culture of the West."

Besides being well-read and intellectually agile, Boyarin can be an amusing *provocateur*. Since he is so much cleverer than the other new Jewish scholars, it is almost possible, despite the kinkiness of his views and his extreme hostility toward Israel, to read him with something approaching pleasure. More often, though, one reads him with something like dread.

The danger is not that such views will conquer Orthodoxy, which is the last bastion that will fall to them. It is rather that, much as one might like to regard the new scholarship as a passing phase in Jewish intellectual life, its proponents are already too strongly entrenched in the academy for this. Given that most of them are young, with long careers still ahead of them in which they will produce many students as their heirs, American Jews will be living with their thinking for decades to come.

For a non-Orthodox American Jewish community that even now is suffering from a loss of boundaries and a deep confusion about its identity, a decline of the family as its core unit, a low birth rate and a high rate of exogamous marriage, falling participation of men as compared with women, a growing distancing from Israel and Jews in other countries and a consequently weakened sense of ethnic solidarity and Jewish peoplehood, and a general uncertainty as to how Jews differ from non-Jews or should want to, this is not good news. Rather than providing such a community with the intellectual leadership it needs, the new scholars will only increase its anomie.

No one can predict the outcome of the sexual revolution that America is now in the throes of, and that dwarfs any of its predecessors in its concentrated assault on fundamentals of male and female behavior that have been taken for granted by nearly all human beings until now. No one can say whether men or women are built to withstand this assault, or what the results may be if they are not. And no one knows what a world lacking firm notions of masculinity and femininity, or of the distinctions between them, would be like. But it is chilling for custodians of the history of a people who taught mankind that it was created, male and female, in God's image to join the serpent of delusory omnipotence in whispering in our ear that we can become like gods, and that we can with impunity remake our pasts and ourselves, sexually and in every other way, as we please.

1998

How Not to Repair the World

A s anyone following the campaign rhetoric of Barack Obama and his supporters will have noticed, this has been a season for "repairing the world." It is also a time, then, for reflecting on the course taken by this ancient Hebrew expression that is uttered three times a day in their prayers by religiously observant Jews; that plays a minor but interesting role in talmudic discourse; that was transformed into an important concept of Jewish mysticism in the late Middle Ages; that has become a buzz phrase of American Jewish liberalism; and that occurs in close to a quarter of the forty short essays by a group of American Jewish intellectuals and social activists, all on the Left, appearing in a new book called *Righteous Indignation*. Among the topics dealt with by these essays are: "Can Social Justice Save The American Jewish Soul?"; "Rereading Genesis: Human Stewardship of the Earth"; "Toxic Waste and the Talmud"; "Judaism, Oil, and Renewable Energy"; "A Jewish Vision for Economic Justice"; "Beyond Same-Sex Marriage: Social Justice and Sexual Values in Judaism"; "Multiracial Jewish Families: A Personal and Political Approach to Justice Politics"; "*Imitatio Dei* and Shared Space: A Jewish Theological Argument for Sharing the Holy Land"; "Once Again: Genocide In Darfur"; and "'Silence is Akin to Assent': Judaism and the War in Iraq."

The Hebrew expression in question—who does not know it by now?—is *tikkun olam*. Traditionally, these were words familiar to the most ordinary Jew, since they occur in a slightly altered form in the *Aleynu* prayer recited at the end of the daily morning, afternoon, and evening services. As translated in the prayer book of the United Synagogue of America, which prefers "perfecting" to "repairing," the second half of the *Aleynu* goes:

> We therefore hope in Thee, O Lord our God, that we may soon behold the glory of Thy might, when Thou wilt remove the abominations from the earth and when all idolatry will be abolished. We hope for the day when the world will be perfected under the Kingdom of the Almighty *[al-ken nekaveh lekha...le-taken olam b'malkhut shaddai]* and all mankind will call upon Thy name.... May all the inhabitants of the world perceive and know that unto Thee every knee must bend, every tongue vow loyalty.... May they all accept the yoke of Thy kingdom and do Thou rule over them speedily and forevermore. For the Kingdom is Thine and to all eternity Thou wilt reign in glory, as it is written in Thy Torah.... The Lord shall be King over all the earth; and on that day the Lord shall be One and His name One.

Its final line taken from the prophet Zechariah, this is a grand prayer, a majestic call for messianic redemption and for humanity's acceptance of the sovereignty of God. It is odd, therefore, that in an essay in *Righteous Indignation* on "What Does *Tikkun Olam* Actually Mean?" by Jane Kanarek, assistant professor of rabbinics at Hebrew College in Boston, the *Aleynu* goes unmentioned. Perhaps this is because discussing it would have obliged Kanarek to reveal that *tikkun olam* means two quite different things in the Hebrew of antiquity, and that the conflation of them is part of contemporary Jewish liberalism's distortion of Jewish tradition.

As Kanarek points out, the concept of *tikkun olam* is invoked, in a variety of situations, "a total of fifteen times" in the Mishnah, the code of rabbinic law that, together with the commentary on it known as the

Gemara, makes up the Talmud. The text in which the phrase occurs most frequently is the tractate of Gittin, which deals with divorce law. From this tractate, Kanarek has chosen two illustrations. The first (in my own rather than in Kanarek's translation) reads:

> If a man sends his wife a writ of divorce and then over-takes the bearer of it, or sends him a messenger, saying, "The writ I sent is canceled," it is canceled. If he himself reaches his wife before the writ's bearer, or sends her a messenger [who arrives first], saying, "The writ I sent you is canceled," then it is also canceled. But if the writ has already been delivered, no cancellation is possible. In former times, the husband could convene a court anywhere to have the cancellation confirmed. But then Rabbi Gamliel the Elder changed this for the sake of *tikkun olam.*

The discussion of this passage in the Gemara makes clear the reason for Rabbi Gamliel's ruling. Once upon a time, if a husband who was separated from his wife and living at a distance from her sent her a writ of divorce and then changed his mind and sent a second, faster messenger to abort the first's mission, the writ was invalidated. If, however, the second messenger failed to overtake the first in time and the writ was delivered to the woman, the divorce took effect—unless, that is, the husband had already convened a rabbinical court to declare it null and void. And yet if he had done so, the danger existed that the woman, unaware of the court's action, might mistakenly believe herself divorced and remarry another man with whom she would live in sinful bigamy and have illegitimate children. To prevent this from happening, Rabbi Gamliel amended the law, "for the sake of *tikkun olam,*" to require the husband to convene the court in the wife's place of residence, thus ensuring that she would know of its decision.

Not all of the cases of *tikkun olam* in Gittin have to do with divorce. Kanarek's second illustration is this:

For the sake of *tikkun olam*, hostages must not be ransomed for more than their normal price. Nor, for the sake of *tikkun olam*, must hostages be helped to escape.

In this case the principle is that, if a Jew is being held for ransom by highwaymen, pirates, or kidnappers, his family, friends, or community must not pay an exorbitantly high sum to free him even if they can afford it. This is because, while there is no basis in Mosaic law for prohibiting such an action, its effect would be to jack up the price of releasing future hostages and encourage attempts to seize more of them. Similarly, even if it is possible to arrange for a Jewish hostage's escape, it is forbidden to do so, because the conditions under which other hostages are held will then be made harsher to prevent more escapes.

Kanarek comments on this as follows:

> In the world of the Talmud, we cannot totally prevent the taking of captives. However, that reality does not imply powerlessness. Rather, existent law must be recalibrated to aim at the formation of a better world.…..
> The Mishnah and Talmud help us ask the big structural questions, forcing us to focus on underlying causes of suffering and to address them—and they also remind us that the goal of *tikkun olam* is not necessarily the world's perfection. As *Pirkei Avot* [*The Ethics of the Fathers*] tells us, "It is not upon you to finish the task, nor are you free to desist from it."….*Tikkun olam* means Jewish social justice. It means having a large vision of the world as it ought to be, and working through and with the Jewish tradition to achieve that vision.

The Talmud's approach to the ransoming of hostages is indeed "structural." But Kanarek glosses rather blithely over the question of suffering. True, reduce the profitability of kidnapping and fewer people will be kidnapped in the long run. In the short run, however, *tikkun olam* calls for an *increase* in suffering, since it condemns Jewish hostages to continued imprisonment and enjoins their families and friends, who could free them, to exercise an excruciating self-restraint in the public interest. Indeed, "in the public interest," rather than for "the sake of repairing the world," might be a better translation of the Mishnaic term.

It is odd, too, that in a book devoted entirely to Judaism's bearing on contemporary social and political issues, Kanarek's contribution totally ignores the truly impressive relevance of this passage. Hostage-taking, after all, is not some quaint ancient custom that has passed from the world. For the past two years, an Israeli soldier has been held captive by Hamas in Gaza, and two more (if still alive) are being held by Hizballah in Lebanon. All this time, Israel's government and public have agonizingly debated the price to be paid for their release—a price that has climbed steeply over the years with previous cases of this sort and that now stands at an exchange rate of hundreds of Palestinian terrorists for every captive Israeli.

It would thus seem that Israel, in its understandable anxiety to redeem its citizens and relieve the distress of their families, has been unmindful of the sort of *tikkun olam* spoken of by the Mishnah. One would think, at the very least, that Kanarek would have remarked on this and on how a more frugal policy of paying for the freedom of Israelis with convicted Palestinians, many of whom have returned to terrorism after their release, would be in line with the Mishnah's recommendation.

And yet she is silent. Thus, she is also forced to be silent about the contradiction between the prophetic *tikkun olam* of the *Aleynu* and the Mishnaic *tikkun olam* of the rabbis, which embody opposite conceptions of change. One—whose goal *is* the world's perfection—is sweepingly utopian and looks forward to a radical transformation in the religious behavior and social relationships of all mankind. The other is cautiously pragmatic and concerned with the management of Jewish reality. (That *tikkun olam* in the Mishnah involves Jewish reality alone is obvious, since even when universal principles are involved, the rabbis' ability to enforce them did not extend beyond Jews.) The first *tikkun olam* is based on the anticipation of a new spiritual consciousness, the second, on the permanence of human nature as we know it.

It can be argued, of course, that the greater and the lesser *tikkun olam*, as they might be called, are complementary, one expansively setting out the final goal and the other tracing a laborious path to it; the first proclaiming the round sum to be striven for and the second counting out the small change by which this sum might be reached in a pilot project involving a single people. But such harmonization is facile, since *tikkun olam* as the perfecting of the world and *tikkun olam* as the public interest of the Jewish people are not always mutually consistent.

To return to the case of hostages, the public interest, as conceived of by the Mishnah, is necessarily imperfect. It involves the difficult task of balancing one set of justified demands against another, the welfare of the community against the happiness or grief of individuals, and it mandates private grief where the public interest requires it. So it is with most laws. They help some by hurting others. It is only in utopia that no one gets hurt at all.

There is a third traditional conception of *tikkun olam*. This comes from the sixteenth-century school of Jewish mysticism known as Lurianic Kabbalah, with its great cosmic drama of a world that is quite literally broken and in need of repair from its inception. At the very moment of creation, according to Lurianic tradition, a universe designed to be perfect fractured like a faulty pot, and the divine light it was designed to contain leaked out, as it were, into the blackness of chaos. From this darkness, it is the mission of every Jew to retrieve the multitude of fallen sparks that must be restored to their source for all to be made whole again. In its fashion, the Lurianic *tikkun* combines aspects of the visionary *tikkun* of the prayer book and the pragmatic *tikkun* of the Mishnah. While it calls for mending the entire cosmos, it holds that this must be done incrementally through the efforts of every Jew. These efforts, in Lurianic Kabbalah, are strictly spiritual, involving prayer, religious ritual, and meditation.

It was not, however, the spiritual aspect of the Lurianic *tikkun olam* but the potential for reinterpreting it politically that appealed to the imagination of Michael Lerner, an ex-student radical of the 1960s who in 1986 founded a magazine called *Tikkun*. Under Lerner's editorship, *Tikkun* embraced social activism and "progressive" politics, frequently sided against Israel in its conflict with the Palestinians, and was largely responsible for transplanting the expression *tikkun olam* from the esoteric soil of Jewish scholarship and liturgy to the wider field of American Jewish discourse, from which it has propagated itself in the vocabulary of liberal politics. "Repairing the world" is now as much of a Jewish contribution to the American language as are chutzpah, schmooze, and schmaltz.

And as repairmen—so the forty essays in *Righteous Indignation* make clear—Jews have their work cut out for them. There appears to be nothing wrong with this world that Judaism does not command us to fix, and nothing needing fixing about which it does not have something to say.

The environment? "The classical Jewish source on conservation," we are told by Shana Starobin, a student in environmental management and public policy at Duke University,

> is the passage in Deuteronomy that introduces the commandment *ba'al tashkhit* [sic! it is *bal tashḥit*] (literally, "do not destroy"), forbidding needless waste and destruction: "When in your war against a city, you have to besiege it a long time in order to capture it, you must not destroy its trees, wielding the ax against them. You may eat of them, but you must not cut them down." …The principle of ba'al tashkhit affirms that our consciousness must be directed toward resources great and small, that the earth and its gifts are not ours to destroy.

Toxic waste? The laws of the Talmud, we learn from Jeremy Benstein, associate director of the Heschel Center for Environmental Learning and Leadership,

> regulate not only injury or harm inflicted by a person or their livestock on another person or their property, but also misuse of the environment as a cause of damages to others. If I dig or uncover a pit in the public domain, I am liable for damages that may ensue. Similarly, if I place a jug or barrel (or thorns or broken glass) in a

communal place and someone is injured…. It is not a far cry from the menace of air pollution and the leaky toxic dumps of our day.

The global AIDS crisis? "The medieval Jewish philosopher Maimonides," say Jacob Feinspan and Julia Greenberg of the American Jewish World Service, "wrote that not only are we permitted to break other commandments to save a life, but that if we fail to act, then we ourselves have transgressed. It is an unsettling fact that there are three times as many HIV-positive people in the world as there are Jews. By raising up their collective voices to say 'Let our people live,' the HIV-positive community is leading a new Exodus."

Transgenderism and sex change? Elliot Rose Kukla, a formerly female Reform rabbi, informs us that the Talmud has a gender category called the *tumtum* (in reality, the Talmud's term for someone born with undeveloped or undifferentiated sexual organs) that provides a "spiritual home" to anyone like himself who "can't or won't conform" to "modern binary gender" classifications. The *tumtum*, Kukla writes, is "a spiritual resource of our tradition."

And so it goes. Health care, labor unions, public school education, feminism, abortion rights, gay marriage, globalization, U.S. foreign policy, Darfur: on everything Judaism has a position—and, wondrously, this position just happens to coincide with that of the American liberal Left.

If it is easy to caricature most of the essays in *Righteous Indignation*, this is because so many of them caricature themselves. They represent the ultimate in the approach, so common in non-Orthodox Jewish circles in the United States today, that treats Jewish tradition not as a body of teachings to be learned from but as one needing to be taught what it is about by those who know better than it does what it *should* be about. Judaism has value to such Jews to the extent that it is useful, and it is useful to the extent that it can be made to conform to whatever beliefs and opinions they would have even if Judaism had never existed.

This is not to say that Jewish tradition has no position on any of the issues discussed in *Righteous Indignation*. The most cogent and dispassionate contribution to the book, "A Jewish View of Embryonic Stem Cell Research" by Elliot Dorff, professor of philosophy at the American Jewish University in Los Angeles, argues persuasively for the halakhic permissibility of such research under certain conditions. Dorff specifies what these conditions are and leaves the reader feeling that tradition has served him as a mentor rather than as a surrogate mother who can be hired to bear any child one wishes. To the extent, moreover, that Dorff's argument is open to qualification or rebuttal on the basis of traditional sources themselves, any such debate would serve further to illuminate the issues and classical Judaism's approach to them.

Jeremy Benstein has a point, too. There is a real parallel between talmudic laws of liability and those brought to bear against latter-day polluters, and a more closely argued essay than Benstein's could have taught us more about this matter. About other matters, however, it would be stretching things to say that there is a definable Jewish point of view. There is nothing amounting to a coherent approach in Judaism toward protecting or not protecting the natural environment, and Shana Starobin's ecological exegesis is downright dishonest, since her citation from Deuteronomy deliberately leaves out the verse, "But the trees which you know are not trees for food, you shall destroy and cut them down; and you shall make bulwarks [with them] against the city that makes war with you until it is subdued." Indeed, if one were to construct an environmental policy on the slender base of Deuteronomy, it would have to be that the Bible sanctions the destruction for utilitarian ends like making siege fortifications of whatever in nature is not, like fruit trees, of direct benefit to mankind.

In still other cases, Jewish tradition is unequivocally opposed to the values that the essayists in *Righteous Indignation* put into its mouth. However many may be the arguments for feminism, the authority of Judaism, which has insisted throughout its history on male dominance and a strict separation of functions between the sexes, is not one of them; just as homosexuality, let alone same-sex marriage, is by any traditional Jewish standard one of the "abominations" that the *Aleynu* prayer would have removed from the earth. "We must be exegetical warriors," writes

Melissa Weintraub, another contributor to *Righteous Indignation*. "We must forcefully weave our values out of the fabric of our living traditions." Forcefully, indeed! To reject a tradition as no longer tenable for one's times can be a form of respect for it. To coerce it into the service of contemporary causes deeply offensive to it is to treat it with contempt.

"It is critical to recognize how central social justice is to Jewish consciousness," writes Sidney Schwarz of the Institute for Jewish Leadership and Values in *Righteous Indignation*'s opening essay. He is, of course, right. In Mosaic law, in biblical prophecy, and in rabbinic jurisprudence alike, the idea that God is well-served by decent and equitable relations among human beings is basic. This is not an invention of American Jewish liberalism, nor of the German Reform and Jewish socialist movements that preceded it and bequeathed to it many of their attitudes.

But there are different conceptions of what social justice is and requires, within Judaism no less than outside of it. In stating that the "prophetic legacy is why the Jewish people were put on this earth . . . to be agents for the repair of the entire world," Schwarz dismisses most of post-biblical Jewish history. For, to a great extent, rabbinic Judaism, though it never openly admitted as much, developed as a means of containing and redirecting the prophetic legacy, whose grand vision of a utopian *tikkun olam* had brought the Jewish people to the verge of ruin.

Rabbinic Judaism emerges into the light of history toward the end of the period of the Second Temple, which was destroyed in the great revolt against Rome of 67–70 C.E. This revolt, and the similarly failed Bar-Kokhba rebellion of 132–135 C.E., were Jewish catastrophes of a magnitude that was not to be repeated until the Holocaust. When they were over, the Jews of Palestine had lost their temple, their last vestiges of independence, hundreds of thousands of lives, and a large number of their homes and villages, and had been banished from Jerusalem, to which they would not return in significant numbers for nearly two millennia.

The root cause of this was precisely the prophetic legacy. It was the apocalyptic messianism of the biblical prophets, particularly the later ones, that encouraged the Jews of Palestine to embark on two courageous but hopeless adventures that challenged the military might of the Roman

Empire. The same Zechariah whose words conclude the *Aleynu*, and who cried out in the name of social justice, "Execute true judgment, show mercy and compassion every man to his brother, oppress not the widow, nor the fatherless, the stranger, nor the poor," envisioned a great military battle in Jerusalem between Jews and Gentiles in which "the Lord will smite all the people who have fought against Jerusalem," after which "it shall come to pass that every one that is left of all the nations which came against Jerusalem shall even go up from year to year to worship the King, the Lord of hosts." The great battle he foresaw indeed took place, but God did not smite the Roman legions.

The rabbis of the period after the destruction of the Temple and the collapse of the Bar-Kokhba rebellion had to rally a beaten and demoralized people. Jewish messianism—the greater *tikkun olam*—had failed on a colossal scale. It was a rabbinic insight to grasp that such a people did not need more and better visions, as Jane Kanarek thinks it does today. It needed laws, organization, authority, routines, a regulating system of halakhah (a literal translation of which might be "a way of doing things") to repair the destruction wrought by the anarchy of dreams. It needed the lesser *tikkun olam*, a conception of the public interest.

And this was necessarily a conception of the *Jewish* public interest. Classical rabbinic thought represents a turning-away not only from utopian thinking about humanity but from the notion that it is the Jews' task to help save humanity—except, that is, insofar as it is their task to build a society that the rest of humanity might someday wish to emulate.

In this, it must be said, the rabbis had key sections of the Bible on their side. When one reads the Five Books of Moses, one is struck by how God changes His mind in them. Up to the time of the Flood, He chooses to work with the entire human race and fails. It is too ambitious a project even for Him. The conclusion He draws is that it is better to start again and to start small, slowly expanding from there on firm foundations: first Noah, then Abraham, then the other Patriarchs, then Jacob's twelve sons, then the twelve tribes of Israel, then the giving to them of a Law at Sinai that they will need to take their time learning to understand and obey.

Meanwhile, the Pentateuch implies, humanity can wait. This is very much the attitude of normative rabbinic Judaism—but not of the prophets, who have no patience with an unredeemed world.

Of course, no period of exilic Jewish history, even the most rabbinically normative, has ever lacked messianic expectancy. Throughout the Exile, rabbinic pragmatism and prophetic utopianism existed side by side in a state of collaborative tension: the one the reality, the other the dream; the first entailing the practical regulation of the innumerable contradictions of daily life, the second representing the faith in a future in which all contradictions would be resolved. This collaboration was only disrupted in times of historical crisis in which, in what is known in Hebrew as *d'hikat ha-ketz*, "the forcing of the end," the "someday" of normative Judaism became the "now" of messianic ferment and the dream rose up to challenge the reality.

This happened when Christianity broke away from Judaism. It happened again in the great messianic eruption of the Lurianically-inspired Sabbatian movement of the mid-seventeenth century—the debacle of which, while leading to the rabbinic repression of messianism in Jewish life, only heightened its unconscious pressures. Ultimately, for many modern Jews, these found their release in the two secular movements of revolutionary socialism and Zionism. The course run by the former in Soviet Russia and elsewhere needs no comment: determined to bring about heaven on earth, it created a hell. Yet its logic was impeccable: men are perfectible; if they refuse to be perfected, that is their own fault; hence, they must be whipped until they stop refusing.

As for Zionism, its fate still hangs in the balance. Early secular Zionism had a strong utopian streak. Many Jews raised in observant homes turned to it after losing their religious faith because it reproduced for them, in secular form, the templates of Jewish thought and feeling that they knew from the prayer book and the synagogue, foremost among them the hope for messianic deliverance. In the land of Israel, they believed, they would construct the perfect society that Jews living under Gentile yoke in the Diaspora could not achieve.

This belief gradually collapsed in secular Israel as the ethos of Zionist pioneering waned and the consumerist values of European and American society took its place. Yet its collapse has been accompanied by a new historical outbreak, in the ranks of the settler movement and its supporters, of the religious messianism of which secular Zionism was a sublimation—an outbreak that, if it is not successfully subdued, could lead to consequences as fateful as did the two uprisings against Rome. Threatened on the secular Left by the cynicism and nihilism that follow the failure of all utopian projects, Israel is today threatened on the religious Right by a belief like Zechariah's that God will come to its rescue no matter how much it disregards the international community or deepens its entanglement with a Palestinian people from whom it needs to extricate itself. Israel's future depends on the same ability to rechannel the greater *tikkun olam* of Redemption into the lesser *tikkun olam* of the Jewish public interest that the rabbis set to work on articulating two thousand years ago.

The Jewish public interest is not a concept that plays a role in any of the forty essays in *Righteous Indignation*. Just as the authors of these essays are indifferent to the state of Israel, apart from chiding it for its various alleged faults of racism, religious intolerance, militarism, and so forth, so they are indifferent to the American Jewish community except insofar as it is prepared to act outside of itself. They want world repair—and they want it now. An end to environmental exploitation! An end to economic injustice! An end to sexual inequality! An end to war! And since the end will not come of itself, Jews must go out into the world and force it.

What is entirely missing from the book and its righteously indignant authors is the slightest sense of the world's complexity or of the fact that repairing almost anything can involve breaking something else. Yes, it is possible to reduce global warming significantly—but only at the cost of also reducing standards of living around the world, including those of the poor. It is possible to let homosexuals marry and raise children like heterosexuals—but only by making heterosexuals wonder what is the point of marrying and raising children. It is possible not to go to war— but only by having condemned the people of Iraq to life under a barbaric and aggressive dictatorship, and by continuing to condemn the people of Darfur to an indescribable misery that nothing but military force can put an end to. There are few cost-free solutions to anything.

This is something that those who bandy the phrase *tikkun olam* might be expected to be aware of. They might, one would think, have learned something from Hillel the Elder.

In the same Mishnah of *Gittin*, there is brief mention of the earliest of rabbinic rulings for the sake of *tikkun olam*. This is the one that has come to be known as the *pruzbul* of Hillel the Elder. Hillel lived while the Temple was still standing, and *pruzbul* is the Hebrew form of the Greek words *pros boulè*, "at the office of the counsel of law." An explanation of the term is found in the Mishnah of Shevi'it that deals with the seventh year of the septennial cycle—a year in which the Jewish farmer in the land of Israel was commanded by the Bible to let his land lie fallow and the Jewish creditor to cancel or release all debts.

The biblical statute, found in Deuteronomy, says:

> And this is the manner of the release. Every creditor that lends whatsoever unto his neighbor shall release it; he shall not exact it of his neighbor or of his brother, because it is called the Lord's release.

The *pros boulè* or *pruzbul* that Hillel the Elder ordained was a way of circumventing this cancellation of debt. As described in Shevi'it, the technique involved a procedure whereby the creditor would turn to a judicial office and authorize it to collect his debt for him *after* the seventh year had passed. The judges could do this without technically violating the biblical commandment because the latter required the creditor to cancel the debt personally; a third party to which the collection had been entrusted would not be so constrained. In this fashion, the biblical law was effectively nullified.

What made Hillel the Elder do this? The Mishnah of Shevi'it tells us, "When he saw that Jews were not lending each other money, and were thus violating the commandment, 'Beware there not be a thought in your wicked heart,' he enacted the *pruzbul*." The commandment referred to comes from the same passage in Deuteronomy and reads in full:

> Beware that there not be a thought in your wicked heart saying, the seventh year, the year of release, is at hand; and your eye be evil against your poor brother, and you give him naught, and he cry unto the Lord against you, and it be a sin unto you.

In other words, foreseeing that wealthy individuals would be reluctant to lend their money to the poor as the seventh year approached, the Bible commanded them to lend it anyway. Yet Hillel, seeing that the wealthy were disregarding this injunction and depriving the poor of badly needed loans, changed the biblical law to ensure that money would be lent by providing a way of recovering it.

This was a watershed in the evolution of Judaism. The biblical law of debt cancellation is motivated by a deep concern, which runs through the Mosaic code and the prophets, for the poor, who are to be periodically forgiven by their creditors in order to prevent their becoming hopelessly mired in debt. One could not imagine a more utopian piece of social legislation. But this, as Hillel the Elder realized, was precisely the problem with it: the regulation was having the paradoxical consequence of only making life for the poor harder by preventing them from borrowing at all.

It is not irrelevant to mention in this context that Hillel knew what poverty was. The story is told of him in the Talmud that once, as a young man, unable to pay the doorman who, for a fee, admitted students to the study house of the great sages Shemaiah and Avtalion, he climbed onto the roof to listen to their lesson through the roof beams and nearly froze to death when buried by a snowstorm.

Hillel was thus well aware of the anguish of the man beset by worry that he has to return a loan he does not have the means to make good on, and of how miraculous a deliverance it would be if, at the last moment, the seventh year would arrive and relieve that man of his distress. He could not lightly have undertaken to abolish the prospect of such deliverance, and he certainly must have realized that his *pruzbul*, enabling the collection of a debt after the seventh year, would cause some proponents of social justice to find him morally callous.

The words in *Gittin*, "Hillel enacted a *pruzbul* for the sake of *tikkun olam*," do not compare in sublimity with the prophet Isaiah's declaration, "When the poor and needy seek water, and there is none, and their tongue faileth for thirst, I the Lord will hear them, I the God of Israel will not forsake them." And yet they reflect no less a passionate caring for the Jewish people. So should a concern for the Jewish public interest today.

2008

If Israel Ceased to Exist

C an Israel, as the prime minister of Iran has bluntly put it, be wiped from the map? Of course it can be. The Iranian nuclear weapons program has only added to the ways in which this can happen. Any small country whose larger neighbors, including those formally at peace with it, would be delighted, with the concurrence of a significant part of the human race, to see it vanish must reckon with its possible mortality. It has never been anything but foolish for Israelis, American Jews, or anyone else to deny this.

If Iran has made a difference, it is that an intermittent anxiety has now become a chronic one. In the past, acute concern over Israel's survival has arisen in times of war—1948, 1967, 1973—and abated once the military threat was over. But the Iranian threat is indeterminate. It has developed slowly and may be slow to go away, if ever it does.

And yet a successful Iranian nuclear attack, although it might effectively obliterate Israel in a matter of minutes, is not the only way in which Israel's military destruction might take place. Should they ever attain conventional military superiority over Israel, Arab armies could also destroy it without actual resort to nuclear arms. It would be enough for them to possess them, or to be allied with their possessors, thus neutralizing Israel's own nuclear arsenal and preventing its deployment as a last-ditch measure were a conventional war about to be lost. And if it were, Israel's conquered Jews would wish only to flee. Presumably, the

United States, the European Union, and other countries would atone for the sins of the Holocaust by taking them in.

These are the envisionable, if not highly likely, cataclysms. But Israel's demise as a Jewish state could also take place less apocalyptically, by means of demographic swamping. There is a faster and a slower way for this to happen.

In the former, an Israel unable or unwilling to withdraw from all or most of the Palestinian West Bank would gradually turn into a binational state. Far from being a utopian solution to the Israeli-Palestinian problem, as it has been touted on the hallucinatory anti-Zionist Left, such a state would be a dystopic horror. Everything we know about countries in which religiously and culturally heterogeneous populations with a long history of enmity are made to cohabit together without the clear dominance of one of them, or of a stronger third party, tells us that permanent and frequently violent conflict is the inevitable result. A binational Israel/Palestine would in all likelihood quickly degenerate into another Lebanon, with a contracting population of Israeli Jews, steadily depleted by emigration, taking the place of Lebanese Christians.

This is the worst-case demographic scenario. Yet even if Israel withdraws to close to its 1967 borders, with or without a peace settlement with the Palestinians, its demographic future will be precarious. In the absence of large-scale Jewish immigration, and even assuming a steady drop in Israeli Arab birthrates such as is already beginning to take place, Israel's Jewish majority, whose ratio to its Arab minority was ten-to-one in the 1950s and now stands at four-to-one, will almost certainly shrink to three-to-one and possibly beyond that before some sort of stasis is achieved.

The greater this shrinkage, the more Arab-Jewish tensions will grow, with Arab demands to do away with Israel's expressly Jewish character becoming more clamorous. At some point the situation could spiral out of control, again leading to endemic violence and the emigration of a demoralized Jewish population. Such an Israel, too, could end in disintegration. Just as the enemies of Zionism predicted, it would have turned out to be a foreign beachhead in the Middle East, unable to hold out forever against the sheer weight of the Arab multitudes ranged against it.

Not even peace with the Palestinians and the Arab world, then, will necessarily ensure Israel's long-term survival. Nor, as desirable as it is for Israel to treat its Arab citizens equitably, is there any reason to believe that, thus treated, they would accept living in a Jewish state once a demographic tipping point were reached. As long as Palestinian and Arab nationalism and Islamic religious militancy persist, Israel will never be like Belgium, in which roughly equal numbers of Walloons and Flemings coexist peacefully despite ethnic tensions between them—and Belgium, too, may one day break apart. Israel's only hope is to stay clear of the tipping point.

And yet here we encounter a curious fact. The same American Jewish community that is so worried about Israel's survival has consistently failed to do the one thing in its power that could most help to assure it.

The statistics speak for themselves. In 2005, 3,005 Jews from France, a country with a Jewish population of a half million, immigrated to Israel; the United States and Canada combined, with roughly twelve times as many Jews, provided 2,987 immigrants. And should it be objected that the comparison is unfair, inasmuch as French Jews have had to live in recent years with a degree of anti-Semitism unknown in America, it is not as unfair as all that. In the sixty years of its existence, during most of which anti-Semitism was not a problem for French Jews, Israel was settled in by seventy-five thousand of them. The figure for North American Jews for the same period was one hundred eighteen thousand, seven times smaller proportionally—or approximately one Jew in three thousand per annum.

What would have happened had American Jewish immigration to Israel since 1948 been proportional to that from France, which itself has not been dramatically high? Nearly a million more American Jews would have gone to live in Israel. Had this happened, the Jewish-Arab ratio in Israel today would be five-to-one rather than four-to-one. The tipping point would be significantly farther away, and the prospect of still more

American Jewish immigrants in the future might have put an Israel within sensible borders out of the demographic danger zone.

The effect on Israel of negligible American Jewish immigration has been more than merely demographic. It has been more than merely socio-cultural and socio-economic, too, though one cannot but think wistfully of the contribution that a million more American Jews with their education, talents, values, and dynamism might have made to Israeli life. It has also been psychological. It has been part of the way in which Israel and American Jewry, although they have been obvious sources of strength to each other, have also been great mutual disappointments. These disappointments go to the core; they strike at the heart of Jewish identity.

Historically, few things have been more basic to this identity than the great narrative of exile and return that is a leitmotif of Judaism—the story of a people, like none other, repeatedly driven from its land and repeatedly dreaming of regaining it, since there alone could it be its true self. Well before the advent of political Zionism, of course, there were Jewish thinkers who suspected that the "true" Jewish self was the false self, so to speak, of the Diaspora. Already in the 12th century we find Yehuda Halevi writing scathingly in his philosophical polemic *The Book of the Kuzari*: "All our prayers [to return to Jerusalem and the land of Israel], such as 'Let us bow to His sacred mount' and 'He who restoreth His presence to Zion' and the like, are merely the prattle of parrots and the caw of starlings, since we do not mean what we say."

Yet not even Halevi was ever shaken in his conviction that the inner striving of Jewish history was homeward. And while even after the inception of the Zionist movement in the late nineteenth century the number of Jews actively seeking to settle in Palestine comprised, prior to the rise of Nazism, a small minority of Diaspora Jews, Zionism could justly claim that it was a revolutionary movement in Jewish life, and that all revolutions, however genuine the aspirations they represent, begin with small, dedicated cadres. They succeed because their founders correctly assess the popular support for them that can be mobilized even if it does not originally exist.

Still, the fact remains that, even after the establishment of a Jewish state, the overwhelming majority of Diaspora Jews have chosen, in the absence of internal pressures to emigrate, to remain where they are—and nowhere more so than in the United States. Considering that there has never been in the Diaspora a better place than the United States for Jews to live, this may be no cause for surprise. Surprising or not, however, only a tiny percent of American Jews have thought, and think today, that the benefits of living in a sovereign Jewish state outweigh the advantages of life in America.

This has delivered a message, however surreptitious, to Israelis. As much as we American Jews are prepared to exert ourselves on Israel's behalf, it has said to them, there is a limit beyond which we will not go. The Jewish narrative of exile and return is a heroic myth; in practice, however, our ordinary lives are good enough for us. Indeed, if we were honest with you we would admit that, while we sometimes complain about Israeli cynicism, no one has done more to make you cynical than we have. Zionism told you that you were the vanguard of a people, and that if you went first and made a home for it, the people would follow. But Zionism lied to you, because we never intended to follow. And since we can read the figures as well as you can, and understand that it would be in our vital interest to reinforce you if we believed that our survival depended on yours, you are right to conclude that we do not believe it. If Israel goes under, we will grieve and get over it, just as Jews have gotten over their grief so many times before in their history.

This statement has been made *sotto voce*. It has not been meant for the ears of American Jews themselves, let alone for those of Israelis. But Israelis have heard it loud and clear. More than that: they have been convinced by it. Not only did they long ago cease to hope that American Jews might join them, they long ago ceased criticizing their fellow countrymen for joining American Jews. There are today an estimated half million Israelis living in the United States—several times the number of American Jewish immigrants in Israel. And why shouldn't there be? If America is the best place for an American Jew to live, why isn't it the best place for an Israeli Jew? And if Jewish life in America will survive Israel's destruction, why shouldn't a prudent Israeli seek a safe haven there now? American Jews should be the last to complain when Israelis forsake Israel for America. It is they who have issued the invitation.

But the disappointment cuts both ways. If the Jews of Israel feel let down, so do American Jews, including many who count themselves among Israel's staunch supporters.

Israel is not the Jewish state these American Jews hoped for. Interminably at war with its neighbors, oppressive toward the Palestinians of the territories conquered in 1967, ridden by internal tensions and political corruption, lacking leaders of stature, out of favor with enlightened opinion everywhere, its people fearful for the future—not only is such a country not, as David Ben-Gurion proclaimed it would be in 1948, a light unto the nations, it is not even a light unto itself.

If American Jews had been like other hyphenated Americans, this might have been of little consequence. But they have been different, as is evidenced by the very term "American Jew," "Jew" being the substantive noun rather than the qualifying adjective that it is in "Italian American," "Polish American," and "Japanese American." Not only are many of them more emotionally involved with Israel than other Americans are with the countries of their ancestors, and not only are they therefore more identified with Israel by other Americans than are Italian and Polish Americans with Italy or Poland, they also have a different image of themselves—and Israel, in recent years, has given this image a beating. It has delivered to the Jews of America a message of its own. It goes like this:

Although we may prefer not to acknowledge it in the presence of Gentiles, we Jews, whether because we have prided ourselves on being chosen by God or on having chosen Him, have always considered ourselves to be more advanced, more rational, and more morally refined than others. Throughout our worst periods in the Diaspora, we have comforted ourselves with the thought that the world's rejection of us was proof, not of our faults, but of its folly—the same folly that caused it to create the cruel and unjust societies we were forced to inhabit. This is what happens, we told ourselves, when Gentiles run the world. How much better a place it would be if Jews could run it. How much better a place it *will* be in religious or secular messianic times when run by Jewish principles!

And yet—so this message continues—we Israelis have for the past sixty years run a tiny part of the world, and look what we have made of it. Although we may have produced more than our share of Nobel Prize winners and hi-tech wizards, we have, when given the full responsibility for managing our own affairs that we never had in the Diaspora, shown ourselves to be no more competent than the Gentiles and less so than some of them. Clearly, we have deceived ourselves, our belief in Jewish superiority having been possible only so long as others were in charge. While we thought of our exile as a misfortune, it alone enabled us to nurture grandiose notions about ourselves that had no basis in reality.

It can be cogently argued that, on both a conscious and an unconscious level, the fear of losing the sense of Jewish specialness explains a great deal of Jewish anti-Zionism, that of the "progressive" Jewish Left no less than that of the "reactionary" ultra-Orthodox Jewish Right. Behind their principled affirmation of the Diaspora, whether as a human opportunity to interact with the world and improve it or as a God-imposed chastisement that must be borne patiently, has lain the understanding that Jews in a Jewish state must of necessity become many things that in the Diaspora were left to others: strutting generals, crooked politicians, mindless bureaucrats, hypocritical diplomats, flag-waving jingoists, provincial intellectuals, parasitic clergymen, bribable policemen, and brawling football fans, joined by millions of ordinary people who have stopped dreaming Jewish dreams because they are living the plebeian fulfillment of one of the greatest of them.

If, then, despite all that American Jews have done for Israel, they have not done what Israel needed most, the reverse is equally true. In fighting Jewish assimilation in America, after all, Israel can offer only limited practical aid. Evenings of Israeli folk dancing and Israel Independence Day parades will not prevent millions of American Jews from marrying out or losing their Jewish identity; neither will bringing them by the chartered planeload to tour Israel, no matter how reassuring its normality may seem to them. On the contrary: the only Israel that could change the self-image of the marginal American Jew would be one that gave him a sense of Jewish uniqueness.

In the years immediately following its brilliant victory of 1967, this was indeed what Israel did. The luster of those years, however, wore off long ago. Today, if Israel has any effect on marginal Jews in America, it is more likely a negative one. Universalist in outlook, liberal in politics, such Jews ask themselves: if this is who the Jewish people turn out to be when left to their own devices, why be part of them? And why cause myself, by living as a Jew, to be associated by other Americans with a country that—at least in the circles I move in—is in growing disesteem and on its way to becoming, as it already is now in Europe, one of the least liked places on earth?

Israel, contrary to what the conventional wisdom has been in the past in the American Jewish community, may today be more of a spur to assimilation than a bulwark against it. One thinks of the Roman Empire after the bloody suppression of the two great Jewish revolts against Rome in the years 67 and 132 C.E. It is a commonplace for historians to observe that many people in this period left Judaism for Christianity, or chose Christianity over Judaism, because of the stigma of being linked in the Gentile mind to a failed and unpopular Jewish nationalism. It may well be that historians of the future will say something similar about Jewish life in our own times.

Of course, deeply religious Jews, who have a transcendent rationale for being Jewish, will not be influenced by such considerations. Such Jews will go on existing in the United States with or without Israel; let it be destroyed and—global weather permitting—they will still be reciting Jewish prayers and studying Jewish texts a thousand years from now. Although assimilation and intermarriage will run their course, and the descendants of most American Jews alive today will disappear from the ranks of the Jewish people, the numbers of ritually observant Jews, for whom alone procreation continues to be a prime commandment of Judaism, may continue to grow.

Should Israel vanish, I would not find the existence of such an American Jewry of any interest. A thousand more years of ritual observance do not strike me as a fit continuation of the great historical adventure that being Jewish has been until now. And while a ritually observant Diaspora Judaism will continue to evolve in the future as it has done in the past, the Jewish people has been *there* before, too. Coming after the immense and open-ended Jewish drama of Israel, such questions of current concern to the American Jewish community as whether women should be rabbis, or homosexuals should be given Jewish weddings, seem trivial.

But even from within—from the perspective of Jewish observance—would there not be something dishearteningly pointless in life after the death of Israel? After all, what is it that Judaism has been telling the world ever since it and Christianity parted ways? Is it not that, unlike Christianity, it is not just a faith but a way of life that seeks to permeate every aspect of existence, and that it can therefore only demonstrate its true worth when every aspect of existence is permeated by it? What then, if not a Jewish state, in which alone this is possible, can be Judaism's ultimate test? And what would be the purpose of a Jewish religious existence that, without having finished taking such a test, its first attempts at which did not earn it high marks, was reduced to facing lesser challenges again? Would it not be a stale anticlimax even to itself?

It is possible to think of Israel as the psychiatrist's couch on which the Jewish people has lain down after long centuries of Diaspora life. Israel forces Jews to surrender fantasies and illusions about themselves that have long been part of their character. It has, literally and figuratively, brought the Jewish people down to earth. As is always the case with punctured ego ideals, this is painful. Still, it is liberating to know who you are, however belatedly, even if it is not who you thought you were.

Except that, at precisely this point, the world has chosen to think otherwise. At the very historical moment when Israel has obliged Jews to come to terms with their ordinary humanity, Israel has more and more impressed ordinary humanity as sui generis. The world declines to see it in ordinary terms.

This is increasingly true of Israel's friends no less than of its enemies. Israel's strongest non-Jewish supporters, especially in America, are now evangelical Christians. Certainly, the discomfort many Jews feel with the backing of evangelicals owes much to the latter's conservative political agenda; certainly, too, it has to do with Christian religious fervor of any kind arousing visceral Jewish fears. But it is also related to the larger-than-life role in which evangelicals have cast the Jewish people and Israel—a role in which, regardless of whether a Christian or a Jewish script is written for it, secular Jews, in Israel and the Diaspora alike, are increasingly unable to recognize themselves.

Yet Christian philo-Semitism, however it may exaggerate Jewish virtues and induce fears of what may happen if its high image of the Jews ever founders, is hardly the greatest problem facing Jews. This distinction continues to be reserved for anti-Semitism, and especially for that variety of it that manifests itself as an extreme hostility to Israel. And because anti-Israelism is now badly infected by anti-Semitism, it, too, attributes qualities to Israel that transcend normal human life. Israel is not just one of many countries ruling another people that wishes to be free of it, it is a reincarnation of Nazism; it is not another nation-state stubbornly trying to make a go of it in an ostensibly postnational age but the very avatar of reactionary tribalism in a new era of global brotherhood; its Jewish supporters are not merely a well-organized political force, they secretly run America, the country on which Israel leans, from their hidden seats of power.

In the face of such and other charges, many Jews feel a mental helplessness greater than in the past because their sense of themselves is more diminished than it was in the past. Once, when Jews believed more in their own exceptionalism, it was possible for them to understand anti-Semitism as the hateful distortion of that belief, its sinister mirror image in which all the good in them was reversed. Did the anti-Semites accuse them of being an infernally arrogant people who refused to mix with the rest of the human race? Yes, they did refuse, but their mission was not infernal but divine. Were they blamed for thinking they were better than others? Of course they thought that—because they were. Was their invisible hand at the center of everything? No, but everything indeed revolved around them, for they were the indispensable ingredient, the magical leaven, that would uplift the entire human race.

Today Jews are left staring at the distorted mirror image alone. The figure that stood before the mirror is gone.

The world, then, continues to miscast the Jews. It has not yet realized that they are not as different or as important as it thinks they are.

Or is it possible that, however distorted its image of them may be, it knows something about them that they no longer do?

This is a question to be asked with trepidation. There is good reason for a religiously skeptical Jew to be dismayed by the thought that his people are forever destined or doomed to the inescapable fate of being singled out. Before picking up the gauntlet that is again being flung at their feet, Jews should be wary of slipping back into the delusions that Israel should have cured them of.

I have in mind those conceptions that would again place Israel and the Jewish Diaspora, linked in common cause and purpose, at the epicenter of history by means of some new, secularized version of Jewish specialness: Israel and the Jews as the front line of democracy, Israel and the Jews as the standard bearers of Western civilization, Israel and the Jews as the world's shock troops against Islamo-fascism, Israel and the Jews as the canaries in the coal mines of the new barbarism and so forth—anything, in a word, but Israel and the Jews as a small country and people that have carried the burden of specialness long enough and paid too heavy a price for it.

This is not to say that all of these things may not, in some sense, be true. It is simply to observe that Jews should not hurry to embrace them without an awareness of the inner need they serve—the need to recover that belief in their own uniqueness, as a people chosen by history if not by God, that they have lost but still crave.

The Jews are a conundrum. When all is said and done—and what hasn't been said and what hasn't been done, to them and by them?—there is something inexplicable about the monumental place assigned to them, by themselves and by others, over the centuries. Israel and America, each in its way, has demystified them; must they now be remystified? If the heavy burden of Jewish history has to be shouldered by them once more, should they at least not know clearly what it consists of?

If Iran goes nuclear, the possibility of Israel's destruction becomes greater. But the possibility is there without Iran, too. How important is it to prevent it? And how important to whom?

A few years ago, I participated in a panel discussion about Israel and the Diaspora held in Washington, D.C. As I generally do on such occasions, I spoke my mind. When the time came for questions from the audience, a man rose and asked me:

"Even if you're right about the inconsequentiality of Jewish life in the Diaspora compared with that in Israel, suppose, God forbid, that Israel should destroyed by a nuclear attack. Wouldn't you be glad then that American Jewry existed, so that it wouldn't be the end of the Jewish people?"

"To tell you the truth," I answered spontaneously, "if Israel were destroyed, I hope it *would* be the end of the Jewish people."

There was a shocked silence before another questioner was called on. When the evening was over, a fellow panelist turned to me and said, "I hope you didn't mean that."

I thought for a moment.

"Yes," I said. "I did."

If Israel should ever go under, I would not want there to be any more Jews in the world.

What for?

Things haven't been this good for the world's Jews in two thousand years. In one respect only are they worse. During that period we were a people that had lost a first temple and a second; yet as great as our misfortunes were, we did not have a third temple to lose. Today, we do. If we cannot safeguard it, it would be as shameless as it would be pointless to want to go on. In Jewish history, too, three strikes and you're out.

2007

Endless Devotion

A first reaction to the deluxe new Siddur or prayer book recently issued in a bilingual edition by Koren Publishers of Jerusalem is that, at 1,244 handsomely printed, imitation stamped-leather-bound pages, it is a bit hefty to be carried to Sabbath and holiday services by the Orthodox users it is primarily intended for, who do not travel on such days. To be sure, the *ArtScroll Siddur*, with which it is meant to compete, has only two hundred pages fewer and, printed on thicker paper, is as bulky. But the *ArtScroll*, the standard prayer book of most American Orthodox synagogues since its publication in 1989, is already on their shelves. The *Koren* must be brought by the congregant—at least until it gains a place on those shelves too, as its publishers clearly hope that it will.

The *Koren Siddur* is so large because, like the *ArtScroll*, it has, facing the Hebrew prayers, an English text and commentary, both the work of its editor, Great Britain's chief rabbi Sir Jonathan Sacks; a generous layout less cluttered than the *ArtScroll*'s, and a comprehensiveness at least as great. Besides the regular weekday morning, afternoon, and evening services, and their Sabbath and holiday variations, which (with the exception of the long Rosh Hashanah and Yom Kippur liturgies) are found in every traditional Siddur, the *Koren* includes numerous items that usually are not. Some of these are for holiday-related occasions like *bi'ur hametz,* the declaring of a house free of unleavened food before Passover, or *ushpizin,* the welcoming of the biblical patriarchs said by Jewish legend to visit on Sukkot; others belong to life-cycle rituals such as *pidyon ha-ben,* the redemption of a first-born son, or *viduy,* the deathbed confession. In addition, the *Koren* has a lengthy introduction by Sacks; the text of all Torah readings for weekday and holiday mornings; a prayer calendar of the Jewish year; a digest of rules and regulations pertaining to Jewish prayer; and a "Halakhic Guide to Prayer for Visitors to Israel," where some customs differ from the Diaspora's. It adds up.

Of course, Jewish liturgy itself has kept adding up over the centuries, continually growing from its earliest origins. These go back, if not as far as is claimed by rabbinic tradition, which ascribes them to Abraham, Isaac, and Jacob, considerably farther than they are held to by the common misconception that Jewish communal worship is strictly a post-Second Temple institution, a response to the abrogation of the priestly sacrifices after the Temple's destruction by the Romans in 70 C.E. There are passages in the Siddur that lend support to this view, such as this one from the morning service:

> Now, because of our sins, the Temple is destroyed and the daily sacrifice discontinued, and we have no priest at his service, no Levite on his platform, no Israelite at his post.... May it be Your will, Lord our God and God of our ancestors, that the prayer of our lips be considered, accepted and favored before You as if we had offered the daily sacrifice at its appointed time and place, according to its laws.**

Yet in actuality, the synagogue was central to Jewish life long before the Temple's destruction and coexisted for centuries with the sacrifices from which it evolved. Its revolutionary significance was pointed out by the German-Jewish historian Ismar Elbogen in his magisterial 1923 study, *The Jewish Liturgy and Its Historical Development*:

** All translations of prayers in this essay are taken from the Koren Siddur, with occasional minor modifications on my part.

...it was the first time in human history that regular assemblies for worship were held at sites that had no other sanctity than what was bestowed upon them by the community of the faithful. It was a liturgy that freed itself from the practices theretofore customary among all peoples, relinquishing all such accessories as sacrifices and other offerings and intermediation by priests, and placing man and his spiritual life at the century of the liturgy. It is the same kind of liturgy as came to prevail in the European religions, and thus became familiar to all of civilized humanity.

As Elbogen observed, Christianity and Islam took not just the forms of regular prayer from Judaism but the very idea of it. Paradoxically, however, it was the supreme importance to biblical Judaism of animal sacrifice in the Temple that led to this idea's development. This was because, by the time the First Temple was razed by the Babylonians in the sixth century B.C.E., all sacrifice to the God of Israel on altars other than the Temple's had been stamped out in the name of the Temple's exclusivity. Worshipers living far from Jerusalem, whether in Palestine or in exile in Babylonia, were compelled to find alternate modes of religious behavior. The two they settled on were public readings from the Torah on Sabbaths, holidays, and the market days of Monday and Thursday, when rural residents flocked to towns, and prayer gatherings held at the hours at which Temple sacrifice took place, originally conceived of as vicarious participations in sacrifice rather than as substitutes for it.

These gatherings began in Second Temple times with members of the priestly caste in Palestine, which sent semiannual delegations from outlying districts to Jerusalem in order to assist for a week in the sacrificial ministrations; since not all priests could join these missions, those staying behind expressed their identification with them by sessions of daily worship synchronized with the morning and afternoon sacrifices and the evening locking of the Temple's gates. When, eventually, these sessions were opened to the general public, made year-round, and combined with readings from the Torah, Jewish prayer as we now know it emerged. By the time of the redaction of the Mishnah over a hundred years after the Second Temple's destruction, the core of the three daily services of *shaharit, minhah,* and *ma'ariv* was nearly the same as it is today.

This core included basic prayers well-known even to many nonobservant Jews, such as the *sh'ma yisra'el,* the "Hear O Israel," and the *amida* or *shmoneh esreh,* the silent "standing prayer" or "Eighteen Benedictions" (so called because its weekday version had eighteen—later enlarged to nineteen—repetitions of the formula "Blessed are You, Lord"). Numerous other familiar prayers, however, only came later. Until the eighth or ninth century, when the Siddur (the Hebrew word means "ordering," i.e., of the liturgy) was first committed to writing, the daily, weekly, and holiday services had to be brief enough to be memorized, if not by the entire congregation, at least by its leader, to whose recitations it answered "Amen." Only once a written Siddur existed was it possible to add new prayers freely, the sole limit on them now being the congregation's time and patience.

It was then that the Siddur's long period of expansion commenced. It has continued right up to modern times. The hymn *adon olam,* "Lord of the Universe," for example, which opens the daily *shaharit* and—heartily sung to a variety of melodies, the oldest originally a seventeenth-century German drinking song—concludes the Sabbath and holiday additional service or *musaf,* is attributed to the eleventh-century Hispano-Hebrew poet Shlomo ibn Gabirol. The solemn *aleynu l'shabe'ah,* "It is Our Duty to Praise," the coda of all three daily services, was restricted to the High Holidays until roughly 1300. This is also approximately when the mourner's kaddish entered the liturgy (other forms of the kaddish are older), while the favorite Sabbath hymn *lekha dodi,* "Let us go, my love," was composed by the sixteenth-century Palestinian kabbalist Shlomo Alkabetz. Part of the prayer for the state of Israel recited by many congregations today derives from nineteenth-century prayers by European Jews for their governments. A Siddur inherited by me from my father, printed in Vilna in 1909, asks God to "protect, assist, elevate, exalt, and raise high our lord Tsar Nikolai Alexandrovitsh, his wife the esteemed

Tsarina Alexandra Fyedorovna, his mother the esteemed Tsarina Maria Fyederovna, and the crown prince Alexei Nikolayevitsh, along with all the royal family, long may it live in glory."

The Siddur is thus not a single text but a compilation of texts, differing (although generally only slightly) from one part of the Jewish world to another. Until the first attempts to streamline it were made by the German Reform movement in the early nineteenth century, it never stopped absorbing new hymns, poems, biblical and rabbinic passages, doxologies, confessional formulas, and pleas for divine aid and intercession. Its original order became a disorder that still seemed orderly to Jewish worshipers because anything repeated day after day, year after year, and century after century will be perceived by its repeaters as the natural—indeed, the only conceivable—way of doing things.

Nevertheless, the original core of Jewish prayer is still intact and tightly structured. Located some two-thirds of the way through *shaharit*, it begins with the *barkhu* or "Bless ye," a call to worship that once marked the morning service's commencement, just as it still does that of the evening service:

> Prayer leader: Bless ye the Lord, the blessed One!
> Congregation: Blessed the Lord, the blessed One for ever
> and all time!
> Prayer leader: Bless the Lord, the blessed One, for ever
> and all time!

Anyone familiar with the traditional synagogue service knows the feeling of snapping to attention that the *barkhu* produces. Until now the congregation has behaved like an undisciplined aggregate, some of its members barely moving their lips as they pray, others whispering, murmuring, or declaiming the words out loud; some keeping up with the prayer leader and some not; the latecomers striving to catch up with the earlier arrivals; no one paying much heed to anyone else. With the *barkhu*, the atmosphere changes. The prayer leader takes command; his chant grows louder and more emphatic; the congregation becomes a single body and responds in unison. The *barkhu* still functions as a call to prayer, even if those called by it have been praying for quite some time.

From the *barkhu*, the *shaharit* proceeds to the *yotser*, a paean to God, the creator of light, who "great in knowledge, prepared and made the rays of the sun." This section builds up to a description of the different orders of God's angels chanting His praises in words taken from the epiphanies of the prophets Isaiah and Ezekiel:

> All accept on themselves,
> one from another,
> the yoke of the kingdom of heaven,
> granting permission to one another
> to sanctify the One who formed them,
> in serene spirit,
> pure speech and sweet melody.
> All, as one,
> proclaim his holiness,
> saying in awe:
>
> Holy, holy, holy is the Lord of hosts:
> the whole world is filled with His glory!
> Then the Ophanim and the Holy Hayot
> with a roar of noise,
> raise themselves toward the Seraphim and,
> facing them, give praise saying:
>
> Blessed be the Lord's glory from His place!

From here the service proceeds to the *boher b'amo yisra'el b'ahava,* a prayer thanking God for His love in choosing Israel; next, to the tripartite "Hear, O Israel," Judaism's great declaration of faith that *adonai eloheynu, adonai ehad,* "the Lord is our God, the Lord is One"; then to the *ga'al yisra'el,* the theme of God's salvation as evinced by the parting of the Red Sea; and on to the silently recited Eighteen Benedictions, which, as explained by Sacks in emphasizing the numerical "fractals" of the liturgy, repeat the triads that have preceded them with "three blessing of praise at the beginning... three of acknowledgment at the end," and in between, "six individual requests, followed by six collective ones, each divided into two groups of three."

The climax of this progression comes in the prayer leader's repetition of the Eighteen Benedictions, now recited aloud with the addition of the *kedushah* or "Holiness." In it, the congregation rises and the prayer leader intones:

> We will sanctify Your name on earth,
> as they [the angels] sanctify it in the highest heavens,
> as is written by Your prophet,
> And they call to one another saying:
>
> Congregation: Holy, holy, holy is the Lord of Hosts,
>   the whole world is filled with His glory!
>
> Prayer leader: Holy, holy, holy is the Lord of hosts,
>   the whole world is filled with His glory!
>
> Congregation: Blessed is the Lord's glory from His place!

Kadosh, kadosh, kadosh: the prophet Isaiah's three "holies" are customarily exclaimed while each congregant rises on the balls of his feet, as if he were in a throng of angels and seeking to catch a glimpse of God's throne over the heads of those in front of him. It is, as Jonathan Sacks writes in his thoughtful introduction, a moment of "astonishing drama." Angels and men in rabbinic midrash are often portrayed as rivals, men striving for the angels' closeness to God, angels jealous of God's fascination with men, and there is an undercurrent of this competition in the morning prayer too, which describes how

> All of his [angelic] servants stand in the universe's heights,
> proclaiming together,
> in awe, aloud,

the words of the living God,
the eternal King.
They are all beloved, all pure, all mighty,
and all perform in awe and reverence the will of
their Maker.
All open their mouths in holiness and purity,
with song and psalm,
and bless, praise, glorify,
revere, sanctify, and crown [Him].

What mortal can vie with such creatures of perfection? Yet in the *kedushah*, men and angels join together, serenading God with the same words. As it is above, so it is below. For a brief moment every morning, the universe is unified as it was at the time of its creation, of which *shaharit* is a recurring commemoration.

It is wonderfully poetic—even more so in Hebrew, to which Sacks's English does not always do full justice.

Often, it does. "Bless the Lord, the blessed One" for *barkhu et adonai ha-mevorakh,* with its response of "Bless the Lord, the blessed One, forever and all time" for *barukh adonai ha-mevorakh l'olam va'ed,* strikes just the right note. How easy it is to strike a wrong one can be seen from the *ArtScroll's* "Bless Hashem, the blessed One"/ "Blessed is Hashem, the blessed One, for all eternity;" the United Synagogue of Conservative Judaism's *Siddur Sim Shalom's* "Praise the Lord, Source of Blessing"/ "Praised be the Lord, Source of blessing, throughout all time"; and the Reform movement's *Mishkan T'filah's* "Praise Adonai to whom praise is due!"/ "Praised be Adonai to whom praise is due, now and forever!"

All three of these are ill-conceived, each in a way that is characteristic of its denomination of Judaism. "Hashem"—literally, "the Name"—is a Hebrew circumlocution commonly used by Orthodox Jews in obedience to the biblical prohibition on taking God's name in vain; as a rendition of *adonai,* "Lord," in the *barkhu,* it suggests that a translated Hebrew prayer is a vain thing itself. *Sim Shalom's* "Praise" instead of "Bless," coupled with "Source of Blessing" (an epithet for God borrowed from the thirteenth-century kabbalist Bahya ben Asher) in place of "the blessed One," are meant to sidestep the question of how God can be blessed by man; yet a good translation transmits questions (this one already embedded in the language of the Bible), it does not conceal them. *Mishkan T'filah*, which also bowdlerizes blessing to praising, seeks a bold immediacy by going to the opposite extreme from the *ArtScroll* and incorrectly treating Adonai as if it *were* the name of God rather than a translatable Hebrew word *for* God. The *Koren* alone is faithful to the *barkhu's* gravity and simplicity.

In other places, however, the *Koren* seems wrong, too. "With a roar of noise" for Ezekiel's *b'kol ra'ash gadol*—literally, "with a great sound of noise"—is clunky. It evokes a revved car engine more than the clamor of angels. Although the King James Bible's "with a noise of a great rushing" may also leave something to be desired, it at least calls to mind waterfalls, not exhaust pipes.

On the whole, Sacks makes little attempt to reproduce the Siddur's poetry. Take the lines in the *yotser* beginning with "All of His servants." In Hebrew they are:

> *Va'asher m'shartav kulam omdim b'rum olam*
> *u'mashmi'im b'yir'ah yahad b'kol*
> *divrey elohim hayyim u'melekh olam.*
> *Kulam ahuvim, kulam b'rurim, kulam giborim,*
> *v'khulam osim b'eymah uvyir'ah r'tson konam.*
> *V'khulam pothim et pihem bikdushah uvtaharah,*
> *b'shirah uv'zimrah, umevarkhim umeshabhim umefa'arim*
> *uma'aritsim umakdishim umamlikhim*
> *et shem ha'el ha-melekh ha-gadol.*

Like all good poetry, this passage depends on its fusion of sense and sound—that is, of its chorus of singing angels and its humming Hebrew *mem*. This consonant already dominates the first line, whose last four words end with it. Lines one, three, and five rhyme in *–am*—twice in *olam*, "world" or "universe," and once in *konam*, "their Maker"—while the same syllable occurs three more times in *kulam*, "all." Even more insistent is *–im,* the masculine plural ending of Hebrew nouns and present-tense verbs, which is repeated fifteen times, reaching a crescendo in the concluding "bless, praise, glorify, revere, sanctify, and crown," all double-*mem*med verbs that, culminating in the triple *mem* of *mamlikhim,* swell like a grand musical chord.

None of this is conveyed by the *Koren Siddur.* Yet Sacks was wise, I think, not to attempt it—and not only because the task might well have been beyond him. Even Orthodox Jews who do not completely understand the Siddur's Hebrew are not, after all, going to recite the *shaharit* in English. Their God expects them to worship Him in Hebrew alone. It is, as it were, His native tongue in which He converses with His angels, and He appreciates the effort to speak to Him in it, however lamely. Sacks's translation is not meant to be prayed in, nor does it aim to create a literary equivalent that would vie with the Hebrew and draw attention away from it. It is there solely as an aid to understanding the Hebrew, a kind of interlinear (though not printed that way) gloss. This is also the logic behind its counter-intuitive printing of the right-to-left-written Hebrew on each left-hand page, and the left-to-right-written English on each right-hand page, thus arranging the two languages back-to-back rather than face-to-face. As explained over the internet by the Koren Siddur Website, this placement is meant to allow the Hebrew and English texts "to align at the center of the Siddur," so that, as both "flow to the margins," they are symmetrical and more easily compared.

But are even Orthodox synagogue goers who fully understand the *shaharit*'s Hebrew moved by its poetry or drama? An outside observer might be permitted to doubt it. Although these worshipers may show a bit of emotion in the *sh'ma* (drawing out the last syllable of *ehad* as did the martyred Rabbi Akiva who, exclaiming it as he was tortured to death by the Romans, "lingered on 'One' and surrendered his soul with it"), and may raise their voices for the "holy, holy, holy" of the *Kedush,* they then take their seats again and help the prayer leader hasten through the rest of the service with a half-swallowed "Blessed is He, blessed is His name" after each "Blessed are you, O Lord" and a quick "Amen" at its end.

They have reason to hurry. Most are men with jobs to get to and have already been praying for close to half an hour, having managed to recite before the *barkhu*—to give a partial list—the blessings for donning their prayer shawls and phylacteries; a lengthy passage from the book of Exodus; the *adon olam*; the *yigdal*, a versification of the thirteen dogmatic beliefs declared by Maimonides to be incumbent on every Jew; the fourteen "Blessings of the Dawn;" a passage from the book of Genesis; long descriptions of the daily sacrifices from the Pentateuch; a section of the Mishnah detailing the ingredients and preparation of the *k'toret*, the incense burned in the Temple; more long descriptions of sacrifices; the thirteen logical principles by which the Mishnaic sage Rabbi Yishma'el taught that the Torah should be expounded; a non-mourner's kaddish; a mourner's kaddish; a dozen different Psalms and compilations of verses from the book of Psalms; excerpts from the books of Chronicles and Nehemiah; the prophetess Miriam's song about crossing the Red Sea in the book of Exodus, and another non-mourner's kaddish.

Nor are the Eighteen Benedictions the end. Still to come are the *tahanun* or plea for God's forgiveness, of which an even longer version is said on days the Torah is read; one more non-mourner's kaddish; the ceremony of removing the Torah scroll from the Ark if it is a Monday or a Thursday; the reading from it; the ceremony of returning it to the Ark; more Psalms and biblical passages; yet another non-mourner's kaddish; *aleynu*; the mourner's kaddish; a special Psalm for the day of the week; and a final non-mourner's kaddish, after which the worshiper strips off his tefillin, quickly removes and folds his *tallit*, and departs—unless, that is, he has chosen, like many Orthodox Jews (the non-Orthodox rarely bother with daily prayer), to say *shaharit* at home and reserve his synagogue going for Sabbaths and holidays. This saves not only travel time but the prayer leader's repetition of the Eighteen Benedictions with the *kedushah*, the reading of the Torah, and the many kaddishes, all of which are performable only in a *minyan* or prayer quorum of ten.

And indeed, Sabbath and holiday prayer in a typical Orthodox congregation is less rushed. There is more singing on the congregation's part and a slower, more melodic delivery on the prayer leader's. Yet the overall impression remains one of casualness. Worshipers pray silently or out loud as they wish, sometimes joining the prayer leader for a phrase or two, sometimes calling out words on their own. Some hold themselves upright, others *shokkel*, to use the Yiddish word for rocking back and forth or swaying from side to side with a motion that can be contemplatively slow or almost sexually frenetic. Men may converse in the middle of the prayer; at the end of the silent *shmoneh esreh*, which is recited at different speeds, those who are done stand chatting while waiting for the others to finish. Small children run unhindered in the aisles. As the Torah is read, the sexton strolls around the synagogue assigning ritual tasks: being called to the Torah; lifting it from the lectern when the reading is over; rolling it tight, restoring its drapery and silver crown, and putting it back in the Ark. On returning to their seats, the recipients of these honors stop to shake the hands held out to them. If a congregant is reading something rather than praying, no one minds. He may be immersed in a page of Talmud or *The Ethics of the Fathers,* a Mishnaic tractate of rabbinic epigrams that is included in the Siddur because it is studied in some congregations on the Sabbath but that also serves as an intellectual refuge for those bored with the prayer itself.

In any congregation, of course, there are also likely to be worshipers praying with genuine fervor. On the whole, however, if prayer is, as Sacks says, "the most intimate gesture of the religious life and the most transformative," there is more intimacy than transformation in most Orthodox services. Although the synagogue may be the house of God, one can't expect to have a fresh or deep experience each time when dropping in on God so often. Nor, perhaps, can one expect God to. There is a joke about the Jew who complains, "O Lord, my next-door neighbor is a Conservative Jew; he prays once a week and he's a millionaire. Down the street lives a Reform Jew; he prays once a year and he's a billionaire. And I pray three times a day, every day, and have nothing but debts."

"That's just it," God replies. "I hate nudniks."

The Baal Shem Tov, the founder of Hasidism, might have said that this Jew's prayers never reached God at all. Once, it is told, the Baal Shem came to a synagogue and balked at entering it. To his entourage he explained that it was crammed full with perfunctorily said prayers whose failure to rise to the heavens left no room for him to set foot inside.

The struggle to keep prayer—"the language of the soul in conversation with God," to quote Sacks again—from becoming a routine activity is intrinsic to every religion that makes praying a regular duty. In *The Ethics of the Fathers* is the saying, attributed to the first-century sage Shimon ben Netanel, "Be punctilious in reciting the 'Hear O Israel' and the other prayers, and when you pray, make your prayers not rote but mercy cries to God"; yet punctiliousness without roteness is not easily achieved. The fourth-century church abbot Agatho, when asked what the hardest part of the religious life was, replied that it was prayer, since the demons who hated God put more effort into thwarting it than into anything else.

Whoever has ever prayed regularly and not just at rare moments of personal crisis knows what these demons are. They range from difficulty in concentrating and the disturbance of distracting thoughts to religious doubts and the inability to identify with the words one is saying. The observant Jew is tempting prey for them. A devout Catholic attends a once-a-week mass that has a great deal of pageantry to hold his attention and in which his role is limited to brief responses to the longer utterances of the priest. In most Protestant services, congregational participation consists largely of hymn singing, an expansively enjoyable activity. Though Muslims pray five times a day, each prayer is brief, a few pithy formulas declaring God's greatness accompanied by frequent changes of physical position. Only Jews must recite every morning, "The incense contained eleven kinds of spices: balsam, onycha, galbanum, and frankincense...myrrh, cassia, spikenard, and saffron... twelve manehs of costus, three of aromatic bark, nine of cinnamon," or, every evening:

Blessed are You, Lord our God, King of the Universe,
who by His word brings on evenings,

by His wisdom opens the gates of heaven,
with understanding makes time change
        and the seasons rotate,
and by His will
orders the stars in their constellations in the sky.
He creates day and night,
rolling way the light before the darkness,
and the darkness before the light,
the Lord of Hosts is His name.

This is a beautiful prayer—there are many others in the Siddur—but the demons are not awed by beauty. Jews have developed ways of dealing with them. They learn the daily services by heart so that they can shut their eyes while saying them and keep the outside world at bay; a few may even wrap their prayer shawls around their heads to be alone with God. They *shokkel,* letting the steady rhythm of their bodies concentrate them as breathing does in meditation. They enter the prayers imaginatively: a list of the ingredients in the Temple incense is different if you picture yourself as the incense maker. (The early nineteenth-century Hasidic master Avraham Yehoshua Heschel of Apt is said to have recited the Yom Kippur service's description of the High Priest's ministrations in the Holy of Holies entirely in the first person because he believed he had performed the rites in a former life.) They seek out the prayers that speak most to them. Someone who is ill or has illness in his family will, in the Eighteen Benedictions, put all his feeling into "Heal us, Lord, and we shall be healed.… Blessed are You, Lord, Healer of the sick of His people Israel." A person conscious of having done wrong will dwell on "Forgive us, our Father, for we have sinned.… Blessed are You, Lord, the gracious One who repeatedly forgives."

Concentrating on the liturgy by endowing its words with maximal meaning, personal significance, or special intensity is known in Jewish tradition as *kavvanah,* a Hebrew word meaning "intention." But the word also has a more technical significance, designating in kabbalistic practice a specific mystical meditation designed to heighten prayer's effect on the

Upper Spheres. Although in some Orthodox circles they may be making a comeback, such *kavvanot,* of which the *Koren Siddur* has only two, have on the whole fallen into disuse, perhaps because they make a long service even longer. While as capable of degenerating into mere words as anything else, the cosmic significance with which they endow the act of prayer can heighten the worshiper's sense of the need to pray with an unwavering single-mindedness.

Nothing, however, can keep one focused on one's prayers when one loses faith in the God one has been praying to. This happened to me midway through adolescence. Although since then I have attended many synagogues services, I have never really been able to pray. A part of me still yearns for the days when I could. It misses the thrill of the leather straps of the tefillin biting into my arm each morning as I bound them to my arm and said, "I will betroth you to me forever; I will betroth you to me in righteousness and justice, loving-kindness and compassion; I will betroth you to me in faithfulness; and you shall know the Lord." It misses the soul-throb of God's bringing on the evening while the last light goes out in the west, the spheres rolling out darkness over the face of the earth. It misses the devotion of bowing low like a servant leaving the room of his master, "the King of all kings of all kings, the Holy One blessed be He," in the concluding *aleynu.*

There were times when I prayed mechanically then, too. There were times when I didn't pray at all. But there were times when I felt like a priest in the Temple, binding my soul to the altar and offering the daily sacrifice at its appointed time and place. It was the intensity of that experience that makes me feel like an imposter when I take part in a synagogue service today. Like anyone skilled at playing a role, I alone know I am playing it. I go through the motions of davening, the Yiddish word for praying that is regularly used by Orthodox Jews, as proficiently as do the men around me. You don't forget such things any more than you forget how to swim or ride a bicycle.

And yet I sometimes wonder how many of these men are having an experience more intense than my own. Not a large number, to judge by outward appearances. Most seem to be engaged in what they are doing without overly troubling themselves about it. They take pleasure in being together, as people take pleasure in any group activity—folk dancing, say, or a sing-along. I do not say they have no feeling of uplift. Clearly they do. But it is an uplift that could also be mine if I allowed it to be, which may be why I place no great value on it.

I acknowledge my snobbery. There is, as Émile Durkheim was perhaps the first to observe in his *Elementary Forms of Religious Life*, a social dimension to worship that may be mistaken for something else. Praying in a *minyan* is different from praying alone, less because of the additional prayers said by the worshipers than because of the human solidarity established among them. Precisely this, though, is its spiritual danger. Judaism, to be sure, is about community. The God of Israel made His covenant not with individuals but with a people, of which a congregation of worshipers is a microcosm. But a congregation can lift its voices more to itself than to God. Communal worship then becomes reflexive, a form of self-celebration. Of all prayer's demons, this may be the subtlest.

A sociologist like Durkheim might remark that it is altogether too subtle to be concerned with, since group prayer is by nature an act in which the social and spiritual are indistinguishable. A woman I know would agree. She has a religious history similar to my own except for the fact that she has continued to attend regular Orthodox services all her life. "It's my way of connecting with what is beyond myself," she has said to me. "Whether that's human or divine, I can't say. I only know that nothing else brings me into the same contact with it."

My father, who davened with great *kavvanah* yet was adamant about having no religious beliefs whatsoever, had a different answer for why he prayed. "It's what a Jew does," he would say. He once told me a story about a man standing in the street outside a *shtibl,* a little synagogue, looking for a *tseynter,* a tenth Jew to add to the nine waiting inside to say the afternoon prayer. Spotting a likely-looking candidate, he asks:

"Excuse me, mister. Are you Jewish?"

"Yes, I am," says the Jew. "What can I do for you?"

"You can join a *minyan* for *minhah,*" the man says.

"I'm afraid that's impossible," answers the Jew.

"Why?" asks the man.

"Because I'm an atheist," says the Jew.

The man gives the Jew a withering look.

"And where," he inquires, "is it written that an atheist doesn't have to say *minhah*?"

In fact, it's written nowhere. As far as Jewish law is concerned, an atheist has to pray like anyone else.

Maybe my snobbery, then, has less to recommend it than I think. I have always considered it a form of respect for the God I once believed in to refuse to dishonor either of us by mouthing empty words to Him. But the God of Judaism, Jewish tradition tells us, would rather have empty words than none. *Mitokh she-lo lishma ba lishma,* the rabbis said: the deed not initially performed for its own sake will come to be for its own sake if persisted at.

Is it only a foolish pride, then, that makes me insist on my impostership? The Hasidic rabbi Yisro'el of Koznitz is said to have let out a cry of illumination upon hearing the verse, "And thy carcasses shall be meat unto all the birds of the air," read in the *tokhehah,* the chapter in Deuteronomy describing the curses God will bring on the people of Israel if disobeyed by them. Afterwards, he shared his insight with his disciples:

> Prayers said without fear or love are like carcasses. But
> He who hears every prayer has mercy on His creatures.
> From above He awakens men's hearts, so that at long last
> they can pray with their souls as they should, and then
> their prayers grow great and devour the carcasses and fly
> like birds to the gates of Heaven.

On Sabbaths, holidays, and days of the new moon, an extra sacrifice was offered in the Temple, which led to the institution of the *musaf,* a fourth, additional synagogue service after the Torah reading. It centers on the silent prayer, whose weekday benedictions are now replaced by a passage about this sacrifice. On Sabbaths, for instance, one says:

May it be Your will
Lord our God and God of our ancestors,
       to lead us back in joy
to our land and to plant us within our borders...
And the additional offering of this Sabbath day
we will prepare and offer before you in love,
in accord with your will's commandment
as you wrote for us in Your Torah....
"On the Sabbath day,
make an offering of two lambs a year old
       without blemish,
together with two-tenths of an ephah of fine flour
mixed with oil as a meal-offering and its appropriate
       libation.

Among the earliest changes in the traditional liturgy made by the Reform movement in Germany, one found in its first prayer book printed by the *Neuen Israelitischen Tempelverein* of Hamburg in 1818, was the elimination of this passage. The motives for deleting it were obvious. Apart from wishing to disassociate themselves from the dream of returning to Zion, the new synagogue's founders regarded even lip service to the reinstitution of animal sacrifice as an embarrassment, the expression of an atavistic desire to revert to a more primitive stage of Judaism that had been happily outgrown.

Contemporary Reform synagogues in America have gone further by eliminating the Musaf service entirely. In the *Mishkan T'filah,* as in its predecessor, the Central Conference of American Rabbis' *Union Prayer Book,* the Sabbath morning service ends with the Torah reading. There is not so much as an editorial note to indicate the Musaf's absence.

The Conservative movement, though it, too, renounces the hope for sacrifice's renewal, has been less radical. Its 1947 *Sabbath and Festival Prayer Book* contains the traditional *amida* of the Musaf, with the passage on sacrifice emended to:

May it be Thy will, O Lord our God and God of our fathers, to lead us joyfully back to our land, and to establish us within its borders where our forefathers prepared the daily offerings and the additional Sabbath offerings, as is written in Thy Torah, through Moses, Thine inspired servant.

Its 1989 *Siddur Sim Shalom* has two Musaf services, the emended traditional one and an "alternative" one. The traditional one modernizes the language of "May it be Thy will" and adds, "And there [in our land] may we worship You with love and reverence as in days of old and ancient times." The alternative one gives the worshiper a choice of four different *amidas*, all ignoring the subject of sacrifice entirely.

One could easily make sport of these two Musafs, the first for the tougher-minded who don't shrink from the fact that their forefathers slit the throats of bullocks, rams, lambs, goats, and doves in the Temple, the second for the squeamish who would rather not think about it. Yet when it comes to animal sacrifice, we are all squeamish today. It is a practice so foreign to us that we scarcely have any notion of what its sacredness was about or of why, for most of human history, religious ceremonies all over the world revolved around it.

Historically, if communal prayer took the place of animal sacrifice, animal sacrifice, as the Bible reminds us in the story of the binding of Isaac, took the place of human sacrifice. Early humanity worshiped its gods with the taking of human life because human life was the most precious thing it could give them. Animal life came next. And because, as the book of Deuteronomy tells us, *ha-dam hu ha-nefesh*, the blood is an animal's life, it commands us: "Only be sure that you eat not the blood.... thou shalt pour it upon the earth as water." The meat of the sacrifice is to be eaten and enjoyed. The blood is for God alone.

The flow of blood always shocks. It mesmerizes. Even cutting a finger sends a shiver of horror and excitement through us that no pain or ache can duplicate. The few drops that are quickly staunched by a Band-Aid are the life beginning to leave us. The blood gushing from an animal's throat at an altar needs no words. It is wordless prayer, just as prayer is bloodless sacrifice.

There is a logic in the absence of the Musaf in *Mishkan T'filah*. We are beyond all that now, so why mention it?

There is a logic in the emended Musaf of *Siddur Sim Shalom*, too. Our forefathers did what they did and we are not ashamed of it, but it would be absurd to want to do it ourselves. Let us therefore mention it—in the past tense.

There is only tradition in the Musaf of the *Koren Siddur*. All but the more hallucinatory Orthodox Jews know that the Temple will not be rebuilt in historical time and that animals will not again be slaughtered in it. And the great majority of them, if honest, would admit to being thankful that this is so.

But the traditional Musaf expresses a passionate wish. *And the additional offering of this Sabbath day we will prepare and offer before You in love*: it is the wish to be able to offer to God what is most precious—and what is most precious is not the words that we say day in and day out. Words are what the Siddur has accumulated, more and more of them, as though in the fear that there can never be enough. Some move us more and some move us less, but none grabs us and shakes us until we feel faint. We yearn for the prayer that cuts to the quick like a knife.

2010

The Robert Alter Version

R obert Alter's *The Hebrew Bible* is a stupendous achievement. The result of decades of work and consisting of over three thousand pages of translated text and commentary, it encompasses every one of the Bible's thirty-five books from Genesis to Chronicles. One might call it the translator's equivalent of a solo circumnavigation of the globe were it not that sailing a boat around the globe takes far less time.

Of the over one hundred English translations of the Bible (many revisions or adaptations of previous ones), almost all have been done by teams or committees. The 1611 King James Version, which was *the* Bible for generations of English readers and retains for many a hallowedness that no other English Bible has, was the work of forty-seven scholars pooling their knowledge, skills, and judgments. All of the better-known modern English Bibles—the *Revised Standard Version of the Bible* (1901), the *Jewish Publication Society Bible* (1917), the *New English Bible* (1946), the *Good News Bible* (1976), the *New International Version of the Bible* (1978), the *New Jerusalem Bible* (1985), the *New Living Translation Bible* (1996), the *Holman Christian Standard Bible* (2004), the *New Jewish Publication Society Bible* (1985), the *ArtScroll English Tanach* (1996), and the *Anchor Bible Series* (initiated in 1956 and now nearing completion), to mention some—have been joint efforts. Not even the King James's two great predecessors that were named for single translators, the fourteenth-century

Wycliffe Bible and the sixteenth-century Tyndale Bible, were actually done single-handedly.

What English Bibles before Alter's were? The brief list includes Robert Young's *Young's Literal Translation of the Holy Bible* (1862), Julia E. Smith Parker's *The Holy Bible* (1876), Ferrar Fenton's *The Holy Bible in Modern English* (1903), James Moffat's *The Old Testament: A New Translation* (1924), George Lamsa's *Lamsa's Bible* (1933), and Eugene H. Peterson's *The Message: The Bible in Contemporary Language* (2002). I know of no others.

Each of these translators had his or her reasons for undertaking the task. Young, an autodidactic Scotsman and Christian missionary, thought that all prior translations of the Hebrew Bible had strayed from its wording and misunderstood its tense system; in fact, the one to misunderstand Hebrew tenses was Young himself. Smith, also self-taught, was the daughter of a Connecticut congregational minister. She said of the Bible, "I do not see how anyone can know more about it than I do," and produced a grotesquely unreadable version of it.

Lamsa, an Assyrian Christian, espoused the dubious theory that the Peshitta, the ancient Syriac version of the Bible, was more accurate than the Hebrew Masoretic text and should be relied on instead. Fenton was a London businessman with a belief in the compatibility of the Bible and science, an interest in Oriental poetry, and the conviction that he had discovered the metrical principles behind "the varied and beautiful forms of ancient Hebrew versification." Some of his translations of biblical poetry were quite good. Those of biblical prose were less so. The King James begins, "In the beginning God created the heaven and the earth. And the Earth was without form and void, and darkness was upon the face of the deep. And the Spirit of God moved upon the face of the waters." Fenton rendered these verses, "By periods God created that which produced the Solar Systems, then that which produced the Earth. But the Earth was unorganized and empty, and darkness covered its convulsed surface while the breath of God rocked the surface of its waters." "Convulsed surface" for the Hebrew *tehom,* "abyss" or "depths," presumably alludes to volcanic activity in the Precambrian Era.

Petersen's *Message Bible* is no less bizarre. A Presbyterian minister and popular author with an MA in Semitic languages, he intended it to be English's first thoroughly colloquial Scripture. In this, he may have succeeded only too well. His Genesis starts: "First this: God created the Heaven and Earth—all you see, all you don't see! Earth was a soup of nothingness, a bottomless emptiness, an inky blackness."

Of all these figures, Moffat alone was an academically trained scholar, a professor of Greek and Bible at Oxford, Yale, and Union Theological Seminary. His goal, as he put it, was a modern translation in "effective, intelligible English" that would reflect the latest advances in biblical source criticism. Seeking, for instance, to harmonize the so-called Elohistic strand of chapter 1 of Genesis with the Jehovistic strand of chapter 2, he wove them into a single account with the editorial introduction: "This is the story of how the universe was formed. When God began to form the universe, the world was void and vacant, darkness lay over the abyss." "This is the story," sounds suspiciously like, "This is *a* story—rest assured that there are others just as good."

And now we have Alter. Today a professor emeritus at the University of California in Berkeley, he has, like Moffat, the most solid of academic backgrounds, though not in biblical studies but in Hebrew and European literature, on which he has published widely. His writings on the Bible began with several essays in *Commentary* in the 1970s, which led to his *The Art of Biblical Narrative* (1981) and *The World of Biblical Literature* (1991); then came translations of Genesis in 1996 and the two books of Samuel in 1999, followed by the rest of the biblical corpus. A leading advocate of the view, rarely voiced before the mid-twentieth century, that the Bible needs to be read as great literature and not just for its religious or historical content, he has sought to bring this perspective to bear on its translation.

The authors of the great works of the Bible, Alter has consistently argued (most recently in his new book *The Art of Bible Translation*), were highly self-conscious poets and prose writers whose artistry has been ignored or inadequately dealt with by nearly all their modern translators. Their choice of words, the construction of their sentences, the cadences of their language, their use of word play and sound play—attention to these and other literary elements has been unjustly subordinated to the truths these authors are thought to have been seeking to convey and to our understanding of the times in which they sought to convey them.

The first two lines of Alter's Bible are, "When God began to create heaven and earth, and the earth then was welter and waste and darkness over the deep, and God's breath hovering over the waters." They illustrate several of his main points about biblical language and its translation. He preserves, because he thinks it stylistically crucial, the Bible's repetitive use of the paratactic "and" instead of varying it with other conjunctions like "while," "then," and "but," or eliminating it completely, as many modern translations do. He translates *ru'ah elohim* as "God's breath" rather than "God's spirit" because "breath" has more of what he calls the "Bible's extraordinary concreteness" (*ru'ah* also means "wind") and better evokes the mysterious force blowing over the depths. He alliterates "welter and waste" to parallel the Hebrew rhyme of *tohu-va'vohu,* the King James' "without form and void." He seeks to reproduce the Hebrew's strong cadences, as in "and the éarth then was wélter and wáste and dárkness over the déep." He eschews all rhetorical paraphrases like Petersen's "soup of nothingness" and "inky blackness," which he considers a bane of modern Bible translation.

All this works well. Yet by now there are so many translations of the Bible that it is impossible to be terribly original. Alter's decision, based on grammatical considerations already discussed by the medieval exegetes, to translate the Hebrew's initial words of *b'reshit bara* by revocalizing them as *b'reshit b'ro,* "When God began to create," has its English predecessors, of whom Moffat may have been the first. Moffat's alliterative "void and vacant" anticipates Alter's "welter and waste." Alter's principled retention of the biblical "and" was also the policy of the King James. His "breath" instead of "spirit" is found in Fenton. And Fenton, while his opening verses of Genesis are laughable, insisted on the importance of rhythm in translating biblical Hebrew long before Alter did.

The merit of Alter's Genesis 1:1-2, therefore, lies less in any single feature than in its overall configuration. This is true of his entire translation.

It is sensitive to the flow and texture of the Bible's language; its choices are judicious; there are no egregious lapses of taste in it; no translator's "Look at me!" or "Can you beat this?" It pays the Bible the respect of treating it as the work of great writers whose mastery needs to be conveyed by literary stratagems that are devoid of whims and eccentricities. To call it the best solo English Bible to date may not, given the competition, be saying much. But one is also tempted to call it the best modern English Bible, period—an opinion with which Alter himself appears to agree. While he states his admiration for the King James often, his criticisms of all the English Bibles that have come after it are unsparing.

Can the Alter Bible compete with the King James? This is not an entirely meaningful question because, like most other English Bibles, it owes so much to the King James that comparing the two is often comparing the King James to itself. Moreover, the contemporaneity of Alter's language as opposed to the King James's can be simultaneously a plus and a minus. Suppose, for example, we set the King James translation of Psalms 8:4, "What is man that thou art mindful of him? And the son of man, that thou visitest him?" alongside Alter's, "What is man that you should note him, and the human creature, that you should pay him heed?"

Since "son of man" is a literal rendering of the Hebrew *ben-adam* and not idiomatic English, and the verb "to visit" has lost its seventeenth-century meaning of "to attend to" or "to succor," the Alter translation makes more sense to us. Yet at the same time, "son of man," whose "man" is both the separate father of each of us and the first father of us all, gives the verse a poetic depth that "human creature" does not have, and there is a wondrousness about God's "visiting" someone even if we no longer use the verb in this fashion. After all, the Hebrew *ki tifkedenu,* the King James's "that thou visitest him," is archaic today, too. Why should we read the Bible in an English that is more comfortably up-to-date than the Hebrew?

On the whole, there are places where the Alter Bible surpasses the King James and places where it falls short of it, frequently in close proximity. Take the well-known theophany in chapter 6 of Isaiah. Here is the King James version of it:

> In the year that king Uzziah died I saw also the Lord sitting upon a throne, high and lifted up, and his train filled the temple. Above it stood the seraphims: each one had six wings; with twain he covered his face, and with twain he covered his feet, and with twain he did fly. And one cried unto another, and said: Holy, holy, holy, is the Lords of hosts: the whole earth is full of his glory.

And here is Alter:

> In the year of the death of King Uzziah, I saw the Master seated on a high and lofty throne, and the skirts of his robe filled the Temple. Seraphim were stationed over him, six wings for each one. With two it would cover its face, and with two it would cover its feet, and with two it would hover. And each called out to each and said: "Holy, holy, holy, is the Lord of armies. The fullness of all the earth is his glory."

Several things strike one as superior in Alter's translation:

1. "In the year of the death of King Uzziah," suggests a memorable year more than does, "In the year that king Uzziah died." Uzziah ruled over Judah for four decades. Isaiah speaks of the year of his death as a milestone. Alter conveys this better.
2. There is no good reason for the "also" in the King James's, "I saw also the Lord." It is not in the Hebrew text and Alter's omission of it is justified.
3. "On a high and lofty throne," is better than, "upon a throne, high and lifted up." "Lifted up" implies a lifter. There is no such implication in the Hebrew.

4. The monosyllabically metrical, "And éach called óut to éach," has a more powerful impact than does, "And one cried unto another."

Such improvements, however, are offset by other things. Alter's choice of "Master" instead of "Lord" is a poor one. Though formed from *adon,* "master," Hebrew *adonai* can only (and regularly does in the Bible and Jewish prayer) refer to God, and the awesomeness of Isaiah's divine vision is ill-served by a word whose referents—one thinks of slave masters, schoolmasters, housemasters, Hasidic masters, Zen masters—are purely human.

Even more unfortunate is Alter's "Lord of Armies" for the Hebrew's *adonai tsva'ot,* in place of the King James's "Lord of hosts." True, the plural Hebrew noun *ts'va'ot* literally means "armies." But the army in the biblical expression *ts'va ha-shamayim,* "the army of heaven," is not a military force. It is a corps of celestial bodies and beings, from stars to angels, enlisted in the service of God, and "the host of the heavens" or "the heavenly host" is the traditional term for it found in almost every English Bible starting with Wycliffe.

Alter's rejection of this term with its aura of solemn mystery is difficult to fathom, especially because it is opposed to his own guidelines. With its driving rhythm and alliteration of "holy" and "hosts," "Holy, holy, holy, is the Lord of hosts," is acoustically faithful to the Hebrew's *kadósh, kadósh, kadósh, adonái ts'va'ót,* whose stressed final *o*-vowel in *tsva'ot* echoes the same vowel in *kadosh.* "Holy, Holy, Holy, is the Lord of armies," goes lame at the end. And why, though it can be justified grammatically, "the fullness of the earth is his glory," when the King James's simpler, "the whole earth is full of his glory," is both more intelligible and more communicative of the Seraphim's excitement? Perhaps the best explanation of such choices is what might be called translator's ennui—the feeling that, it being dull work always to adopt a universally followed precedent, one should sometimes try something different. There is no need to be a partisan of committees to observe that, had Alter been on one, a fellow member would have raised a red flag at this point.

In an even better-known passage—given the contemporary attention that has been paid to it, it may be the Bible's best-known of all—Alter cites precedent for breaking with precedent. Here is his Genesis 22:1-5:

> And it happened after these things that God tested Abraham. And he said to him, "Abraham!" and he said, "Here I am." And He said, "Take, pray, your son, your only one, whom you love, Isaac, and go forth to the land of Moriah and offer him up as a burnt-offering on one of the mountains which I shall say to you." And Abraham rose early in the morning and saddled his donkey and took his two lads with him, and Isaac his son, and he split wood for the offering, and rose and went to the place that God had said to him. On the third day Abraham raised his eyes and saw the place from afar. And Abraham said to his lads, "Sit you here with the donkey and let me and the lad walk ahead and let us worship and return to you."

By way of contrast, this is the New Jewish Publication Society translation:

> Sometime afterward, God put Abraham to the test. He said to him, "Abraham," and he answered, "Here I am." And he said, take your son, your favored one, Isaac, whom you love, and go to the land of Moriah, and offer him there as a burnt offering on one of the heights that I will point out to you." So early the next morning, Abraham saddled his ass and took with him two of his servants and his son Isaac. He split the wood for the burnt offering and he set out for the place of which God had told him. On the third day Abraham looked up and he saw the place from afar. Then Abraham said to his servants, "You stay here with the ass. The boy and I will go up there; we will worship and we will return to you."

A comparison of these two versions demonstrates how right Alter is about the biblical "and," which the New JPS version, while retaining in some places, omits in six others and changes in still others to "so" and "then." The "ands" create a series of discrete events, none of which governs the next one. All are equal links in a terrible chain that Abraham is free to break at any point. When the New JPS gives us, "So early the next morning, Abraham saddled his ass," it is telling us: *Well, of course. Abraham has decided to go to Mount Moriah to sacrifice his son, so he has to saddle up.* When the Alter Bible opts for the more literal "And Abraham rose early in the morning and saddled his donkey," what we hear is: *No! Abraham does not have to do this. Each time he proceeds, he makes a choice. Each time he can say, "I'm not going ahead with this."* The "ands" expand each moment to its maximum extent. At each, Abraham has a chance to turn back. At each, he must firm up his resolve all over again. At each, he comes closer to killing his son. At each, every step becomes harder.

Father and son reach Mount Moriah. The Alter translation continues:

> And Abraham took the wood for the offering and put it
> on Isaac his son, and he took in his hand the fire and the
> cleaver, and the two of them went together.

The *cleaver*? Other English Bible translations have "the knife." With a knife, Abraham will slit Isaac's throat as one slaughters an animal. With a cleaver...but let's look at Alter's always helpful commentary, which is one of his Bible's best features:

> *the cleaver:* E.A. Speiser notes, quite rightly, that the
> Hebrew term here is not the usual biblical term for knife
> and makes a good argument that it is a cleaver. Other
> terms for butchering, rather than sacrifice, are used [fur-
> ther on in the story].

The scholar Ephraim Avigdor Speiser, in his translation of Genesis in the Anchor Bible series, indeed gives us "cleaver" and observes in a note that it is the right term for "the pertinent Hebrew noun (see also Judges 19:29 and Proverbs 30:14)."

The "pertinent noun" is *ma'akhelet,* formed from the verb *akhal,* to eat or devour. Let us turn, as Speiser suggests we do, to Judges 19:29. This verse comes at the end of a chapter narrating the rape of a traveling Israelite's concubine by the townsmen of Gibeah. In Alter's translation of it:

> And he... took a cleaver [*ma'akhelet*] and held his concubine and cut her up limb by limb into twelve pieces, and he sent her through all the territory of Israel. And so whoever saw her would say, "There has not been nor has there been seen such a thing from the day the Israelites came up from the land of Egypt."

This is frightful. The traveler wishes to incite the tribes of Israel against the inhabitants of Gibeah and succeeds, whereupon a war breaks out between them and the tribe of Benjamin, in whose territory Gibeah is located.

And Abraham, who has staked his own and his son's life (for in the context of the story, the two are inseparable) on his faith that somehow, in some way he does not understand, God will keep His promise that "through Isaac your seed will be acclaimed?"

Alter doesn't ask in his commentary why Abraham should have brought along a cleaver instead of a knife, nor does Speiser. This forces us to do it. Is it Abraham's plan that, if not stopped from going through with the sacrifice of Isaac, he will then butcher and dress him, arrange the pieces on the altar, and burn them as the offering he was told to make for their pleasing or sickening smell to pierce God's nostrils?

Or will he do what the traveling Israelite did? There are no tribes of Israel to send the pieces of Isaac to. Will he send them to the seven peoples of Canaan, the Canaanites, the Hittites, the Jebusites, the Amorites, the Perezites, and the Girgasites, for them to say, "There has not been nor has there been seen such a thing from the day crazy Abraham listened to his crazy God and came to this land from Ur of the Chaldees?"

In all likelihood, *ma'akhelet* does not mean "cleaver" in the story of Abraham and Isaac, although it may have that meaning in the book of Judges or be a general term for a large cutting instrument. Contrary to Alter's assertion, there is no "usual" biblical word for a knife. *Sakin,* the rabbinic and modern word that Hebrew shares with Aramaic, occurs in the Bible only once. The earliest Bible translation, the Greek Septuagint, renders *ma'akhelet* as *mákhaira,* a large knife or dagger. The next earliest, the rabbinic translation into Aramaic known as the Targum, has *sakin.* Jerome's Latin Vulgate has *glaudium* or "sword," but Jerome was probably thinking of a long slaughterer's knife with a curved tip such as is portrayed in the sixth-century C.E. synagogue mosaic of the binding of Isaac at the Israeli archeological site of Bet Alfa. This certainly seems more plausible than a cleaver. As Alter writes in *The Art of Biblical Translation,* "You cannot determine the meaning of biblical words without taking into consideration their narrative or poetic contexts." He might have profitably heeded his own advice in this case.

But the problem of determining what the Bible is telling us so as to be able to convey it in translation goes beyond the meaning of specific words. Alter makes an important point when he writes in his introduction to *The Hebrew Bible,* "Beyond issues of syntax and local word choice lies a fundamental question that no modern translator I know of has really confronted: What level, or perhaps levels, of style is represented in biblical Hebrew?"

Though the Bible is the most studied book in history, we often simply don't know.

Consider another biblical story thematically related to the binding of Isaac, that of Jephthah's sacrifice of his daughter. It, too, occurs in the book of Judges, in which Jephthah is an Israelite warrior, or perhaps one should say gang leader, living east of the Jordan, beyond the mountains of Gilead; the son of a prostitute, he has gathered around him a fighting force of "no-account men." When the Gileadites, his fellow Israelites, appeal to him to rescue them from their Ammonite enemies, he agrees and leads this force into battle. First, though, in Alter's translation,

> Jephthah made a vow to the Lord and said, "If you indeed give the Ammonites into my hands, it shall be that whatever comes out of the door of my house to meet me when I return safe and sound from the Ammonites shall be the Lord's, and I shall offer it up as a burnt offering."

Like every translator of this passage, Alter had to make a hard call, because the words rendered by him as "whatever comes out of the door of my house"—*v'hayah ha-yotsey asher yetsey mi-daltey veyti*, literally, "the comer-out that comes out of the doors of my house"—can also be translated, as he notes in his commentary, as "*whoever* comes out of the door of my house." This ambiguity, on which the story hangs, cannot be preserved in English, in which a translator must come down on one side or the other. Wycliffe opted for "whoever" and "I shall offer him up"; Tyndale for "that thing that cometh out" and "I will offer it"; the King James for "whatsoever" and "it"; modern translators have gone both ways, with Alter following Tyndale and the King James.

Jephthah wins his battle against the Ammonites and returns triumphantly home. Alter's Judges relates:

> And Jepthah came to his house at Mizpah, and, look, his daughter was coming out to meet him with timbrels and with dances, and she was an only child – besides her, he had neither son nor daughter. And it happened when he saw her, that he rent his garments, and he said, "Alas, my daughter, you have indeed laid me low and you have joined ranks with my troublers, for I myself have opened my mouth to the Lord, and I cannot turn back." And she said to him, "My father, you have opened your mouth to the Lord. Do to me as it came out from your mouth, after the Lord has wreaked vengeance for you

from your enemies, from the Ammonites." And she said to her father, "Let this thing be done for me: let me be for two months, that I may go and weep on the mountains and keen for my maidenhood, I and my companions." And he said, "Go." And he sent her off for two months, her and her companions, and she keened for her maiden-hood on the mountains. And it happened at the end of the two months, that she came back to her father, and he did to her as he had vowed, and she had known no man.

This is heart-wrenching. Our hearts go out to them both, the virginal daughter who must die and the grieving father who must put her to death. It is only on second thought that we think: "Just a minute! *Must* he? And does he grieve for her at all?"

Let us consider his situation. It is not like Abraham's. Jephthah has not been commanded by God to take his daughter's life. He has made a mindlessly phrased vow, his intention (giving him the benefit of the doubt) having been to sacrifice a "what," not a "who," a farmyard animal rather than a human being. Only when his daughter is the first to emerge from the house does he realize he has been trapped by his own words.

But there is a difference between being mindless and being mon-strous. Which is the Jephthah who says, "Alas, my daughter, you have indeed laid me low and you have joined ranks with my troublers?"

You have indeed laid me low and you have joined ranks with my trou-blers? What kind of language is this? Who talks this way to a daughter when telling her he is going to kill her?

In the Hebrew, Jephthah's exclamation is, *"Aha, biti! Hakhre'a hikhra'tini, v'at hayit b'okhrai."* This is difficult. If one were to try trans-lating it literally, one might arrive at something like, "Ah, my daughter! To bring to knee have you brought me to my knees, and you have been one of my troublers." The "to bring to knee you have brought me to my knees" construction, formed in this case from the verb *kara',* "to kneel," is a common biblical one known as the infinitive absolute; consisting of a twice-repeated verb, first in its infinitive form and then in an inflected

HILLEL HALKIN

one, it makes it more emphatic and is often translated with the help of "surely" or "indeed," as Alter does here. As for *okhrai*, it comes from the verb *akhar*, to muddy or trouble, as in the muddying or "troubling" of water; hence, "one of my troublers." Yet when Ahab says to Elijah in the book of Kings, "Is that you, you *okher* of Israel?" he is clearly calling him a trouble*maker*, which is what Jephthah appears to be calling his daughter, too. And he is also engaging in word play, since *hakhre'a, hikhra'tini*, and *okhrai* echo each other's consonants.

How to translate this?

As Alter does?

As, "Ah, my daughter, you are my undoing! Look at what you have done"?

As, "Damn it, child! You've tripped me up and trouble is all you are"?

To answer the question, we would have to be able to say what "level of style" Jephthah is resorting to—and we can't speak with any confidence about styles of Israelite speech three thousand years ago. Jephthah could be talking "high" or "low," in stilted rhetoric or in the spontaneous language of the street. His utterance could be the literary flourish of an author or the outburst of a man blurting words whose sounds lead him unthinkingly from one to the next. It's anyone's guess—and rather than guess, translators faced with such dilemmas have often preferred the safety of following in their predecessors' footsteps. Thus, we have Tyndale ("Alas, my daughter, thou hast made me stoop and art one of them that trouble me."), the King James ("Alas, my daughter! thou has brought me very low and thou art one of them that trouble me."), and Alter, with little difference between them, although the potential for difference is great.

The Bible is often like this. Its translators work in a closed circle. To understand the nuance of a line, they must understand the passage in which it occurs, but they cannot understand the passage without understanding each line's nuance. Before objecting that "Damn it, child!" can't possibly be the tone in which Jephthah is speaking, we need to consider how self-centered he is depicted as being. He has made a rash vow that his daughter had no way of knowing about—she runs excitedly out to greet him when he returns from battle—for this he decides she must die—and all he can do is blame her while thinking of his own predicament. It's her fault! How could she have done this to him? Just look at what she's gotten him into!

Jephthah's subsequent behavior would seem to reflect no better on him. When his daughter asks for a two month stay of her sentence so that she may mourn in the mountains with her friends, all he can manage is a gruff, "Go!" Not once during those months are we told that he attempts to see her. He simply waits for her to return, confident that she will, and when she does, "he did to her as he had vowed." It never occurs to him that he needn't keep his vow—that he can swallow his pride or sense of honor, admit he has made a foolish mistake, and spare his daughter's life. He won't have been the first Israelite to have broken a vow and he won't be the last.

But that, you say, is the whole point! Jephthah isn't just another Israelite. He is a God-fearing one, and he has made a promise to God that he must keep. He is a tragic victim of fate, not a monster. He stresses his own feelings because he is devastated by them—that's why we are told he rends his clothes. He says "Go!" and no more because he is too choked by emotion to say another word. He lets his daughter wander for two months in the mountains in the hope that she will flee and not return. She comes back anyway because she is her father's child and thinks, like him, that a vow is a vow. Our hearts go out to them both.

The ancient rabbis thought that Jephthah had misunderstood the story of Abraham and Isaac by not realizing that its test was meant for Abraham alone. God's relationship with Abraham is unique. The two have gambled everything on each other. This has nothing to do with Jephthah, whose situation is entirely of his own making. In the Midrash Tanchuma we read:

> Because Jephthah the Gileadite had no knowledge of Torah, he lost his daughter.... When he sought to sacrifice her, she wept and said: "Father, I came out joyously

to greet you and you would slaughter me? Did God say in his Torah that we should sacrifice human life to him?"

The misunderstanding was not just Jephthah's. Pretending to go with her friends to the mountains, his daughter, according to Tanchuma, went to Jerusalem to ask the Sanhedrin (which historically, of course, did not exist at the time) to absolve her father of his vow but could not get it to do so because it, too, failed to interpret the law correctly. When she was offered up on the altar,

> God's Holy Spirit cried, "Did I ask for human sacrifice? I never commanded it... I never intended Abraham to slaughter his son... .nor asked Jephthah to sacrifice his daughter.

Much of the Bible is about God's commandments and the human judgment that must be exercised in obeying them. Many of them are purely ritual. Alter translates these faithfully, even though one would be hard-pressed to find literary merit in passages like,

> And you shall do a burnt offering, a fragrant odor to the Lord, one bull from the herd, one ram, seven unblemished yearling lambs. And their grain offering mixed with oil, three-tenths for the bull, two-tenths for the ram. And one-tenth for each lamb of the seven lambs.

But what about this?

> And it happened on the third day as it turned morning, that there was thunder and lightning and a heavy cloud on the mountains and the sound of the ram's horn, very strong...And God spoke all these words, saying: "I am the Lord your God who brought you out of the land of Egypt, out of the house of slaves. You shall have no other gods beside Me.... You shall not take the name of

the Lord your God in vain, for the Lord will not acquit whoever takes His name in vain.... You shall not murder. You shall not commit adultery. You shall not steal. You shall not bear false witness against your fellow man. You shall not covet your fellow man's house. You shall not covet your fellow man's wife, or his male slave, or his slave girl, or his ox, or his donkey, or anything that your fellow man has."

Jephthah must decide which commandment matters more, "You shall not take the name of the Lord your God in vain" or "You shall not murder," and he decides badly. This is a story that can be read as literature. But can the Ten Commandments themselves be read that way? And why do they not affect us as powerfully in Alter's translation as they do in the King James Version? There we read:

And it came to pass on the third day in the morning, that there were thunders and lightnings, and a thick cloud upon the mount, and the voice of the trumpet exceeding loud.... And God spake all these words, saying,
I am the Lord thy God, which have brought thee out of the land of Egypt, out of the house of bondage.
Thou shalt have no other gods before thee...
Thou shalt not take the name of the Lord thy God in vain; for the Lord will not hold him guiltless that taketh his name in vain....
Thou shalt not kill.
Thou shalt not commit adultery.
Thou shalt not steal.
Thou shalt not bear false witness against thy neighbor.
Thou shalt not covet thy neighbor's house, thou shalt not covet thy neighbor's wife, nor his manservant, nor his maidservant, nor his ox, nor his ass, nor anything that is thy neighbor's.

One reason that Alter's rendering is weaker is that it does not, as does the King James, allow each commandment its own space. Such spacing goes back to the Masoretic text and the traditionally written Torah scroll, in which every commandment, while not occupying a separate line as in the King James, is set off by an empty half line on either side of it. Into this emptiness, a moment's lull, as it were, in the roar of the thunder and the bellowing of the ram's horn, God's voice comes crashing. *Thou shalt not kill.* Lightning! Thunder! The ram's horn! *Thou shalt not commit adultery.* Lightning! Thunder! The ram's horn! The people are terrified. "Speak you with us that we may hear," they say to Moses, "and let not God speak with us lest we die."

There is no reason why Alter could not have followed the King James in this or reproduced the Masoretic format. Even if he wanted to, however, he could not have compensated for English's loss of the pronoun "thou," the intimate form of "you" still possessed by most European languages. "You shall not steal" and "Thou shalt not steal" are not quite the same thing. "You" can be either singular or plural and addressed to everyone. "Thou" is addressed to me alone. I am the person in the crowd at whom it points its finger and says, "You there, I'm talking to *you!*"

The Bible points to each one of us. It says, *I may be masterfully written, but this is only a means to an end. The end is your obedience. Do not mislead yourself into thinking it is anything else.*

No one has put it better than Erich Auerbach. It was Auerbach, then a Jewish refugee from Nazi Germany living and teaching in Istanbul, who wrote, in the 1940s, the first serious literary analysis of biblical narrative style. In his great book *Mimesis,* the opening chapter of which compares the prose of Homer's *Odyssey* to that of the story of the sacrifice of Isaac, he writes:

> One can perfectly well entertain historical doubts on the subject of the Trojan War or of Odysseus' wanderings, and still, when reading Homer, feel precisely the effects he sought to produce; but without believing in Abraham's sacrifice, it is impossible to put the narrative

of it to the use for which it was written. Indeed, we must go even further. The Bible's claim to truth is not only far more urgent than Homer's, it is tyrannical—it excludes all other claims.... The Scripture stories do not, like Homer's, court our favor, they do not flatter us that they may please us and enchant us—they seek to subject us, and if we refused to be subjected, we are rebels.

Reading the Bible as literature remains an act of rebellion today, if not against a divine giver of it who no longer commands our credence, then against the Bible itself, which does not wish to be read in this way. It is to read the Bible not so much without faith as in bad faith, although what better faith can be hoped for from the faithless than the faith in literature, which alone holds that every word in the Bible counts even if it is not God's, would be hard to say.

2019

Sailing to Ithaca

I first set foot on the island of Ithaca by swimming ashore. This was not how it was done by Odysseus, who was carried from a ship in early dawn by the sailors conveying him on the final leg of his long journey home. "Then they stepped forth on the land," Homer tells us, "and first they lifted Odysseus out of the hollow ship… and laid him down on the sand, still overpowered by sleep." He would have had to be sleeping quite soundly not to awake, for we have just been told that, in beaching, the ship "ran full half her length on the shore in her swift course, at such a pace was she driven by the arms of the rowers." That must have given her a powerful jolt.

One cannot beach a modern yacht, which has a keel to give it stability in the water. Ancient Greek ships lacked true keels and so—at least to judge from Homer—they often capsized in rough seas. Nor did ancient Greek harbors have docks or piers. The Greek coast is rugged and its mountains continue their plunge beneath the water line, making the drop-off too steep to allow for the sinking of pilings in Homer's time. And while one could always moor or anchor offshore, this made loading and unloading cumbersome. The best harbor was a protected spot with enough sand or gravel for oarsmen to put a ship on.

Our yacht, chartered on the nearby island of Levkos, had cast anchor in a little cove. It was morning and the turquoise transparency of the water, through which the anchor seemed to ripple on the bottom, was still unruffled by the day's breezes. The first to dive into it, I swam to land.

The little beach was small and pebbly, boxed in by the headlands of the cove. At its rear, where it ran for a few yards before starting up the mountainside, grew an olive tree and some mastic and burnet bushes, typical scrub of the eastern Mediterranean. I could have been anywhere on the Greek or Turkish coast. But I wasn't. I was dripping wet on Ithaca, as excited as on the day when, a twenty-one-year-old student of English literature from New York City, I stepped off the *Queen Elizabeth* onto English soil.

What does a twenty-one-year-old student of English literature do upon disembarking at Southampton on a summer day in 1960? He takes a train to London and another to Cambridge, where he is going to study; stows his luggage with the trunk that has arrived in advance; returns to London with a backpack in which is a copy of *The Canterbury Tales*; and walks, like Chaucer's pilgrims, fifty miles to the cathedral in Canterbury, arriving with blisters on his feet and a sour stomach from too many unripe apples picked and eaten along the way.

Actually, English literature didn't have to wait that long. On the London underground, on my way to King's Cross Station and thence to Cambridge, I struck up a conversation with a young man from the Caribbean. Hearing that these were my first minutes in London, he surprised me by asking, "If there was one place in this city you would like me to take you to, what would it be?"

"You wouldn't have heard of it," I told him.

"Try me."

"Keats's cottage."

"In Hampstead? Let's go!"

And so, lugging my suitcase, I got off at the next station and followed him to the home of John Keats. O blessed land in which even the immigrants on your underground are versed in the lives of your great poets!

I have always been a book-driven traveler. When I was eighteen, two weeks after obtaining my driver's license, I talked a friend into buying an old Dodge and setting out with me for Mexico on the sole strength of having read D. H. Lawrence's *The Plumed Serpent*. *The Plumed Serpent* had as much to do with the real Mexico as the *Bagavad-Gita* has to do with the real India, but I was quite sure that it and a Spanish grammar were the only guidebooks we needed. More precisely, I thought of Mexico as a guide to *The Plumed Serpent*. To my mind, countries existed as illustrations for books.

This was why, when one of my two partners in the twenty-four-foot sailboat we own asked if I would join a group planning to cruise in the Ionian islands off the west coast of Greece, I agreed despite not caring much for yacht trips. After a day or two of them, I'm starved for solitude. Although you might think there would be plenty of that out on the water, a yacht is basically a small, floating apartment shared with several roommates—the difference being that if you quarrel with one of them, or weary of their small talk, you can't go out for a walk. It takes a nature more gregarious than mine to look forward to that.

But the Ionian islands meant Ithaca, and Ithaca meant *The Odyssey*, and *The Odyssey* is a book I have cherished. Several years ago I made a list of the things I most wanted to do before I died. One of them was learning enough Greek to read *The Odyssey* in the language Homer wrote it in. Poetry, not just as language heightened, but as language transformed, its particles fused into rare new elements, begins with Homer. The wine-dark sea! The rose-fingered dawn! No book has lovelier phrasing. How could I have been so foolish in college as to major in English, which I needed no instruction to read, when I could have been studying Greek? How not sail to Ithaca now?

When Odysseus awakes on shore, the sailors are gone and he does not know at first where he is. He has been away for twenty years—ten fighting before the walls of Troy and ten striving to return to the island he once ruled and left a wife and infant son on, detained by the sea-god Poseidon whose wrath he has incurred. "Therefore," Homer says, "all things seemed strange... He sprang up and stood and looked upon his native land...and said, 'Woe is me, to the land of what mortals am I now come?'"

Could the beach I was on be the very spot he was carried ashore at? That one also had "two protecting headlands sheer to seaward" and "a long-leafed olive tree," plus a "pleasant, shadowy cave sacred to the nymphs that are called Naiads." But it wasn't likely. Although Ithaca is a small island barely twelve miles long, its two halves joined by a narrow isthmus, we had already passed, sailing up its eastern coast from Levkos, several coves with beaches like this one. And from where I sat, there wasn't a cave in sight.

Indeed, it turns out that there isn't a cave corresponding to the Naiads' within easy walking distance of any of Ithaca's beaches. Nor, apart from Mount Neritos, the island's dominant peak, is it possible to identify a single place from Homer's descriptions, some of which are manifestly wrong. Take the nearby and much larger island of Cephalonia, itself of literary fame since the publication of Louis de Bernières's best-selling 1994 novel *Captain Corelli's Mandolin*, subsequently made into a star-studded movie. So close a neighbor is Cephalonia that its higher mountains literally cast their evening shadows over Ithaca. Yet whereas Ithaca is due east of Cephalonia, lying between it and the Greek mainland, Homer, after observing correctly that Ithaca "lies low in the sea by comparison," positions it "further toward the dark" and away from "the dawn and the sun"—that is, to Cephalonia's west.

Two schools of thought have arisen to account for such errors. One holds that Homer knew whereof he wrote but that names have shifted in the course of history, so that the Ithaca of Homer's age, which is generally assumed to have been the eighth century B.C.E., is not the Ithaca of today and should be identified with somewhere else in the vicinity. The second school holds that present-day Ithaca, whose demotic name of Thiaki shows every sign of having been handed down from antiquity, is indeed the Ithaca of Homer—who, however, was never there and had only a hazy idea of its geography. He set much of his epic poem on an island he hadn't been to because tradition held that his hero came from there, and he researched his work by asking travelers for information. One need only suppose that some of this was inaccurate, misremembered or garbled by him, to account for his mistakes.

The second explanation is more parsimonious, it being simpler to assume that Homer was never on Ithaca than that Ithaca was never on Ithaca. Not that, if Odysseus had lived on Cephalonia or Levkos, one's impressions of his native environment would differ greatly. While Ithaca's size seems better suited to the intimate, one-town island described by Homer, its "quivering-leaved" mountains, so much greener than those of the Aegean, and its "rock-girt" coast, banded above sea level by a belt of bare limestone as if to keep it from sliding into the water, are just as typical of its neighbors—"not one of which of those that slope abruptly to the sea," as Odysseus' son Telemachus remarks of their terrain, "is fit for driving horses, or rich in meadows, and Ithaca least of all."

Why care, then, if one is on the real Ithaca? And yet one does. It would make as much sense to tell someone searching for a grave in a cemetery that its exact location doesn't matter, since most tombstones look alike. The search is not for a different-looking grave, but for the right one.

Deep down, the dead live mysteriously on for us; this is the oldest layer of human religion and perhaps its sole ineradicable one. But like Odysseus' mother—who, when encountered by him in the underworld, proves ignorant of his wanderings while knowing everything about recent events on Ithaca—the dead cannot visit new places and return as ghosts only to where their memories can take them. This is why houses aren't haunted by those who haven't lived in them; why it mattered to think I was on Homer's Ithaca.

Apart from the episode in Hades, the dead are not prominent in *The Odyssey*. Although many of Odysseus' comrades and shipmates have perished, whether at Troy or on the journey home, the steady focus of the story is on him, his wife Penelope, and his son Telemachus—now a young man of twenty who sets out, even as his long-missing father nears Ithaca's shores, in search of some trace of him.

And yet *The Odyssey* is about loss, and as death is the ultimate loss, all other loss is its symbol. A man is gone from his home for twenty years. No known person has seen him for the last ten of these. The island's bachelors lounge insolently in his palace, drinking his wine and feasting on his flocks while wooing his wife, each determined to wed her and be king in his place. Although only she and her son, born on the eve of her husband's departure, still believe he may be alive, they, too, are on the verge of giving up hope as Homer's story begins. Surely, his return is as unlikely as a dead man's.

Every culture has its iconic story about the acceptance of death's finality. Ancient Greece had the myth of Orpheus, who travels to the dark underworld to retrieve his wife Eurydice, killed by a snakebite. His love for her is so great that he is given permission to return with her to the land of the living, on the condition that he not look back as she follows him. Yet at the last moment, as he is about to step into the sunlight, he turns to make sure she is there and at once she vanishes. Who of us has not been Orpheus in our dream-lives, reunited in sleep with the dead we have loved only to lose them again to the light of day?

The Odyssey, by comparison, is a fully awake book. Despite its man-eating Cyclops, its fatal Sirens, and its other mythological figures, it takes place in a Mediterranean sunlight so strong that even the gods who are ostensibly the puppet masters of its plot fade into insubstantiality. Homer's gods are dramatic characters whose sometimes comic, sometimes petulant speeches he grants himself full poetic license to invent; often they appear to be no more than the externalized embodiments of human moods or thoughts. It's hard to say whether he believed in them. Perhaps it would be better to call *The Odyssey* an almost fully awake book, written in that state after waking when one's dream images, though understood to be false, still exert a powerful impression.

Odysseus, in any case, is perfectly human. He has been away for twenty years, he is desperate to get home, and he is worried that when he gets there he will find his wife remarried or no longer in love with him, and his son a stranger. How will he appear to them? How will they appear to him? In every age men returning from long absence have had the same fears.

Twenty lost years, full of adventures. And this, too, is a reason for concern, because of adventures in those same years Penelope has had none. She has spent them in her chamber, weaving at her loom, listening to the carousing of the suitors in the great hall of the palace. What can she still feel for the man who has been away for so long? What can they still have in common?

When one speaks of loss, one speaks of things from the most trivial to the most terrible. The first thing I can remember losing in my life was a children's book that I loved. One day it disappeared. Nothing was more important than finding it. For years, long past the time when I would have deigned to read it, I dreamed of its reappearance. These were joyous dreams, and I awoke from them like Orpheus, clutching a ghost. Although I could easily have obtained another copy, that never occurred to me. Life had taken my book, and life, if it wished to prove its good intentions, would return it unprompted.

There is a phenomenology of loss that goes far beyond the value of what is lost. Everyone has had the experience of misplacing an everyday item—a cheap watch, a favorite pen, an old pocketknife—only to be stricken by a feeling of true grief. Presumably this is what we mean by ascribing to such things a "sentimental value," although we rarely reflect on the nature of the sentiment.

It is the same should we happen to come across one of them. Suddenly, long after we have given up the search, there it is, in the one drawer we neglected to look in, the pocket of the winter coat we stuck it in on the last cold day of the year. Naturally we are glad. But whence the disproportionate flood of gratitude that overwhelms us, as if we had found something of inestimable worth?

Loss has its hierarchies. These may start with a children's book. Then a family heirloom. Next, a disappointment in love or at work. Higher still, a home abandoned, a ruined marriage, a child estranged from its parents. And at the top, always, death itself. But because rung leads to rung, the lowest prefigures the highest. The lost book is the child's first premonition that there is nothing life cannot take from him; the dream of finding it his first hope that there is nothing it cannot restore.

I don't know what made a particular child grow up with this hope so much a part of him. Of major loss he knew, having had outwardly a very ordinary childhood, only the symbols. When he put aside children's books for real ones, however, he found that those that spoke to him most deeply were, or seemed to be in one way or another, about the restoration of loss.

And of these none more than *The Odyssey*, in which an exile strives to return, a woman unreasonably believes that he will, a boy who never knew him trusts he will reappear. And so he does, arriving in Ithaca to slay the insolent suitors and regain the wife he loves. Twenty years have not come between them. His son fights by his side and proves as worthy of him as he proves worthy of the boy.

Time and age are vanquished. Nothing has dulled Penelope's beauty or Odysseus's youthful looks and strength. They meet again as if parted for a month. "And when the two," Homer relates, "had had their fill of the joy of love, they took delight in tales, speaking each to the other. She, the fair lady, told of all that she had endured in the halls. But Zeus-born Odysseus recounted all the woes that he had brought on men, and all the toil that in his sorrow he had himself endured, and she was glad to listen, nor did sweet sleep fall upon her eyelids, till he had told all the tale."

Today, looking back, I am embarrassed to admit how a book like *The Odyssey* shaped me. By this I do not mean merely that I have been, though hardly of a serene cast of mind, an optimist for most of my life. While this is true, it is not saying much. Optimists believe in happy endings, not in the restoration of loss.

What is the difference? If the child were to get a new book, one he loved more than the first, this would be a happy ending. But it would not be the restoration of loss.

If Odysseus were to return to Ithaca and find Penelope, now the mother of many children, happily wed to a man whom Telemachus adores as his father, he would be desolate. He might rage, sink into a depression, even decide to resume his wanderings. Yet suppose that, just as he was about to set despairingly out again, he met a charming young widow, fell in love, and remarried. That would be a happy ending, but not the restoration of loss.

When I was in my twenties, I had a long, torturously romantic affair with a young woman that lasted, on and off, for seven years. It should have ended long before that. We were only making each other more and more unhappy. But so much had passed between us—so much love, anguish, perseverance, guilt, anger, reconciliation, and remorse—that it seemed inconceivable to have to cut our losses. Like a desperate gambler, the greater these grew, the more I doubled my bets. The wager was less on the two of us than on life itself. I would not let life be a thief. I would make it honor its debts to me.

—⁂—

Largely destroyed, like parts of many of the Ionian islands, in the great earthquake of 1953, Vathi, Ithaca's main town, consists of several streets running back from its port, which was deserted in midafternoon. The ports of the Greek islands fill up toward sunset, the yachts flocking to them like starlings to a roost. At night the crews crowd their restaurants, all with similar candlelit tables spread around similar waterfronts and offering similar menus. By midmorning the next day, the roosts are empty again.

The archeologists have found no signs of a Trojan War-period palace in Vathi, which—a naturally fortified spot at the sandy head of a bay entered by a narrow channel easily blocked from a small island in its middle—seems the logical place for a town to have stood in Odysseus's day. Possible royal ruins from the Homeric age have been unearthed near Stavros, in the island's interior, but this does not jibe with Homer's account. Besides, the taxi driver who took me to Stavros on a winding road along mountains that dropped abruptly to the sea, lifting his hands alarmingly from the steering wheel between one hairpin turn and the next to snap his fingers to the Greek music on the radio, explained, after pointing out a modern bust of Odysseus in the town square, that the ruins were on a distant hilltop that it would take hours to reach by foot. I would have to forgo them.

This bust was the only awareness of *The Odyssey* that I saw on the island. There was mercifully no Odyssey Café, no Calypso's Tavern, no

"Ithaca: Home of Homer" baseball caps or T-shirts on sale. Ithaca was not like Toledo, its souvenir stores stocked with endless figurines of Don Quixote, or Stratford with its Shakespeariana, all those tacky evocations of the past that frighten its real ghosts away. The yacht crews came in the evening and left in the morning. They sought quiet beaches, good winds, and a cold beer with their moussaka or fried calamari at the end of the day. They sat in the cockpits of their yachts after dinner, conversing in low voices, as in a summer bungalow colony in which, porch after porch, men and women talk far into the night to avoid the hot, sticky bedrooms that await them.

"Corelli's Ice Cream" said a sign in Poros, our first anchorage in Cephalonia, clear evidence that Nicolas Cage and Penelope Cruz can do more for an island than all the classics courses in the world. Yet *Captain Corelli's Mandolin*, which I had taken to read on our cruise, is a marvelous book. It gazes down at *The Odyssey* as Cephalonia gazes down at Ithaca. I finished it in Poros, reading its last chapters on deck, where I preferred to sleep, by the dawn light.

Its plot is simple. An Italian captain, a talented mandolinist named Antonio Corelli, is billeted during World War II in the home of a village doctor on—as the latter puts it in a local history he is writing—"the half-forgotten island of Cephalonia," then under Italian military occupation. Corelli and the doctor's young daughter Pelagia fall shyly and tenderly in love. When the German army brutally takes over the island after the anti- fascist uprising that overthrows Mussolini, the captain, saved from a close brush with death, is smuggled out of it. Before he leaves, he swears to Pelagia that he will return.

And return he does at the book's end—forty years later. He is by now an old, white-bearded man of seventy, and for years he has sent Pelagia mysterious, unsigned postcards from his wanderings all over the world. She, too, is bent and weary after a hard life. While she has a married daughter, a war foundling she raised, she has never married or even had a lover. Her memories of Corelli have usurped all else. Now, forty years later, she is furious. Her first words to him are Italian curses: "*Sporcaccione! Figlio d'un culo! Pezzo di merda!* All my life waiting, all my life mourning, all my life thinking you were dead. *Cazzo d'un cane!* And you alive, and me a fool. How dare you break such promises? Betrayer!"

It is a tragicomic moment. And to add to it, Corelli has actually been back to Cephalonia long before this. He has come as soon as the war ended, keeping his promise, only to catch sight of Pelagia, as he rounds the bend of the road to her house, holding the infant she adopted in her arms; wrongly assuming that she has married in his absence and had a child, he departs brokenheartedly. Throughout the years, he has never stopped loving her. Although they are now together again, they have been robbed of the life they might have had by a ridiculous twist of fate.

An ending more bitter than sweet, this was, it struck me, a scathing commentary on *The Odyssey*. Homer, *Captain Corelli's Mandolin* proclaims, is the liar that Plato long ago, for reasons of his own (Plato thought all poets lied), accused him of being. The warrior who comes home to his wife after twenty years, his comrades-in-arms dead, his crew drowned or slain, his ships repeatedly wrecked, cannot possibly be the man described in *The Odyssey* as going off to bed with Penelope "in form like unto the immortals." Or rather, he must be exactly like the man described in *The Odyssey*—who, when he awakes on the shores of Ithaca, is informed by his patron goddess Athena that she will disguise him and "shrivel the fair skin on thy supple limbs, destroy the flaxen hair from off thy head, and dim thy two eyes that were before so beautiful, that thou mayest appear mean in the sight of all the wooers, and of thy wife." It is not Athena who has done this to Odysseus but twenty years of war and wandering. The gods of *The Odyssey*, we have said, are often projections of human states.

And Penelope? She, too, must have been not "like unto Artemis or golden Aphrodite," as Homer calls her, but old and gray herself, embittered by the wasted years of her womanhood. What happiness can she have with this bald old man who has now come back, puckered by sea brine and wrinkled by the sun, to erase even her dearest memories of the handsome young husband who went off to war? What "fill of the joy of love"? The truest words spoken at *The Odyssey*'s end are hers when, responding to her husband's crestfallen anger at her initial failure to recognize him in his disguise, she says: "Be not vexed with me, Odysseus, for... it is the gods that gave us sorrow, the gods who begrudged that we two should remain with each other and enjoy our youth."

The Odyssey is a fairytale, the most wonderful ever written. What distinguishes a true fairytale, after all, is not its fairies, much less the good luck of getting something for nothing, but, on the contrary, the principle of getting something for something: of love, faith, and steadfastness always having their commensurate reward. *Lefum tsa'ara agra*, the ancient rabbis said: "As is the suffering, so is the recompense." But the rabbis were thinking of the World to Come. In *The Odyssey*, there is only this world.

—◊◊◊—

In the well-known opening chapter of Erich Auerbach's masterwork of modern literary criticism *Mimesis*, there is a comparison of an intricate passage from *The Odyssey* with the brief narration of the sacrifice of Isaac in the book of Genesis. Writing in the early 1940s, Auerbach made the claim—astonishing for a time when biblical prose was still considered too crude to merit the attention of literary critics—that the terse minimalism of the Bible was more sophisticated in its representation of human reality than all the sumptuous detail of Homer. He wrote:

> Each of the great figures of the Old Testament, from Adam to the Prophets [is chosen and formed by God] to the end of embodying His essence and will—yet choice and formation do not coincide, for the latter proceeds gradually, historically, during the earthly life of him upon whom the choice has fallen. How the process is accomplished, what terrible trials such a formation inflicts, can be seen from our story of Abraham's sacrifice. Here lies the reason why the great figures of the Old Testament are so much more fully developed, so much more fraught with their own biographical past, so much

more distinct as individuals, than are the Homeric heroes. Achilles and Odysseus are splendidly described in many well-ordered words… but they have no development…. Odysseus on his return is exactly the same as he was when he left Ithaca two decades earlier. But what a road, what a fate, lie between the Jacob who cheated his father out of his blessing and the old man whose favorite son has been torn to pieces by a wild beast!—between David the harp player, persecuted by his lord's jealousy, and the old king surrounded by violent intrigues….

Or between, one might add, the Abraham and Isaac who set out for Mount Moriah and the Abraham and Isaac who return from it several days later. True, the Bible says nothing about their having changed; but then, as Auerbach observes, speech in the Bible "does not serve, as does speech in Homer, to manifest, to externalize thoughts—on the contrary, it serves to indicate thoughts which remain unexpressed." Their expression is left to us.

Abraham has, at the last minute, been given back his son: the boy's life, which God commanded him to take, has been spared. While dreadful loss has not actually taken place in this story, but only been anticipated, in all of literature there is no more dramatic case of its restoration. Not even Odysseus's return to Ithaca can vie with it.

But what, or who, has been restored? The terrified boy who lay bound while the father he loved prepared to slaughter him is no longer the same person. Never again will he look at Abraham without a shudder; never again will he laugh or smile as he did before. He has been restored only for Abraham to lose him more profoundly. It is no accident that the "God of Abraham" is also called, in a startling verse in Genesis, "the Fear of Isaac," or that Sarah, Abraham's wife and Isaac's mother, dies immediately after this incident; no accident that Isaac, upon marrying and having sons himself, favors the down-to-earth Esau over Jacob, who follows his grandfather's God. This God, for Isaac, is the memory of a knife blade on his throat.

Jacob, the God-destined son loved by his mother Rebecca, favors Joseph, the God-destined son of Rachel, the wife Jacob loves most. Joseph's brothers revile him for being his father's favorite as Esau reviles Jacob for stealing his birthright. Because of this, they sell him into slavery in Egypt. Because he grows wealthy and powerful there, they descend to Egypt themselves in time of famine. Because they do, their progeny is enslaved as Joseph was...

In the Bible, as opposed to *The Odyssey*, there is nothing, as Auerbach observes, without its consequences. There is no returning to what was. Even when you think you have gotten back what was taken from you, you have gotten back something else.

—◊—

Like just about everywhere, the offshore winds in the Ionian islands begin to blow in late morning and reach their peak in midafternoon. Turning into the narrow strait between Ithaca and Cephalonia on our way back to Levkos, we caught a brisk northwest breeze. The sails stiffened and the boat heeled sharply as it headed up, close-hauled, into it.

These are the best moments of sailing. Everything is taut, aquiver. You feel the force of the sea on the rudder and resist with a will of your own. Because you are facing into the wind, its speed is increased by your speed, making it seem stronger and your boat faster than they are. There is the thrill of slight danger. If the wind gusts, forcing you over further on your side, so that the bottom of your jib dips to meet the waves sloshing over the deck, you have to decide quickly whether to trust your keel to right you or to slacken the mainsheet and lose momentum so as to relieve the pressure on the sails. The boat takes the waves as if galloping beneath you.

Homer had it just right when he said, describing Odysseus's homeward journey, "And as on a plain four yoked stallions spring forward all together beneath the strokes of the lash, and leaping on high swiftly accomplish their way, even so the stern of that ship leapt on high, and in her wake the dark wave of the loud-sounding sea"—*polyphleuisboio thalasses*, the loveliness of it!—"foamed mightily, and she sped safely and surely on her way."

Every decision has its consequences. By the time one is not in one's twenties but in one's sixties, the consequences of what one has done—or not done, it's all the same—leave a wake stretching to the horizon.

What's lost is lost.

Yet the wake continues to lengthen. Because Israel multiplies in Egypt, Pharaoh orders its male sons killed. Hence, the newborn Moses is hidden in the bulrushes. Hence, he is found by an Egyptian princess and raised in the royal house. Hence, he cannot tolerate his people's enslavement when he reaches manhood. Hence, Israel is redeemed by him...

The redemption of loss—the idea that, although nothing can be restored, everything that has happened can be changed by adding to it, so that the past is always with us and continually still taking place—is a biblical concept. You won't find it in *The Odyssey*.

This, too, is different from a belief in happy endings. The life of the real Abraham and Sarah is even more unlikely to have ended happily than that of the real Odysseus and Penelope. The consequences of a man trying to kill his own son are too great. But there is an interconnectedness of things that extends beyond Homer's ken. Because a knife was laid on Isaac's throat at Mount Moriah, Israel receives the Torah at Mount Sinai.

Quite a few years ago, a close friend of my wife's and mine, a woman who lived in the United States, died of cancer. A frequent visitor to Israel, she loved our home, and having decided to be cremated, she asked us to bury her ashes beneath a favorite olive tree on our property. Not far from the tree was a stone wall with a gateway, beyond which a footpath led into town, and in one of our last conversations with her she said, "I don't know how long it will take, but one day you'll pass through that wall and I'll be there."

More than once, on my way into town, I have half-expected to see her in the sunlight. It hasn't happened yet. Nor did I encounter any ghosts on Ithaca. It was just a small, pleasantly undeveloped Greek island, and while something in me was fulfilled by being there, I did not learn much about *The Odyssey* that I couldn't as well have learned from books.

It was fitting, then, that a book's was the only ghost that did appear. It was the ghost of the same book I had lost when I was a child. For years, it had been a blank in my memory. Apart from having lost it, I couldn't remember a thing about it. And then, as I was writing this essay, a small part of it came back to me. It was a Donald Duck book. That is, Donald Duck was its main character; I couldn't recall even now who else of his comic book entourage was with him. But he must have been on a sea voyage, because the scene that suddenly flashed into my mind was of a ceremony in which he and his fellow passengers underwent a mock trial for having crossed the Equator without asking the permission of King Neptune and were sentenced to a dunking. There was, I was quite sure of it, a colorful illustration of the captain gotten up as Neptune with a trident, prodding a reluctant Donald in full dinner dress off the diving board of the ship's swimming pool.

Now the odd thing, which must be what stirred this memory from its depths, is that Neptune, the Roman god of the seas, is the Greek Poseidon, Odysseus's nemesis. Poseidon thwarts Odysseus's return to Ithaca because Odysseus has blinded his son, the one-eyed Cyclops, who prays to him for vengeance. Consequently, as Homer has Zeus say, "From that time forth Poseidon, the earth-shaker, has not indeed slain Odysseus, but has beaten him off from his native land."

So I had to sail to Ithaca to find a fragment of a children's book lost sixty years before. Things turn up where you least expect them to.

2005

Law in the Desert

Talk of failed New Year's resolutions! Three or four times over the years, come Rosh Hashanah, I've promised myself that this year, *this* year, I'll study at home each week, with its standard commentaries, the *parshat ha-shavu'a,* the weekly Torah reading recited in synagogue on the Sabbath. Three or four times, I've started out a few weeks later with high hopes. Three or four times, I've worked my way through the ten weekly readings of Genesis and the first five of Exodus. Three or four times, I've stopped there.

Studying the weekly Torah reading with its commentaries is an old Jewish custom and many Jews—most, unlike myself, regular synagogue goers—repeat the entire fifty-two-week cycle of the Chumash, the Five Books of Moses, year after year. Although different editions of the Chumash have different commentaries, the more complete sets include, at a minimum, the second-century-C.E. Aramaic translation of the Bible known as Targum Onkelos, the eleventh-century commentary of Rabbi Shlomo Yitzhaki or Rashi, the twelve-century commentary of Rabbi Abraham ibn Ezra, and the thirteen-century commentary of Rabbi Moses ben Nahman or Nahmanides, known acronymically as the Ramban. Together with the voluminous corpus of the Midrash that they frequently draw on, these are the main pillars of Jewish biblical exegesis, on which all subsequent commentators have built.

Each has its distinctive traits. The Targum, though on the whole highly literal, occasionally introduces free rabbinic interpretations into the text. Rashi, a meticulous Hebraist, is pietistic in outlook and a faithful transmitter of rabbinic tradition. Ibn Ezra, no less scrupulous a grammarian, is a rationalist with a preference for naturalistic and sometimes philosophical explanations. The Ramban likes to rely on his predecessors for the plain meanings of verses while focusing on broader contextual issues.

They complement one another. Their interplay isn't always explicit. "Your brother has come in deceit and taken your blessing," says Isaac to Esau in the sixth weekly reading of Genesis upon realizing that he has been tricked by Jacob. Onkelos, like the ancient rabbis, is disturbed by this—how can one revered Patriarch call another a deceiver?—and translates the Hebrew *b'mirmah*, "in deceit," as the Aramaic *b'hukma*, "with wisdom." Rashi echoes Onkelos without citing him. Ibn Ezra demurs without mentioning either man. "He told a lie," he says tersely of Jacob, tacitly rebuking Rashi and Onkelos for whitewashing the text. The Ramban seeks to adjudicate. Yes, he says, Isaac does call Jacob a deceiver—but Isaac realizes the deceit is justifiable, having had the insight that Jacob, though not his own choice, is God's, thus making him a *wise* deceiver.

The Patriarchs! Often I have thought of them as great, lawless spirits taken captive by moralistic minds. Of course Jacob lies. He has to, precisely because his father does not have the insight the Ramban attributes to him. If anyone has it, it's Jacob's mother Rebecca, who masterminds the deceit. Jacob goes along with her willingly. He knows that the stakes—the legacy of the blessing first given by God to Abraham—are too high to allow for the rules of fairness. He grasps the enormity of this legacy better than does Esau and so is worthier of it. In Genesis, the worthiest strive to fulfill a destiny whose grandeur they are conscious of even if they, too, fail to fully comprehend it.

But Esau is himself a wonderful character—wonderful in grief when he cries out, "Bless me, Father, too," and wonderful in forbearance when he and Jacob meet again years later. The rabbis, painting him in dark colors to highlight Jacob's virtue, begrudge him any acknowledgment of this. Does the Bible tell us he was a capable fellow, "a man skilled in hunting?" Hunting, writes Rashi, refers to Esau's shameless stalking of his father's favors. Did he sell his birthright because he came home one day "weary" and desperate for refreshment? He was weary of all the murders he had committed. Drawn with great sympathy by the biblical text, he gets none from the classical commentators.

They flatten the text, these commentators, so as to re-elevate it on their own terms. I preferred my Patriarchs to theirs: lawless, unbridled, freely camping and decamping, putting up and taking down their tents, always on the move with their wives, their children, their concubines, their flocks and camels, their bitter family quarrels passed down from generation to generation, always restlessly seeking, carrying with them the destiny not fully understood: Abraham, the reckless gambler; timid yet tenacious Isaac; wily Jacob, tricking and being tricked; suave, diplomatic Joseph, lowering the curtain on Genesis with a happy ending just when it has come to seem the most tragic of books. Joseph the divine impresario!

The curtain stays down for hundreds of years. When it rises again, the Patriarchs' descendants are slaves in Egypt, ignorant of the legacy their ancestors fought over. Moses appears—impetuous, self-doubting, unyielding, long-suffering Moses! He encounters the God of his forefathers. He and his brother Aaron confront Pharaoh. They inflict ten plagues on the Egyptians. They lead the Israelites to a mountain in the desert. Moses ascends it to receive the Law. "And Mount Sinai was all in smoke because the Lord came down on it in fire, and its smoke went up like the smoke from a kiln, and the whole mountain trembled greatly." Onkelos, anxious as always to avoid physicalizing God, translates "came down on it" as "was revealed on it." Rashi, having no such compunctions, tells us that God spread the sky over the mountain "as though covering a bed with a sheet" and lowered His throne onto it. Ibn Ezra remarks that Mount Sinai only trembled metaphorically. The Ramban explains that the Israelites did not *see* God descend in the fire but heard His voice saying, "I am the Lord your God.... You shall have no other God beside me…. You shall make no graven image of what is in the heavens above or on the earth below…."

It's a page-turner, the *parshat ha-shavu'a*. I can't wait for the next installment.

It comes. It's called Mishpatim, "Laws." It begins:

> These are the laws you shall set before them. Should you buy a Hebrew slave, six years he shall serve and in the seventh he shall go free…. And should an ox gore a man or a woman and they die, the ox shall surely be stoned and its flesh shall not be eaten, and the ox's owner is clear…. And should a man open a pit, or should a man dig a pit and not cover it and an ox or donkey fall in, the owner of the pit shall pay silver, and the carcass shall be his…

Next comes Terumah, "Donation." It concerns the construction of the Tabernacle. It begins:

> And the Lord spoke to Moses, saying: "Speak to the Israelites, that they take me a donation from every man…. And this is the donation you shall take from them: gold and silver and bronze and indigo and purple and crimson and linen and goat hair and reddened ram skins and ocher-dyed skins and acacia wood…"

After Terumah comes Tetzaveh, "You Shall Command." It's about the garments and sacrifices of the priests serving in the Tabernacle. It begins:

> And you shall command the Israelites… and these are the garments they shall make: breastplate and ephod and robe and checkwork tunic, turban and sash.

So this is the legacy! The grand narrative flow of Genesis and the first half of Exodus is over, though it still will burst forth in trickles here and there. It couldn't have happened soon enough for Rashi. In his commentary on the first verse of Genesis he approvingly quotes the fourth-century Rabbi Yitzhak as saying that little would have been lost had the Bible begun with the middle of Exodus, since "the crux of the Torah is only its commandments."

Three or four times over the years, I reached the commandments. Three or four times, I got no further.

———

Last Rosh Hashanah, I resolved, after a long hiatus, to try again. I'm now nearing the end of Exodus and going strong.

What made this year different? In part, my deciding to read the biblical text not in Hebrew but in the Latin Vulgate of the Christian church father Jerome. This added the stimulation of novelty.

Jerome translated the Bible while living in Palestine in the late fourth and early fifth centuries. An accomplished author in his own right, he studied Hebrew and Aramaic and regularly consulted Onkelos's Targum, the Greek Septuagint (a Jewish translation of the Bible, the world's first, done in Alexandria in the third and second centuries B.C.E.), and diverse rabbinic sources. Even more faithful than the Targum to the literal meaning of the biblical text, he was far freer with its form and took frequent liberties with its Hebrew syntax, whose extreme simplicity, with its repetitive reliance on short, independent clauses linked by paratactic "ands," fell short of his standards of Latin elegance. Often, he subordinated clause to clause, as we do in English with all our "whens," "whiles," "befores," and "durings" that biblical Hebrew eschews.

Jerome translated the legal and ritual sections of the Chumash out of a sense of duty; he could not but have been rather bored by them. While they, too, were a part of God's word, they were the part that God had abrogated. Both Jerome's Christian faith and his taste in prose would have inclined him more to the structured rhetoric of a Pauline epistle like Romans that declares, "Now we know that whatsoever things the

Law says, it says to them who are under the Law, that every mouth may be stopped and all the world may become guilty before God. Therefore, by the deeds of the Law there shall no flesh be justified in His sight, for by the Law is the knowledge of sin."

Dutiful Jerome, laboring faithfully through the laws of goring oxen, the measurements of the Tabernacle, and the vestments of its priests when they only led to the knowledge of sin!

Not that Paul was against laws. His epistles counsel adherence to those of Rome. But those were the laws of secular authority. Breaking them made one a criminal in the eyes of the state, not a sinner in the eyes of God. God had not promulgated them. He *had* promulgated the Law given at Sinai—and He had done so, paradoxically, knowing that its statutes were too numerous and complicated to be obeyed, so that anyone seeking to do so would be ultimately reduced to a helpless sense of his inability to perform God's will. This, as Paul saw it, was the Law's ultimate purpose: to produce in its adherents an overwhelming consciousness of sin, alien to the pagan world, that would compel them, followed by the rest of humanity, to throw themselves on the mercy of God's grace as manifested through the son sent to atone for them.

I've always sympathized with Paul. He was raised, as I was, in the world of Jewish observance, and while he felt, like me, too cramped by it to remain in it, he was too attached to it to let go of it without a prolonged inner struggle. He longed to link up with the rest of humanity while remaining the Jew that he was, and by repudiating the Law in the name of the Law he found a brilliant if tortured way of doing so. Long before Spinoza, he was the prototype of a certain kind of modern Jewish intellectual.

As a child, I, too, knew the difference between the laws of Rome and the laws of God. When I was six or seven, sent by my mother to buy a newspaper, I picked up two papers by mistake from a pile at the kiosk while paying for only one; but although I lived for a while in great fear of being arrested for theft, I got over it as soon as I realized that my crime had gone undetected. It was different when I unwittingly placed a meat fork in the dairy silverware drawer in our kitchen. Then I had a consciousness of sin, which lasted longer. God was no kiosk owner.

All around me were sins waiting to be committed. If I forgot to say my bedtime prayers, I had sinned. If I unthinkingly switched on a light on the Sabbath, I had sinned. I envied the Patriarchs who lived before the Law. Hadn't Abraham served his guests in Mamrei milk and butter with their meat? That was why Rashi was in such a hurry to get past him to the commandments. Yet three or four times over the years, I groaned when I reached them. So must have Jerome. *Haec sunt iudicia quae propones eis*: these are the laws you shall set before them. I did not want them set before me.

—⟊—

The second half of Exodus can be read as a study in the institutionalization of religion. No longer a small roaming band to whom God can appear anywhere and at any time, the Israelites leave Egypt as twelve tribes. They need what any large group needs if it is not to degenerate into a mob: clear rules of conduct, recognized penalties for breaking them, established forms and places of worship, trained specialists to mediate between them and the divine. Mishpatim, Terumah, Tetzaveh: these lay the foundations for a code of civil behavior, a centralized cultus, a priestly class. They mark, in the biblical narrative, a transition from an era of spontaneity between man and man, and between man and God, to one of regulated order. This is necessary. It is part of God's plan. But like all institutionalizations of originally spontaneous relationships, it leaves one yearning for what has been lost.

It is part of God's *second* plan. His first is to create in six days a world that is all good and let human beings made in His image run it by themselves. This works out badly. The first humans disobey Him and are driven from Eden. By the tenth generation of them, the generation of Noah, "God saw the earth, and it was corrupt, for all flesh had corrupted its ways on the earth."

God wipes out everything with a great flood and starts anew. This time He will do it differently. He will ignore most of the human race; it is too large, too unruly, for Him to work with. He will proceed slowly, methodically. And so He begins with a single individual, Abraham. Carefully, lest He make another mistake, He tests Abraham again and again to make sure He has chosen correctly, satisfied only by the last, pitiless trial of the sacrifice of Isaac. From there He moves on to a family, carefully winnowing it as it grows until it consists of twelve brothers. Taking time out to let their offspring multiply and be enslaved in Egypt, He is now ready for the next stage: He will take the descendants of these brothers out of bondage and make them a model people—"a kingdom of priests and a holy nation," as He tells them when they are assembled before Him at Sinai. They will be His pilot project on earth. Once it succeeds, He can extend it to the rest of humanity.

A model people needs model laws. God goes about it pedagogically, starting with the laws that He knows will be of greatest interest. As the Ramban puts it: "God began with the laws of the Hebrew slave because freeing him in the seventh year was a reminder of the exodus from Egypt." More than a reminder: a promise to an anxious people that it will not be re-enslaved by the more powerful of its own brethren. One imagines the stir in the desert. Six years of servitude and no more! So this is law! Slaves until now have had no laws but the whims of their masters.

There follow laws of property, laws of damages and restitution, laws of theft and murder, laws of sexual relationships: the basic norms that a functional society must have. All else is in abeyance. Moses is on the mountain receiving the Law, and we, the Bible's readers, are given a preview of it while the worried Israelites camped below await Moses's return. We know the Law's contents before they do.

The narrative only resumes with the weekly reading of Ki Tisa. Afraid that Moses has abandoned them and left them leaderless in the desert, the Israelites say to Aaron, "Rise up, make us gods that will go before us, for this man Moses who brought us up from the land of Egypt, we do not know what has happened to him." And so Aaron collects their gold jewelry and fashions from it a calf—a graven image—and the people worship it and revel around it. High on the mountain, Moses is told by God, "Go, go down, for your people, which you have brought out of

Egypt, have been corrupted." Moses descends after first persuading a wrathful God not to wipe out the Israelites as He threatens to, sees them dancing around the calf, angrily smashes the tablets of the Law that he is carrying, and commands the Levites to commit a punitive massacre in which thirty thousand of the calf-dancers are killed. God, though calmed, remains hurt and withdrawn. No longer, He tells the people, will He lead them through the wilderness; an angel will take His place, lest "I consume you on your way." The Israelites—"And the people heard these evil tidings and mourned"—are depressed.

"For your people have been corrupted," *ki shihet amkha*: Rashi's comment on the cutting "your"—that of a father who comes home to find his son misbehaving and tells his wife it's her child, not his—is to assure us that God is not disassociating Himself from the Israelites but scolding Moses for having permitted idolatrous heathen to join them and lead them astray. Well, that's Rashi for you: always sticking up for the Jews. But why does neither he nor any of the other commentators in my Chumash point out that the verb *shahet*, to act corruptly, is the very same verb used in Genesis to describe the human race on the eve of the Flood? Why does no one dwell on the obvious parallel between the two stories? In both, God sets out to create or recreate the world. In both, all goes well for a while. In both, the illusion of success soon collapses. In both, God resolves to destroy what He has done and begin again, the second time with Moses as a second Noah or Abraham. ("And now leave me be," God tells Moses, "that my wrath may flare against them, and I will put an end to them, and I will make you a great nation.") In both, He repents of His fury and offers its survivors an eternal pact—a promise not to repeat the Flood, a reaffirmation of His covenant with Israel. There must be commentators on the *parshat hashavu'a* who have noticed this. The Zohar, itself a mystical commentary on the Chumash written shortly after the time of the Ramban, does notice it. When the Israelites sinned with the golden calf, it says, they fell from the heights of Sinai to the lower depths, for the same serpent that poisoned Adam poisoned them, so that *g'rimu mota l'khol alma*, they brought, like Adam and Eve, death upon the whole world. The debacle at Sinai is a cosmic catastrophe, comparable only to the sin in Eden.

I was wrong then to think that the narrative flow of Exodus had ever stopped. Mishpatim, Terumah, and Tetzaveh were a continuation of it. They were needed, not only as a contretemps to create a sense of lapsed time, the forty days spent by Moses on the mountain, between two contiguous events, but because the drama lost much of its intensity without them. Their detail was necessary to illustrate the effort God had put into designing a Law flouted by His chosen people as soon as Moses turned his back on them—to illustrate the extent of God's failure. His second at forging order out of chaos, it is even more galling than the first, since the lesson learned from the first has not kept it from being repeated.

This realization—*parshat ha-shavu'a* students would call it a *hidush*, a new way of looking at things—carried me excitedly through the last six Torah readings of Exodus that had always stymied me before. Suddenly, God's effort needed to be understood. It was an integral part of the story. "And should a man open a pit, or should a man dig a pit and not cover it, and an ox or donkey fall in, the owner of the pit shall pay silver, and the carcass shall be his...." Did that mean that if an ox wandered onto my property and fell into a pit and was killed, I, the pit's owner, was responsible?

No, said Rashi. My property was my property. The Torah was referring to a pit dug in the public domain.

But if I dig a pit in the public domain, how am I its owner?

By "owner," Ibn Ezra explains, the Torah designates the pit's user, since it must have been dug for some use.

Then I have no liability at all if the pit is dug on my own property?

My *parshat ha-shavu'a* commentators weren't clear about this. I looked at the third-century-C.E. Mishnah, the earliest systematic explication of biblical law. Yes, said the first chapter of Bava Kama, the opening part of the treatise of Nezikin or "Damages": only if, in digging a pit on my own property, I cross the line separating it from the public domain, or from someone else's property, is anyone falling into it from the other side my responsibility, too.

But it was more complicated than that. The sixth-century Gemara, the systematic explication of the Mishnah, stated that according to Rabbi Akiva, even if the pit was entirely on my property, I was still liable if I hadn't made clear that trespassing was forbidden. Rabbi Ishmael disagreed. The Gemara's discussion of their disagreement was long and intricate, and I had trouble following it.

Nor would following it in the Gemara have been enough to know the outcome. For that, I would have had to consult the Ge'onim, the seventh- to eleventh-century talmudic scholars of Babylonia; and after them, the Rishonim, the eleventh- to sixteenth-century scholars of North Africa and Europe; and after them, the Aharonim, the scholars who came later—in short, the whole vast edifice of Jewish law. It suddenly towered above me, this edifice, in all its architectural immensity, dizzyingly tall—explication upon explication, disagreement upon disagreement, complication upon complication—and for the first time, though I had never gotten beyond its bottom floors, I felt that I grasped its full grandeur—the indomitable scope of its determination to make up for the golden calf. Century after century, the Jews had labored to convince God that He was right not to have given up on them at Sinai—that His pilot project could still work, that they would devote themselves to it endlessly, tirelessly, even if it took thousands of years, even if the rest of humanity went its own way in the meantime—even if the rest of humanity agreed that the Law only led to the knowledge of sin.

I've been thinking about the knowledge of sin.

Over the years, I've been involved, sometimes alone and sometimes with others, in more court cases than I'd have liked to be in. Nothing major. A case involving my father, then ill with Alzheimer's, who was defrauded by his neighborhood grocer. A case involving a mobile phone antenna erected illegally opposite our home. A running battle with the town we live in about building rights on our land. A consequent suit for damages filed by us. A fight with the local planning commission over a road planned to run through our and our neighbors' property. Another fight to stop a nearby wedding hall from blasting loud music into the night. All trivial stuff.

On the whole, the courts have performed creditably. I can't complain too much about the judges. The sad thing has been the deceit they've had to deal with. Corrupt authorities. Secret, illicit deals. Law enforcers looking the other way. Manipulation of evidence. Lies on the witness stand. Suborning of witnesses.

I suppose it's that way everywhere. Why wouldn't it be? It's only the laws of Rome. If you think you can get away with it, you break them. I've broken my share of them myself and hoped I wouldn't be caught, just as I did as a boy when I came home with an extra newspaper.

Wouldn't we better off with the Law of God? If every bribe taker, perjurer, and tax evader knew he was sinning?

Not that you can't know that you're a sinner and sin some more. In one way or another, that's what most believers in the Law do. That's Paul's whole point. It's why I don't say a God-given Law is a solution. I only say I've come to believe that if God had a plan for humanity, He would give it a Law, nor would He abrogate it as Paul thought He did.

That hasn't always been my opinion. But neither was it God's. The first time around, He waited ten generations before deciding He was wrong.

I'm not happy with that. I have an anarchistic streak. I've never liked being told what to do. I've always wanted to do the right thing because I wanted to, not because I had to. I've wanted to do it Paul's way, without the Law, "for when the Gentiles, which have not the Law, do by nature the things contained in the Law, these, having not the Law, are a law unto themselves."

Like the Patriarchs.

It's a nice idea. It was clever of Paul to have thought of it. It just doesn't work. It didn't work before the Flood and it won't work now. There isn't enough of mankind—there isn't enough of *me*—that, having no Law, will do by nature the things contained in the Law. We need a sense of sin to bridle us. If it's taken me most of a lifetime to realize that, then that's what lifetimes must be for.

This week was Pekudei, the last Torah reading of Exodus. Before it came Vayakhel. Together they are two of the most tedious *parshot ha-shavu'a* in the Chumash. Vayakhel relates how the Israelites built the Tabernacle according to the instructions in Terumah; Pekudei, how they made the priests' vestments according to the instructions in Tetzaveh. Both repeat the language of Terumah and Tetzaveh almost to a word. "And they shall make an Ark of acacia wood, two and a half cubits its length, and a cubit and a half its width, and a cubit and a half its height," says Terumah. "And Bezalel made an Ark of acacia wood, two and a half cubits its length, and a cubit and a half its width, and a cubit and a half its height," says Vayakhel. The commentators fall silent. What's there to add?

But a *hidush* is a *hidush*—and now I read even Vayakhel and Pekudei with fresh eyes, starting with the former's opening verses, which describe how the Israelites, called upon to donate "gold and silver and bronze and indigo and purple and crimson and linen and goat hair and reddened ram skins and ocher-dyed skins and acacia wood," respond with such enthusiasm that Moses has to tell them to stop, there being already more than enough. If it occurred to any of the commentators in my Chumash that behind this outpouring of public-spiritedness was a post-depression euphoria, they kept it to themselves. I can't say it didn't occur to me.

There is a cheerfulness in Vayakhel and Pekudei that would hardly have seemed possible a short time before. Everyone is bringing gifts to the Tabernacle; everyone is measuring, making, fitting. Bezalel runs around giving orders. We hear the sounds of saws and hammers; there is a smell of freshly cut lumber, the crisp colors of newly died fabrics. "And they made the boards for the tabernacle, twenty boards for the southern end...." "And they made the curtain of indigo and purple and crimson, designer's work they made it...." "And they made tunics of twisted linen, weaver's work, for Aaron and his sons...." It's like a huge stage set on which a multitude of workers is racing to get things done in time for the premiere.

It's brilliant. There's nothing better for a depression than a project to work on, something constructive to do, something to keep one from brooding endlessly on one's sinfulness.

The date arrives. It's the anniversary of the exodus, the first day of the first month of its second year. Miraculously, everything is ready on time. The tabernacle is standing. The Ark of the Covenant is in place. The shewbread is on the table. The lamp in the Tent of Meeting is lit. The golden altar is ready for its offerings. Moses enters and offers up the burnt offering and the grain offering as commanded. The audience holds its breath.

And then it happens:

"And cloud covered the Tent of Meeting and the glory of the Lord filled the Tabernacle."

God is back. It's a mini-Sinai, His glory in cloud is like fire in smoke. All that light and dark mixed together, the brightest sunshine and the blackest gloom!

"And when the cloud went up from over the Tabernacle, the Israelites would journey onward in all their journeyings. And if the cloud did not go up, they would not journey onward until the day it went up. For the Lord's cloud was over the Tabernacle by day, and fire by night was in it, before the eyes of all the house of Israel in all their journeyings."

Explicit, says Jerome, *liber Ellesmoth id est Exodus.*

Bring on Leviticus!

2011

Working One's Way Out

Half inch crust of frozen snow on hills facing south
toward Pownal Valley and the Berkshire hills beyond—
blinding blue of winter sky and sun glare on the icy
crust—sensations of exposure and abandonment—
desolation of the sublime.

Steve Kogan, *Winter Vigil*

There was a time when a senior editor at a good publishing house
who read a manuscript that began with such a sentence and
didn't falter for the next 200 pages would have snapped it up at
once. This was before he or she would have said, "I loved the book. Let me
consult my colleagues about it." Before "My colleagues are enthusiastic.
We're going to run it past our marketing department." Before "We're terribly sorry, but marketing says memoirs by unknown authors don't sell."
Before twenty such rejection letters were received by Carol Rusoff, Steve
Kogan's widow, until in 2018, three years after his death, she published
Winter Vigil at her own expense.

When I first read *Winter Vigil* over a year ago, I was as swept away as
that once-upon-a-time editor might have been. I hadn't read any contemporary writing as good in a long time. I hadn't known Steve Kogan could
write like that. I hadn't, it turned out, known very much about him.

The two of us were classmates at Columbia in the late 1950s and early '60s, first as undergraduates and then as graduate students. I don't remember if I knew Steve as an undergrad, although we were both English literature majors, and *Winter Vigil* describes courses that I took. We certainly didn't sit in the same classes in graduate school because I didn't go to any during the year in which, on my way to dropping out of academic life, I picked up an MA on the strength of a thesis written in utter solitude. To this day I smile sheepishly when someone says to me, "You were at Columbia in the early sixties? It must have been wonderful going to lectures by men like Lionel Trilling and Jacques Barzun." I never attended a lecture by either man.

In this respect, I was different from Kogan, who gladly took what formal studies had to offer and wrote about Trilling and other professors appreciatively. In the end, though, he dropped out, too. "I have come here," he tells us, recalling his stay in the cabin he built overlooking Pownal Valley,

> from libraries and lecture rooms and the dread that came over me at twenty-nine that I was heading straight for death in the academic world, with the doctorate as the sealing of the tomb. On a winter break in '67, I walk along the edge of Candlewood Lake in Connecticut one early morning and hear the ice crack and shift beyond the shore. I think about my divorce after six years of a graduate school marriage and about my students' papers and my unfinished dissertation on Elizabethan theater and decide I've had enough. Two months later, I'm living among radicals in Oakland and losing myself in one sixties' scene after another from California to the Lower East Side, ending up in a "commune" just above the Southern Vermont Apple Orchards, where I finally come to rest.

By the time all this had happened, I hadn't seen Steve for a while. Before that, though, we had gotten to know each other through a circle of mutual friends in which we found ourselves together on many occasions. The ones I recall best were the musical ones. These were nights at off-campus apartments in which people drifted in and out while four musicians played and sang and put down their instruments and picked them up to play some more. There was Art Rosenbaum from Indianapolis, a wonderful banjoist with whom I had biked around Brittany the summer after our college graduation; Art went on to become a professor of art at the University of Georgia and a painter of colorfully rhythmic, WPA-style canvases and murals. There was Tam Gibbs, who came from California and played a funky blues guitar. (He later became the disciple of a Chinese Tai Chi master, fell unhappily in love, it was said, with the master's daughter, and died from either suicide or drink, depending on whom you heard it from.) There was a fiddler, Brooks Adams Otis, a tall, thin, quiet young man directly descended from John Adams, the second American president. And there was Kogan on the mandolin. When the four of them got up a full head of steam on "Swannanoa Tunnel" or "Old Joe Clark," the drifting out stopped.

For sheer volume, a mandolin can't compete with a banjo or violin. I remember Steve looking down from time to time at his instrument as he played, as if seeking reassurance from it that they were being heard, and back up with a nod and shy smile. Perhaps I imagined those being his thoughts. But the shyness was real. You felt it when you spoke with him. He wasn't a stutterer. He didn't stumble over words. But the words, when they came, seemed to come with difficulty, as if there were some impediment in their way. As if they had to be searched for in a place he had no easy access to, dredged up from the depths of silence.

Silence, Kogan tells us, was the "root experience" of his childhood. It emanated from his mother, a "long-haired, beautiful woman inhabited by the past [who] lived in a state of low-intensity possession, as if she were a daily medium for ghosts, " communing with her lost youth in the

Ukraine and talking aloud to the photographs in her family albums, most of relatives killed in the Holocaust. At such moments, she was "nearly motionless, lost inside her memories, absorbing me into her world.... Identifying with my mother's moods, I felt threatened by change of any kind, and beginning with those afternoon photo séances of hers, stillness and passivity became a way of life for me." Writing in English about her, and about being the only child in an immigrant home whose main languages were Russian and Yiddish, "kills the emotions and events I am describing," Kogan tells us, "by translating them out of their living context, making me want to be silent—in other words, to be with mother and remain a child."

Carol Rusoff has written me that Kogan originally thought of calling *Winter Vigil* "Queen Lear in Brownsville," which is now the title of the book's fourth chapter. Indeed, Lear goes mad and Kogan's mother is described by him as "gently, almost spiritually psychotic." Yet read Shakespeare's play and there is more to it than that. "What shall Cordelia speak? Love, and be silent" are the first words uttered by Lear's youngest and, in the end, only remaining daughter. And in the play's last act Lear says to her, now a crazed old man:

> Come, let's away to prison.
> We two alone will sing like birds i'th'cage
> ....So we'll live,
> And sing, and tell old tales, and laugh
> At gilded butterflies.

We two alone. Long parts of *Winter Vigil* are about a New York childhood that, though crammed with model trains and airplanes and erector sets, was dominated by a mother who, when not in one of her withdrawn states, sang her son Russian songs, and read him Russian fairytales about snow maidens and talking animals and forest witches, and spent days with him at her side making jams and cooking borscht and sewing and stuffing little pouches of chicken skins, weaving around them a magic spell that he was unable to cast off no matter how many

Brooklyn streets he rode his bike down, or pink rubber Spaldings (was it only in Manhattan that we called them "spaldeens?") he fired at strike zones chalked on the walls of buildings, or CO_2-propelled rockets he and his friend Marty Maisel shot into the air with seltzer cartridges. Everything about his mother, Kogan writes, "seemed bewildering, and since she was both oppressive and detached, being in her presence was like being absorbed into a prison and an endless distance all at once."

Only partly balancing her was Kogan's father. An outgoing man, he was a connection to the world outside the home, though in it, Kogan writes, "he left me exposed to mother in far too many ways" and was himself subjugated by "his spirit of sacrifice to her [which] led me into being absorbed by her illness, so that throughout my childhood I had the vague sensation of having been born somehow ill—some vague but permanent condition of never being well." Originally hailing from Kishinev, Kogan's father added Hebrew to his Russian, Romanian, and Yiddish while living in Tel Aviv as a construction worker in the 1920s before coming to America, where he worked in an aircraft plant and then as a salesman. A combative and adventurous spirit (he once cowed a ruffian in a bar by threatening to slash him with a water pitcher he smashed, and another time came home from a walk in the park with a snake he had caught), he was a lover of classical music, an ethnic Jew who hated religion and wouldn't let his son have a bar-mitzvah, a Zionist with a liking for Arabs, and an ardent Communist until devastated by the Party's post-Stalin revelations. Yet he was also given to dark broodings. "Sometimes," Kogan writes,

> I think that this troubled side of him was his deepest bond with my mother and that in some sense he too was disturbed, not in any conventional way, and certainly not in the unbalanced condition of my mother, but nevertheless disturbed, so that both of them appear to me as orphans of the storm. I know that he used her illness as a way of hiding his own insecurities, which were only proper to himself (the current term is "co-dependency");

yet I also know that he loved her, as best he could, that they shared an exquisitely personal sense of loss and nostalgia, and that he was convinced that if he left her, she would simply drown, that no amount of family support could rescue her, and that in some strange and fatal way, he was responsible for her life. It is at this point that their relationship becomes so filled with darkness that I no longer know what to think.

Loss and nostalgia. In reading *Winter Vigil*, I felt them too.

That's not surprising. Kogan and I were born within a year of each other. *Winter Vigil*'s pages are full of the New York and America that we grew up in and went to school in and left school in. The erector sets, the model airplanes, the cap pistols, the stamp collections, the Good Humor man and the knife grinder's truck, the automats, the telephone numbers that started with Academy 2 and Haverfield 4, *Life* and *Junior Scholastic* magazines, the Yankee, Dodger, and Giant games traveled to on the IRT and the IND and the BMT in cars packed with fans like troop carriers ("friends of mine who grew up in Brooklyn," Kogan writes, "remember seeing ballplayers coming out of the subway along with the people"), the summer bungalow colonies in the Catskills: childhood!

And then the high school years with their discoveries. Of a world beyond the confines of home, neighborhood, and early schooling. (Kogan escaped Brownsville by going to Manhattan's High School of Music & Art, one of five special New York City schools that gave admission exams, while I fled my Jewish day school for another of the five, the Bronx High School of Science.) Of intellectual and aesthetic experience—the books, the museum visits, the concerts, each capable of making you feel you had just begun a new life. Of girls and the torments of dating. ("I would end up standing," Kogan writes about the carless New York boy's duty to escort his date home, "on some God-forsaken avenue near Utopia Parkway at two in the morning waiting for a bus to take me to a train." He neglects to mention that the night was bitter cold, and the bus ran once an hour.)

Of America itself, the unknown continent across the Hudson with which Kogan "finally made contact... coming into my own, coming down to earth," on a summer job with Black migrant workers on a chicken farm in New Jersey just as I did the summer I baled hay and drove fence posts at an outpost of integration in the Jim Crow south in the company of left-wing organizers, early civil rights activists, southern Negroes, and Tennessee hillbillies.

And then Columbia and the sixties and the call of the road. Kogan writes:

> By 1968, I had driven, hitch-hiked, flown, and taken trains and buses around the country a dozen times or more—once in late winter with a couple of friends in an old New York City taxi cab to sell to an Indian in Butte. He met us on a snow-covered street with a hundred and fifty silver dollars in a sack. We had a steak dinner at nine in the morning, bought some old work clothes in a general store... and we headed out of town—Mark in hiking gear, Jenkin in sneakers reciting Whitman while standing in a foot of snow. Somewhere in Idaho, they hitched a ride and caught a freight train to Chicago, freezing all the way. I went south on a passenger line to Salt Lake City, sleeping the night before in the Pocatello railway station and in the morning looking through my railway window at the winter vastness of the west—gray sky turning brilliant blue in Utah, where I took a jet that night to make it back in time for my doctoral exams.

Had I not, too, stood on a street corner in a Black neighborhood of Baton Rouge with my friend Nicky Goldman and a New York abstract expressionist painter whose name I've forgotten, auctioning off an old semi-automatic Dodge that sprang an oil leak and died in billows of smoke on our way back from Mexico City, the proceeds from which barely paid for three Greyhound tickets to New York? Mark and Jenkin!

That's Lennie Jenkin and Micky Solomon, who writes a foreword to *Winter Vigil*—Micky of the golden, nearly shoulder-length locks (now Mark and bald) that drew jeers from the passing cars that wouldn't stop for him, his wife Kathy, and me when we were marooned for a day outside Lordsburg, New Mexico while trying to thumb our way to California.

That was a continuation of a second Mexican adventure. We had agreed to meet in Tehuantapec because it was both on the map and in a Wallace Stevens poem, and we had set aside three days to rendezvous there in the marketplace at five in the afternoon, after which, if I or they didn't show up, they or I would move on. I had worked on a banana boat that left me off at the Panama Canal on its return trip from Ecuador and hitchhiked most of the way to the Mexican border, which I only reached at noon of the third day because I had lingered to climb a volcano in Guatemala, and all the way I leaned forward in my seat and said, *"Mas rápido, mas rápido,"* to the taxi driver, who got me to Tehuantapec at 4:45, a straw sombrero on my head and a dagger inscribed with the words *Amor Perdido* tucked into my belt, feeling like Phileas Fogg in *Eighty Days Around the World*.

The sixties and the lure of a life on the land! After studying in England for a year, returning to New York for my MA, spending half a year in Israel, teaching for another year at a Black college in Alabama, returning again to New York and heading out for a while to California, I bought land in Maine on which I planned to live in a log cabin. This was about the time that Kogan came to rest, as he says, in his cabin in southern Vermont. A few months later, I married. My wife and I spent the summer of 1967 tenting on our land while the dust from the Six-Day War was settling over the Middle East, and in 1970, just in time to round out the decade, moved to Israel. After that, my life and Kogan's, which had in some ways run parallel, took different directions.

I was talking about nostalgia the other day with my eldest daughter. She's an expert on it. When she was six, she once burst into tears because she realized she would never again be five.

"It's not the erector sets or the telephone numbers," she said. "It's being young. My generation will feel nostalgic for Lego and landline phones."

She was right, of course. I romanticize. Those years weren't quite like that. Our memories pass through a filter of forgetfulness that coats them with colors they may not originally have had, that may derive from stories told long afterwards to ourselves or to others, from a self-image we wish to promote, even from books we have read. Kogan speaks of the influence of Kerouac. Who of us wasn't exposed to it?

Still, I told my daughter, there's a difference. Erector sets came with screwdrivers, wrenches, nuts, and bolts. They prepared you for a world of real tools. And "even the loss of supposedly trivial things like the names of subway routes or telephone exchanges," as Kogan writes,

> has repercussions in the way we come to feel and live our lives. The substitution of "the number 1," the number 2," "the number 3" for names of subway routes or of area codes for neighborhoods on the old telephone lines destroys a small but identifiable sense of community and leaves an abstraction in the place of a living thing. And with the loss of all these focal points of human association comes a weakening of social ties, so that when we're faced with new tasks and responsibilities, there's less and less to rely on in the way of continuity.

I agree. But one of the challenges of growing old is the need to distinguish between nostalgia and valid social criticism. One doesn't want to be a grouchy old man. Things may seem to have been better when we were young—but were they better because they were better, or were they better because we were young?

You can argue either side of it. The thing about social change, especially when it's technologically driven, is that the good always comes with the bad. It's a package deal. Modern medicine can cure an array of once untreatable diseases, but where are the days, remembered by Kogan and me, when family doctors routinely made house calls and came when you needed them? The automobile shrank distances, relieved the isolation of millions, clogged roads and streets, exfoliated cities, poisoned their air. Television educated and entertained generations of viewers while reducing large numbers of them to stupefaction. Air travel, computers, smartphones, social media—you can say the same for them all.

Winter Vigil doesn't say it by arguing. Mostly, Kogan makes the case for the times he grew up in by describing their rich texture and leaving us to compare them with being young today. Model airplanes, for example:

> The history of flight was still news in the late 1940s, and a boy could daydream about World War I aces and Lindbergh in a Curtiss-Jenny, the plane in which he gained his expertise before his transatlantic flight in his silver Ryan monoplane. Hanging on a wall in Marty's room was a model of the Jenny's upper wing, the whole assembly still exposed. We sat at a work table covered with X-Acto knives, tubes of glue, drafting pencils, sharpeners, compasses, pins, assorted plastic stencils, a blueprint for the Jenny's underwing, and a light to illuminate details. We spent afternoons enlarging designs from model airplane magazines and testing gasoline and diesel engines by screwing them onto plywood motor mounts and bolting the rig to any convenient fence that we would find. After we installed the engines in our planes, we took the finished models to an empty lot in the neighborhood or vacant fields heading to the Rockaway shore [in order to fly them].

This was not particularly unusual activity for an eleven- or twelve-year-old in the late 1940s, before television, computers, and video and virtual reality games turned childhood into something else. A lot has been said about children once having been more active, more engaged in play and projects of their own invention, more independent, and more often out-of-doors. Kogan makes yet another point: children, or at least some of them, once had an intimation of history—they had historical heroes and a wish to emulate them—that they no longer have. Eleven-year-olds today, to the best of my knowledge, do not build models of 1977 Apple and Digital PCs or dream of being Steve Jobs or Bill Gates.

"What's left of the old forms and structures falls away," Kogan writes, "and we all turn a little bit more into exiles in our own country, adrift and homeless under the bombardment of the mechanical and impersonal—in schools, homes, literature, everywhere." The madness of our times, their progressive destruction of all that is natural without and within (the destroyers of the one and the destroyers of the other, oddly enough, belonging to opposite political camps)—the belief that it is reasonable to scorch the earth, foul the seas, change our sex at will, erase the distinctions between men and women, digitalize our lives, make babies in laboratories, let robots and computers do our work and thinking, hope to communicate by computer chips implanted in our brains, plan to avoid the extinction of our species by founding colonies in outer space: is it mere nostalgia, of which Kogan's mother had a pathological case, to think this has something to do with having cut our moorings to the past?

Our politics, too. We justly complain that we are led by mediocre types unfit to govern us. But the great politicians of former times went to schools that forced them to study the speeches of Pericles and the campaigns of Alexander the Great—were educated, that is, to have some conception of what greatness is.

Kogan was wiser than I was. He understood the importance of education at an age at which I was still rebelling against it. In fact, though he took a time-out from it, he never rebelled against it at all. He not only loved high school and college, he even liked public school. He remembers its "vanished world…. the awe and authority that radiated from the family to the teacher and the flag in the corner of the room—a lost world of democratic excellence and the natural bonding of community," about which he says:

> My home was admittedly unusual, but #233 was simply a
> local Brooklyn public school; yet there was Mrs. Levine,

teaching neighborhood kids like Lenny Tasch, Bonnie Skellet, and Allan Kaganov to parse sentences, draw detailed maps, and read *The New York Times*. Nowadays, learning and imagination are described as if they were conflicting worlds, and it seems almost impossible for me to communicate the combination of strict order and unbounded wonder I experienced at school.... There we were, in the supposedly narrow-minded '50s, in an ordinary working-class neighborhood, under an educational system that has been mercilessly attacked by the academic left, and all the time we were being given an elementary school education that many high school and even college graduates today have not received.

Kogan's gratitude for what schools have taught him is immense. And he knows whereof he speaks in discussing education's decline, because having returned in the end to graduate school and gotten his PhD, he taught for many years at Manhattan Community College and its Writing Center. Half of his students there, he tells us, didn't know the geography of their own city, "let alone its place in the larger world," to say nothing of the place in space and time of other cities, states, and countries. Never having had the "strong and independent teachers" that he had, or "the authoritative and deep curriculum" that public schools, high schools, and colleges once insisted on before they caved in to the demands of cultural relativism and social relevance, such young people are doomed to go about half-blind, unable to see beyond their own immediate experience.

More than about education in our society, however, *Winter Vigil* is about the education of its author, a Jewish boy born in Brooklyn in 1938 who struggled to put together the confusing pieces of a life: his East European immigrant home; his enticing, enslaving mother with her imagined idyll of the Tsar's *ancien régime*; his resourceful but ultimately helpless father and the broken dream of the Revolution; the tough streets of Brownsville; his schooling; his overabundance of talent (Kogan passed the entrance exam to Music & Art not in music but in art); his love of literature and painting; his wanderings in America; his need to be silent; his need to speak. On a first reading, I was overwhelmed by the book's mass of detail, the memories, anecdotes, and sketches that crowd its pages like the parts of a Curtiss-Jenny scattered on a work table. On a second reading, I began the work of assemblage. On a third, the brilliantly coherent structure of it all, the perfect fit of all the parts, came fully into view.

—⚹—

I knew Kogan was Jewish, of course. His family name was enough to tell me that. But how Jewish he was I had no idea until reading *Winter Vigil*, not even after he and his daughter Sonya were my family's overnight guests in Israel in 1982.

To tell the truth, I don't remember that visit very well. Kogan mentions my taking him and Sonya to the archeological site of Megiddo, so I suppose I must have. The clearest memory I have is of him astounding my own two daughters by spearing a piece of pickled herring on the breakfast table, asking for maple syrup, pouring it over the herring, and chewing the improbable morsel with grunts of satisfaction and a straight face betrayed only by the twinkle in his very large and blue eyes—eyes, as I recall, that seemed to open wide at all they looked at, as if the world were an endlessly interesting and puzzling place.

I can't state for a fact that Kogan didn't talk to me during this visit about his childhood, his Yiddish-speaking parents, his father's years as a *halutz* in Palestine and knowledge of Hebrew, or his father's relatives Riva and Solomon who lived in Hadera, a twenty-minute drive from our home, and whose old-time Israeli ethos of simple living and pride in their and their country's accomplishments made a deep impression on him. To the best of my memory, though, I first learned of these things from *Winter Vigil*.

When I think of it, it wasn't just Kogan. Today I'm amazed by how many boys whom I knew in high school and college turned out to have had Jewish sides to them that I wasn't aware of until I found out about it long afterwards, often inadvertently. I didn't even realize Lennie Jenkin was a Jew until he married a girl who wasn't. And when, in middle age,

Micky Solomon became a *ba'al teshuvah,* a newly observant Jew committed to a life of Jewish ritual and study, it was a total surprise for me. I had no idea where it came from. By then he was the poet Mark Solomon who had written

> Can you sing in Arizona? Does that train grinding
> > into town,
> containers of Pacific mildew—Hanjin, Sealand,
> > Evergreen—bolted down on flatcars in Seattle make
> Your bed jangle in the middle of the night?

and who now wrote

> Words are inscribed on my doorposts and
> > on my gates,
> bound for a sign upon my arms, for frontlets between
> > my eyes. Words
> that I speak when I'm sitting in my home, when I
> > travel on a journey,
> to the Land of the Patriarchs.

And who of my friends knew how Jewish *I* was? I must have surprised them by moving to Israel as much as Micky surprised me.

It wasn't that we were embarrassed by our Jewishness or went out of our way to hide it. We just didn't know what to do with it or where to put it. It had no obvious relation to the Americans we were or wanted to be or to that "all-embracing and positive vision of America," as Kogan puts it, that "flowed from the spirit of Whitman's poetry." Whitman, without whom there would have been no *Democratic Vistas,* no "Song of the Open Road" (and no Kerouac), no now-preposterous-sounding lines like

> Singing the song of These, my ever-united lands – my
> body no more inevitably united, part to part, and made
> out of a thousand diverse contributions one identity,
> any more than my lands are inevitably united and made
> ONE IDENTITY.

That identity was a myth. It came out of the Civil War and out of Whitman. You'll find it in him even before the Civil War. In one of his typical catalogues of trades and occupations, written on the war's eve, he lists

> The camp of Georgia wagoners just after dark, the supper-fires and the cooking and eating by whites and negroes....
> These are the negroes at work in good health, the ground in all directioncover'd with pine straw;
> In Tennessee and Kentucky slaves busy in the coalings, at the forge, by the furnace-blaze, or at the corn-shucking,
> In Virginia, the planter's son returning after a long absence, joyfully welcom'd and kiss'd by the aged mulatto nurse.

Today lines like these could get—may already have gotten—Whitman banned from the public libraries. But far from being pro-slavery, they affirm the single identity of the slave and the slave owner. This was the myth of an America of a sturdy, shared camaraderie beyond all divisions of race and class that Steve Kogan was taught at Public School 133, and that brought me and a girlfriend to Alabama in 1964–65, a year that started with freedom songs and the Selma marches and ended with the Watts riots and the myth's beginning to fall apart.

The filter of forgetfulness! The stray memories that slip through it!

Micky and Kathy Solomon came down from New York that winter to spend a few days with us in Alabama. One evening we decided to drive to a small town an hour away to hear Martin Luther King preach at a local church. We had been in Washington for his "I Have a Dream" speech, but this was a chance to hear him in another setting, a Black preacher talking to Black people, not to the nation.

At the last minute, Micky announced he wasn't coming. This wasn't like the March on Washington, he said. It wouldn't be right, the four of us sitting at the back of a Black church. The church wasn't ours. We would be voyeurs.

We argued with him. No one would mind if we were there. The Black struggle was ours, too. The churchgoers would know how we felt.

We went without him and were thankful for the experience, because King was in fact different in a country church than he had been at the Washington Memorial. It was only gradually that I came to understand Micky better. And it wasn't just the church. It was all of it, all of us white northerners, a high proportion of us Jews, who had come south to be part of something. We were idealistic about what we were doing, but that's what it was for us: an *experience*. We had come, and we would go, taking the experience with us so that we could reminisce about it someday as I am doing now, while the Blacks of Georgia and Alabama and Mississippi would remain. We were Americans, and their struggle was ours—but not in the same sense, not in the same way. In that sense and in that way, we *were* voyeurs. My Black students knew it all along. It was in the looks they sometimes gave me, those guarded, curious, almost amused looks that I hadn't known how to interpret and that had said *Yes, we're grateful that you care, grateful for your show of solidarity—but don't think we don't see through you, don't think we don't know why you are here.* As the year moved from Selma to Watts, a radicalized Black civil rights movement let us know that it knew too, that it would continue without us.

In my relationship to America, as in America itself, that year was a turning point. I didn't want to be a voyeur. I had my own people, just as Black Americans had theirs. The myth of Whitman's America was falling apart for me, falling apart for us all.

National myths can be dangerous but they are what make a nation a nation and not just the conglomeration of its citizens that America has since become. It never found anything to replace Whitman with.

I go through memories the way I built my cabin on the hill, finding lost and abandoned things and giving them another home—reading a notice one day in a local paper that I could salvage all the materials I might need by clearing out a basement and helping to tear down an old

and unused barn—and then the lugging of windows and
lumber, a wood stove, roofing tar, and tin.....

Winter Vigil

Building his cabin, it struck me while reading Kogan's book for the
third time, was his first attempt at writing *Winter Vigil*.

"All through the summer of '68," he tells us in the book's penultimate
paragraph, "I worked on my cabin at the end of the woods, while streams
of people from around the country found their way to our communal
house. The whole scene was a heavy dose of the '60s, coming all at once."

He describes that scene: the artists, the drifters, the drop-outs, the
draft resisters on the run to Canada, "one or two professors checking out
the scene, an Indian who had wandered east, walking almost all the way
from Ohio to Vermont, a precocious high school kid from New York
who was looking for the universal language." Then come the final lines:

> December 14, 1968—midnight on the frozen hills. In
> the main house, nearly everyone is gone. I sit inside my
> cabin like a winter animal or dormant seed—a kerosene
> lamp and a candle by the window—a stick of incense
> glowing in the dark. Smoke blows faintly in the icy
> air—a copy of *Walden, The Magus,* and *Raja Yoga* on
> my desk—the yoga of the mind—things and images in
> proper place—my cabin-mother keeps me warm. I watch
> over my thirtieth birthday as my old life slips away.

My cabin-mother!
A whole summer of work, an eager torso bared to the sun,

> The preparatory jointing, squaring, sawing, mortising,
> The hoist-up of beams, the push of them in their places,
> laying them regular,
> Setting the studs by their tenons in the mortise, according
> as they were prepared.

the pausing to brush the sweat from one's eyes, and stepping back to take a look at what has been done and what remains to be done, and again back to work—and to what end?

To build a cabin-mother, a "sacred icon in the woods—the hermit monk's retreat and woodland monastery cell" (that's Kogan, not Whitman), a wintry womb of silence with its "unconscious desire to relive the snow scenes in my Russian book of fairytales and melt the frozen mother-feelings of my heart."

Unconscious desire. Kogan wrote these words years later. That summer in Vermont, he thought he was just building a cabin. He didn't realize it was a womb to retreat to and be reborn from.

The cabin was his dream. *Winter Vigil* is its interpretation.

But the interpretation is modeled on the dream. Kogan's book is constructed from every scrap of memory, every "lost and abandoned thing" from his first thirty years that he was able to find a use for.

A piece of junk ceases to be junk when it is assigned a functional purpose. A stray memory ceases to be stray in the same way.

Winter Vigil, according to Carol Rusoff, didn't consciously start out as an integrated whole. Kogan began it, she has written me, in his cabin that winter. When he left the cabin and returned to New York, "he started thinking about his past in earnest.... He had a manila folder labeled *Sketches*, and he threw whatever he wrote, unedited, in there. There was no order to them during those years." Only in about 2010, Rusoff recalls, did he begin to think of these sketches as the chapters of a unified volume. This was four years before being diagnosed with cancer, after which, she wrote, "he worked on them continually until he couldn't sit up any more. Then he died."

And yet a more integrated whole than *Winter Vigil* could hardly be imagined. The book is a wondrous demonstration of how everything, as Kogan writes, "exists in everything, as we are microcosms that incorporate the world." One can open it at random to almost any page and see the truth of this.

Here, I've just done it:

There is a landscape painting by Jacob Ruisdael that shows a Dutch field stretching out to an infinite horizon, in which the point of view is taken from the rise of a hill, so that one is looking out and down upon a great expanse, with massive clouds moving straight across the sky. There is a late afternoon stillness over the scene, as though it were late afternoon in the universe, in which a solitary figure draws us into that exquisite drama of the infinite.... No one ever painted a landscape like that before the Dutch.... When Columbus found a continent beyond the horizon by pursuing an idea, he was doing what the Dutch did.... They too showed Europe new worlds inside of old.

I read this passage that my finger has blindly fallen on and marvel. Kogan's deep knowledge of art and the Old Masters—the stillness of the scene, like the stillness with which his mother filled their Brownsville apartment—the hilltop view "looking out and down upon a great expanse" as *Winter Vigil* looks back upon a life—the "late afternoon in the universe" (it is late afternoon in this life as Kogan writes)—the solitary figure drawing the viewer into an "exquisite drama," an "endless distance" (the mother again!)—the new world of America, the *idea* of America (Whitman!): all in a brief description of a seventeenth-century landscape. Was Kogan aware of all this as he wrote?

I doubt it. "The unconscious never fails to astonish me," he says.

If I planned a piece of writing from beginning to end, I could never organize it as precisely as free association allows me to do, for I would be imposing an order instead of allowing the material to come up as though by itself, in all its surprising and truly connected detail.

Lumber from here, windows from there, a wood-burning stove from somewhere else, and at summer's end—a cabin!

Whose womb he enters to "melt the frozen mother-feelings" of his heart and from which he emerges to write about them, his silence ended like Cordelia's at the end of *Lear*.

With this melting comes an outpouring of love. For his mother, her witchlike spell cast off at last, now seen as the beautiful, haunted soul that she was, a fairy princess transformed into a Baba Yaga by her obsessive need to preserve and control. For his father, whose vital spirits were crushed by the burden of an ill wife and the terrible failure of a faith. For the vanished New York and America that he grew up in. For his teachers and friends. For the past, the smallest remembered detail of which he chronicles as though it were something precious.

Which it is if you can find a use for it.

The year I was a student in England, I had a tutor, a poet and a mystic, who once said to me, "You know, you spend the first part of your life working your way into your incarnation and the last part working your way out of it."

I didn't know what she was talking about. How could I? I was still working my way in. Today, I think I get it. I would just phrase it differently. I would say you live a life that's messy with experience and clean up by leaving something complete. You don't do that by throwing anything away. You do it by putting everything in its place.

2021